C# Yellow Book

Rob Miles

Copyright © 2018 Rob Miles
All rights reserved.
ISBN: 9781728724966
Imprint: Independently published
Edition 9.0

Introduction 1
    Welcome 1
    Getting a copy of the notes and code samples 1
1   Computers and Programs 2
    1.1 Computers 2
    1.2 Programs and Programming 5
    1.3 Programming Languages 10
    1.4 C# 11
2   Simple Data Processing 15
    2.1 A First C# Program 15
    2.2 Manipulating Data 23
    2.3 Writing a Program 35
3   Creating Programs 51
    3.1 Methods 51
    3.2 Variables and Scope 61
    3.3 Arrays 64
    3.4 Exceptions and Errors 69
    3.5 The Switch Construction 73
    3.6 Using Files 76
4   Creating Solutions 82
    4.1 Our Case Study: Friendly Bank 82
    4.2 Enumerated Types 83
    4.3 Structures 85
    4.4 Objects, Structures and References 90
    4.5 Designing with Objects 97
    4.6 Static Items 102
    4.7 The Construction of Objects 106
    4.8 From Object to Component 113
    4.9 Inheritance 120
    4.10 Object Etiquette 130
    4.11 The power of strings and chars 135
    4.12 Properties 138
    4.13 Building a Bank 144
5   Advanced Programming 149
    5.1 Generics and Collections 149
    5.2 Storing Business Objects 154
    5.3 Business Objects and Editing 165
    5.4 Threads and Threading 171

- 5.5 Structured Error Handling ... 179
- 5.6 Program Organisation ... 182
- 5.7 A Graphical User Interface ... 188
- 5.8 Debugging ... 198
- 5.9 The End? ... 202

6 Glossary of Terms ... 203

- Abstract ... 203
- Accessor ... 203
- Base keyword ... 203
- Calling methods ... 203
- Class in C# ... 204
- Code Reuse ... 204
- Cohesion ... 204
- Collection ... 204
- Compiler ... 204
- Component ... 204
- Constructor ... 205
- Coupling ... 205
- Creative Laziness ... 205
- Declarative language ... 205
- Delegate ... 206
- Dependency ... 206
- Event ... 206
- Exception ... 206
- Functional Design Specification ... 207
- Globally Unique Identifier (GUID) ... 207
- Hierarchy ... 207
- Immutable ... 207
- Inheritance ... 207
- Interface ... 208
- Library ... 208
- Machine code ... 208
- Member ... 208
- Metadata ... 208
- Method ... 208
- Mutator ... 208
- Namespace ... 209
- Overload ... 209
- Override ... 209

- Portable 209
- Private 209
- Property 209
- Protected 210
- Public 210
- Reference 210
- Signature 210
- Source file 210
- Static keyword 210
- Stream 211
- Structure 211
- Subscript 211
- Syntax Highlighting 211
- Test harness 211
- This keyword 211
- Typesafe 211
- Unit test 212
- Value type 212
- Virtual Method 212

Index 213

The author can be contacted at:

Email: rob@robmiles.com   Blog: www.robmiles.com   Twitter @RobMiles

If you find a mistake in the text please report the error to foundamistake@robmiles.com and I will take a look.

Introduction

Welcome

Welcome to the Wonderful World of Rob Miles™. This is a world of bad jokes, puns, and programming. In this book I'm going to give you a smattering of the C# programming language. If you have programmed before I'd be grateful if you'd still read the text. It is worth it just for the jokes and you may actually learn something.

If you have not programmed before, do not worry. Programming is not rocket science it is, well, programming. The bad news about learning to program is that you get hit with a lot of ideas and concepts at around the same time when you start, and this can be confusing. The keys to learning programming are:

Practice – do a lot of programming and force yourself to think about things from a problem-solving point of view

Study – look at programs written by other people. You can learn a lot from studying code which other folk have created. Figuring out how somebody else did the job is a great starting point for your solution. And remember that in many cases there is no *best* solution, just ones which are better in a particular context, i.e. the fastest, the smallest, the easiest to use etc.

Persistence – writing programs is hard work. And you have to work hard at it. The principle reason why most folks don't make it as programmers is that they give up. Not because they are stupid. However, don't get too persistent. If you haven't solved a programming problem in 30 minutes you should call time out and seek help. Or at least walk away from the problem and come back to it. Staying up all night trying to sort out a problem is not a good plan. It just makes you all irritable in the morning. We will cover what to do when it all goes wrong later in section 5.9.

The book is written to be read straight through, and then referred to afterwards. It contains a number of *Programming Points*. These are based on real programming experience and are to be taken seriously. There are also bits written in a *Posh Font*. These are really important, should be learnt by heart and probably set to music.

If you have any comments on how the notes can be made even better (although I of course consider this highly unlikely) then feel free to get in touch.

Above all, enjoy programming.

Rob Miles

Getting a copy of the notes and code samples

The website for the book is at **http://www.csharpcourse.com** where you can also find the Powerpoint slide decks and laboratory exercises for a C# course based on this text. You can find the C# code samples here too. You can obtain a Kindle ebook version from Amazon.

1 Computers and Programs

In this chapter you are going to find out what a computer is and get an understanding of the way that a computer program tells the computer what to do. You will discover what you should do when starting to write a program, to ensure that you achieve a "happy ending" for you and your customer. Finally, you will take a look at programming in general and the C# language in particular.

1.1 Computers

Before we consider programming, we are going to consider computers. This is an important thing to do, because it sets the context in which all the issues of programming itself are placed.

1.1.1 An Introduction to Computers

One way of describing a computer is as an electric box which hums. This, while technically correct, can lead to significant amounts of confusion, particularly amongst those who then try to program a fridge. A better way is to describe it as:

A device which processes information according to instructions it has been given.

This general definition rules out fridges but is not exhaustive. However, for our purposes it will do. The instructions you give to the computer are often called a program. The business of using a computer is often called programming. This is **not** what most people do with computers. Most people do not write programs. They use programs written by other people. We must therefore make a distinction between users and programmers. A user has a job which he or she finds easier to do on a computer running the appropriate program. A programmer has a masochistic desire to tinker with the innards of the machine. One of the golden rules is that you never write your own program if there is already one available, i.e. a keen desire to process words with a computer should not result in you writing a word processor!

However, because you will often want to do things with computers which have not been done before, and further because there are people willing to pay you to do it, we are going to learn how to program as well as use a computer.

Before we can look at the fun packed business of programming though it is worth looking at some computer terminology:

1.1.2 Hardware and Software

If you ever buy a computer, you are not just getting a box which hums. The box, to be useful, must also have sufficient built-in intelligence to understand simple commands to do things. At this point we must draw a distinction between the software of a computer system and the hardware.

Hardware is the physical side of the system. Essentially if you can kick it, and it stops working when immersed in a bucket of water, it is hardware. Hardware is the impressive pile of lights and switches in the corner that the salesman sold you.

Software is what makes the machine tick. If a computer has a soul, it keeps it in its software. Software uses the physical ability of the hardware, which can run programs, to do something useful. It is called software because it has no physical existence and it is comparatively easy to change. Software is the voice which says "Computer Running" in a Star Trek film.

All computers are sold with some software. Without it they would just be a novel and highly expensive heating system. The software which comes with a computer is often called its Operating System. The Operating System makes the machine usable. It looks after all the information held on the computer and provides lots of commands to allow you to manage things. It also lets you run programs, ones you have written and ones from other people. You will have to learn to talk to an operating system so that you can create your C# programs and get them to go. Windows 10 is an example of an operating system. It gives computer programs a platform on which they can execute.

1.1.3 Data and Information

People use the words data and information interchangeably. They seem to think that one means the other. I regard data and information as two different things:

Data is the collection of ons and offs which computers store and manipulate.

Information is the interpretation of the data by people to mean something. Strictly speaking computers process data, humans work on information. As an example, the computer could hold the following bit pattern in memory somewhere:

    11111111 11111111 11111111 00000000

You could regard this as meaning:

"you are 256 pounds overdrawn at the bank"

or

"you are 256 feet below the surface of the ground"

or

"eight of the thirty two light switches are off"

The transition from data to information is usually made when the human reads the output. So why am I being so pedantic? (pedantic means being fussy about something being exactly right) Because it is vital to remember that a computer does not "know" what the data it is processing actually means. As far as the computer is concerned data is just patterns of bits, it is the user who gives meaning to these patterns. Remember this when you get a bank statement which says that you have £8,388,608 in your account!

Data Processing

Computers are data processors. Information is fed into them; they do something with it, and then generate further information. A computer program tells the computer what to do with the information coming in. A computer works on data in the same way that a sausage machine works on meat, something is put in one end, some processing is performed, and something comes out of the other end:

A program is unaware of the data it is processing in the same way that a sausage machine is unaware of what meat is. Put a bicycle into a sausage machine and it will try to make sausages out of it. Put invalid data into a computer and it will do equally useless things. It is only us people who actually give meaning to the data (see above). As far as the computer is concerned data is just stuff coming in which has to be manipulated in some way. This makes a computer a very good "mistake amplifier", as well as a useful thing to blame.....

A computer program is just a sequence of instructions which tell a computer what to do with the data coming in and what form the data sent out will have.

Note that the data processing side of computers, which you might think is entirely reading and writing numbers, is much more than that, examples of typical data processing applications are:

`Digital Watch`: A micro-computer in your watch is taking pulses from a crystal and requests from buttons, processing this data and producing a display which tells you the time.

`Car`: A micro-computer in the engine is taking information from sensors telling it the current engine speed, road speed, oxygen content of the air, setting of the accelerator etc and producing voltages out which control the setting of the carburettor, timing of the spark etc, to optimise the performance of the engine.

`CD Player`: A computer is taking a signal from the disk and converting it into the sound that you want to hear. At the same time, it is keeping the laser head precisely positioned and also monitoring all the buttons in case you want to select another part of the disk.

`Games Console`: A computer is taking instructions from the controllers and using them to manage the artificial world that it is creating for the person playing the game.

Note that some of these data processing applications are merely applying technology to existing devices to improve the way they work. However, the CD player and games console could not be made to work without built-in data processing ability.

Most reasonably complex devices contain data processing components to optimise their performance and some exist only because we can build in intelligence. It is into this world that we, as software writers are moving. It is important to think of the business of data processing as much more than working out the company payroll, reading in numbers and printing out results. These are the traditional uses of computers.

As software engineers it is inevitable that a great deal of our time will be spent fitting data processing components into other devices to drive them. You will not press a switch to make something work, you will press a switch to tell a computer to make it work. These embedded systems will make computer users of everybody, and we will have to make sure that they are not even aware that there is a computer in there! Note that this "raises the stakes" in that the consequences of software failing could be very damaging.

You should also remember that seemingly innocuous programs can have life threatening possibilities. For example, a doctor may use a spread sheet to calculate doses of drugs for patients. In this case a defect in the program could result in illness or even death (note that I don't think that doctors actually do this – but you never know..)

Programmer's Point: At the bottom there is always hardware

It is important that you remember your programs are actually executed by a piece of hardware which has physical limitations. You must make sure that the code you write will actually fit in the target machine and operate at a reasonable speed. The power and capacity of modern computers makes this less of an issue than in the past, but you should still be aware of these aspects. I will mention them when appropriate.

1.2 Programs and Programming

Programming is a black art. It is the kind of thing that you grudgingly admit to doing at night with the blinds drawn and nobody watching. Tell people that you program computers and you will get one of the following responses:

1. A blank stare.
2. "That's interesting", followed by a long description of the double glazing that they have just had fitted.
3. Asked to solve every computer problem that they have ever had, and ever will have.
4. A look which indicates that you can't be a very good one as they all drive Ferraris and tap into the Bank of England at will.

Programming is defined by most people as earning huge sums of money doing something which nobody can understand.

Programming is defined by me as deriving and expressing a solution to a given problem in a form which a computer system can understand and execute.

One or two things fall out of this definition:

- You need to be able to solve the problem yourself before you can write a program to do it.
- The computer has to be made to understand what you are trying to tell it to do.

1.2.1 What is a Programmer?

I like to think of a programmer as a bit like a plumber! A plumber will arrive at a job with a big bag of tools and spare parts. Having looked at it for a while, tut tutting, he will open his bag and produce various tools and parts, fit them all together and solve your problem. Programming is just like this. You are given a problem to solve. You have at your disposal a big bag of tricks, in this case a programming language. You look at the problem for a while and work out how to solve it and then fit the bits of the language together to solve the problem you have got. The art of programming is knowing which bits you need to take out of your bag of tricks to solve each part of the problem.

From Problem to Program

The art of taking a problem and breaking it down into a set of instructions you can give a computer is the interesting part of programming. Unfortunately, it is also the most difficult part of programming as well. If you think that learning to program is simply a matter of learning a programming language you are very wrong. In fact, if you think that programming is simply a matter of coming up with a program which solves a problem you are equally wrong!

There are many things you must consider when writing a program; not all of them are directly related to the problem in hand. I am going to start on the basis that you are writing your programs for a customer. He or she has a problem and would like you to write a program to solve it. We shall assume that the customer knows even less about computers than we do!

Initially we are not even going to talk about the programming language, type of computer or anything like that; we are simply going to make sure that we know what the customer wants.

Solving the Wrong Problem

Coming up with a perfect solution to a problem the customer has not got is something which happens surprisingly often in the real world. Many software projects have failed because the problem that they solved was the wrong one. The developers of the system quite simply did not find out what was required, but instead created what they thought was required. The customers assumed that, since the developers had stopped asking them questions, the right thing was being built, and only at the final handover was the awful truth revealed. It is therefore very important that a programmer holds off making something until they know exactly what is required.

This is a kind of self-discipline. Programmers pride themselves on their ability to come up with solutions, so as soon as they are given a problem they immediately start thinking of ways to solve it, this is almost a reflex action. What you should do is think "Do I really understand what the problem is?" The worst thing you can say to a customer is "I can do that". Instead you should think "Is that what the customer wants?"

Before you solve a problem, you should make sure that you have a watertight definition of what the problem is, which both you and the customer agree on. In the real world such a definition is sometimes called a Functional Design Specification or FDS. This tells you exactly what the customer wants. Both you and the customer sign it, and the bottom line is that if you provide a system which behaves according to the design specification the customer must pay you. Once you have got your design specification, then you can think about ways of solving the problem. You might think that this is not necessary if you are writing a program for yourself; there is no customer to satisfy. **This is not true**. Writing some form of specification forces you to think about your problem at a very detailed level. It also forces you to think about what your system is not going to do and sets the expectations of the customer right at the start.

Programmer's Point: The specification must always be there

I have written many programs for money. I would **never** write a program without getting a solid specification first. This is true even (or perhaps especially) if I do a job for a friend.

Modern development techniques put the customer right at the heart of the development, and involve them in the design process. These work on the basis that it is very hard (and actually not that useful) to get a definitive specification at the start of a project. You as a developer don't really know much about the customer's business and they don't know the limitations and possibilities of the technology. With this in mind it is a good idea to make a series of versions of the solution and discuss each with the customer before moving on to the next one. This is called prototyping.

1.2.2 A Simple Problem

Consider the scenario; you are sitting in your favourite chair in the pub contemplating the universe when you are interrupted in your reverie by a friend of yours who sells double glazing for a living. He knows you are a programmer of sorts and would like your help in solving a problem which he has:

He has just started making his own window units and is looking for a program which will do the costing of the materials for him. He wants to just enter the dimensions of the window and then get a print out of the cost to make the window, in terms of the amount of wood and glass required.

"This looks like a nice little earner" you think, and once you have agreed to a price you start work. The first thing you need to do is find out exactly what the customer wants you to do...

Specifying the Problem

When considering how to write the specification of a system there are three important things:

- What information flows into the system.
- What flows out of the system.
- What the system does with the information.

There are lots of ways of representing this information in the form of diagrams, for now we will stick with written text when specifying each of the stages:

Information going in

In the case of our immortal double-glazing problem we can describe the information as:

- The width of a window.
- The height of the window.

Information coming out

The information that our customer wants to see is:

- the area of glass required for the window
- the length of wood required to build a frame.

You can see what we need if you take a look at the diagram below:

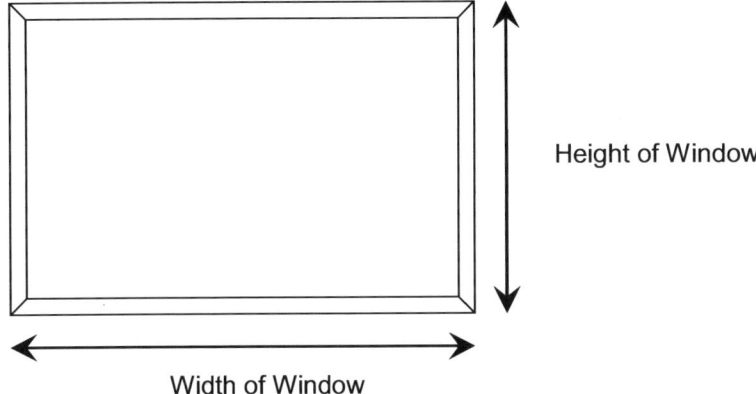

The area of the glass is the width multiplied by the height. To make the frame we will need two pieces of wood the width of the window, and two pieces of wood the height of the window.

Programmer's Point: metadata is important

Information about information is called *metadata*. The word meta in this situation implies a "stepping back" from the problem to allow it to be considered in a broader context. In the case of our window program the metadata will tell us more about the values that are being used and produced, specifically the units in which the information is expressed and the valid range of values that the information may have. For any quantity that you represent in a program that you write you must have at least this level of metadata .

What the program actually does

The program can derive the two values according to the following equations:

```
glass area = width of window * height of window
wood length = (width of window + height of window) * 2
```

Putting in more detail

We now have a fairly good understanding of what our program is going to do for us. Being sensible and far thinking people we do not stop here, we now have to worry about how our program will decide when the information coming in is actually valid.

This must be done in conjunction with the customer, he or she must understand that if information is given which fits within the range specified, your program will regard the data as valid and act accordingly.

In the case of the above we could therefore expand the definition of data coming in as:

- The width of the window, in metres and being a value between 0.5 Metres and 3.5 metres inclusive.
- The height of the window, in metres and being a value between 0.5 metres and 2.0 metres inclusive.

Note that we have also added units to our description, this is very important - perhaps our customer buys wood from a supplier who sells by the foot, in which case our output description should read:

- The area of glass required for the window, in square metres. Remember that we are selling double glazing, so two panes will be required.
- The length of wood required for the frame, given in feet using the conversion factor of 3.25 feet per metre.

Having written this all up in a form that both you and the customer can understand, we must then both sign the completed specification, and work can commence. Note that both you and the customer **must** understand the document!

Proving it Works

In a real world you would now create a test which will allow you to prove that the program works, you could for example say:

"If I give the above program the inputs 2 metres high and 1 metre wide the program should tell me I need 4 square metres of glass and 19.5 feet of wood."

The test procedure which is designed for a proper project should test out all possible states within the program, including the all-important error conditions. In a large system the person writing the program may have to create a test harness which is fitted around the program and will allow it to be tested. Both the customer and the supplier should agree on the number and type of the tests to be performed and then sign a document describing these.

Testing is a very important part of program development. There is even one development technique where you write the tests *before* you write the actual program that does the job. This is actually a good idea, and one we will explore later. In terms of code production, you can expect to write as much code to test your solution as is in the solution itself. Remember this when you are working out how much work is involved in a particular job.

Getting Paid

At this point the supplier knows that if a system is created which will pass all the tests the customer will have no option but to pay for the work! Note also that because the design and test procedures have been frozen, there is no ambiguity which can lead to the customer requesting changes to the work although of course this can still happen! Better yet, set up a phased payment system so that you get some money as the system is developed.

The good news for the developer is that if changes are requested these can be viewed in the context of additional work, for which they can expect to be paid.

Customer Involvement

Note also in a "proper" system the customer will expect to be consulted as to how the program will interact with the user, sometimes even down to the colour of the letters on the display! Remember that one of the most dangerous things that a programmer can think is "This is what he wants"! The precise interaction with the user - what the program does when an error is encountered, how the information is presented etc., is something which the customer is guaranteed to have strong opinions about. Ideally all this information should be put into the specification, which should include layouts of the screens and details of which keys should be pressed at each stage. Quite often prototypes will be used to get an idea of how the program should look and feel.

If this seems that you are getting the customer to help you write the program then you are exactly right! Your customer may have expected you to take the description of the problem and go into your back room - to emerge later with the perfect solution to the problem. This is not going to happen. What will happen is that you will come up with something which is about 60% right. The customer will tell you which bits look OK and which bits need to be changed. You then go back into your back room, muttering under your breath, and emerge with another system to be approved. Again, Rob's law says that 60% of the wrong 40% will now be OK, so you accept changes for the last little bit and again retreat to your keyboard....

Fact: If you expect to derive the specification as the project goes on either you will fail to do the job, or you will end up performing five times the work!

The customer thinks that this is great, reminiscent of a posh tailor who produces the perfect fit after numerous alterations. All the customer does is look at something, suggests changes and then wait for the next version to find something wrong with. They will get a bit upset when the delivery deadline goes by without a finished product appearing but they can always cheer themselves up again by suing you.

Actually, we have come full circle here, because I did mention earlier that prototyping is a good way to build a system when you are not clear on the initial specification. However, if you are going to use prototypes it is a good thing to plan for this from the start rather than ending up doing extra work because your initial understanding of the problem was wrong.

If your insistence on a cast iron specification forces the customer to think about exactly what the system is supposed to do and how it will work, all to the better. The customer may well say "But I am paying you to be the computer expert, I know nothing about these machines". This is no excuse. Explain the benefits of "Right First Time" technology and if that doesn't work produce a revolver and force the issue!

Fact: More implementations fail because of inadequate specification than for any other reason!

Again, if I could underline in red I would: All the above apply if you are writing the program for yourself. You are your own worst customer!

You may think that I am labouring a point here; the kind of simple systems we are going to create as we learn to program are going to be so trivial that the above techniques are far too long winded. You are wrong. One very good reason for doing this kind of thing is that it gets most of the program written for you - often with the help of the customer. When we start with our double glazing program we now know that we have to:

```
read in the width
verify the value
read in the height
verify the value
```

```
calculate width times height times 2 and print it
calculate ( width + height ) * 2 * 3.25 and print it
```

The programming portion of the job is now simply converting the above description into a language which can be used in a computer.......

Programmer's Point: Good programmers are good communicators

The art of talking to a customer and finding out what he/she wants is just that, an art. If you want to call yourself a proper programmer you will have to learn how to do this. One of the first things you must do is break down the idea of "I am writing a program for you" and replace it with "We are creating a solution to a problem". You do not work for your customers, you work with them. This is very important, particularly when you might have to do things like trade with the customer on features or price.

1.3 Programming Languages

Once we know what the program should do (specification), and how we are going to determine whether it has worked or not (test) we now need to express our program in a form that the computer can work with.

You might ask the question "Why do we need programming languages, why can we not use something like English?" There are two answers to this one:

1. Computers are too stupid to understand English.
2. English would make a lousy programming language.

To take the first point. We cannot make very clever computers at the moment. Computers are made clever by putting software into them, and there are limits to the size of program that we can create and the speed at which it can talk to us. At the moment, by using the most advanced software and hardware, we can make computers which are about as clever as a tape worm. Tape worms do not speak very good English; therefore we cannot make a computer which can understand English. The best we can do is to get a computer to make sense of a very limited language which we use to tell it what to do. Programming languages get around both of these problems. They are simple enough to be made sense of by computer programs and they reduce ambiguity.

To take the second point. English as a language is packed full of ambiguities. It is very hard to express something in an unambiguous way using English. If you do not believe me, ask any lawyer or consider just what the following statement really means:

Time Flies like an Arrow.
Fruit Flies like a Banana!

Programmer's Point: The language is not that important

There are a great many programming languages around, during your career you will have to learn more than just one. C# is a great language to start programming in, but do not think that it is the only language you will ever learn.

1.4 C#

We are going to learn a language called C# (pronounced C sharp). If you ever make the mistake of calling the language C hash you will show your ignorance straight away! C# is a very flexible and powerful programming language with an interesting history. It was developed by Microsoft Corporation for a variety of reasons, some technical, some political and others marketing. There are literally hundreds of programming languages around; you will need to know at least 3!

C# bears a strong resemblance to the C++ and Java programming languages, having borrowed (or improved) features provided by these languages. The origins of both Java and C++ can be traced back to a language called C, which is a highly dangerous and entertaining language which was invented in the early 1970s. C is famous as the language the UNIX operating system was written in, and was specially designed for this.

1.4.1 Dangerous C

I referred to C as a *dangerous* language. So what do I mean by that? Consider the chain saw. If I, Rob Miles, want to use a chain saw I will hire one from a shop. As I am not an experienced chain saw user I would expect it to come with lots of built in safety features such as guards and automatic cut outs. These will make me much safer with the thing but will probably limit the usefulness of the tool, i.e. because of all the safety stuff I might not be able to cut down certain kinds of tree. If I was a real lumberjack I would go out and buy a professional chain saw which has no safety features whatsoever but can be used to cut down most anything. If I make a mistake with the professional tool I could quite easily lose my leg, something the amateur machine would not let happen.

In programming terms what this means is that C lacks some safety features provided by other programming languages. This makes the language much more flexible.

However, if I do something stupid C will not stop me, so I have a much greater chance of crashing the computer with a C program than I do with a safer language.

Programmer's Point: Computers are always stupid

I reckon that you should always work on the basis that any computer will tolerate no errors on your part and anything that you do which is stupid will always cause a disaster! This concentrates the mind wonderfully.

1.4.2 Safe C#

The C# language attempts to get the best of both worlds in this respect. A C# program can contain *managed* or *unmanaged* parts. The managed code is fussed over by the system which runs it. This makes sure that it is hard (but probably not impossible) to crash your computer running managed code. However, all this fussing comes at a price, causing your programs to run more slowly.

To get the maximum possible performance, and enable direct access to parts of the underlying computer system, you can mark your programs as unmanaged. An unmanaged program goes faster, but if it crashes it is capable of taking the computer with it. Switching to unmanaged mode is analogous to removing the guard from your new chainsaw because it gets in the way.

C# is a great language to start learning with as the managed parts will make it easier for you to understand what has happened when your programs go wrong.

1.4.3 C# and Objects

The C# language is *object oriented*. Objects are an organisational mechanism which let you break your program down into sensible chunks, each of which is in charge of part of the overall system. Object Oriented Design makes large projects much easier to design, test and extend. It also lets you create programs which can have a high degree of reliability and stability.

I am very keen on object-oriented programming, but I am not going to tell you much about it just yet. This is not because I don't know much about it (honest) but because I believe that there are some very fundamental programming issues which need to be addressed before we make use of objects in our programs.

The use of objects is as much about design as programming, and we have to know how to program before we can design larger systems.

1.4.4 Making C# Run

C# is a compiled programming language. The computer cannot understand the language directly, so a program called a compiler converts the C# text into the low-level instructions which are much simpler. These low-level instructions are in turn converted into the actual commands to drive the hardware which runs your program.

You actually write the program using some form of text editor - which may be part of the compiling and running system.

We will look in more detail at this aspect of how C# programs work a little later, for now the thing to remember is that you need to show your wonderful C# program to the compiler before you get to actually run it. A compiler is a very large program which knows how to decide if your program is legal. The first thing it does is check for errors in the way that you have used the language itself. Only if no errors are found by the compiler will it produce any output.

The compiler will also flag up *warnings* which occur when it notices that you have done something which is not technically illegal, but may indicate that you have made a mistake somewhere. An example of a warning situation is where you create something but don't use it for anything. The compiler would tell you about this, in case you had forgotten to add a bit of your program.

The C# language is supplied with a whole bunch of other stuff (to use a technical term) which lets C# programs do things like read text from the keyboard, print on the screen, set up network connections and the like. These extra features are available to your C# program but you must explicitly ask for them. They are then located automatically when your program runs. Later on we will look at how you can break a program of your own down into a number of different chunks (perhaps so several different programmers can work on it).

1.4.5 Creating C# Programs

Microsoft has made a tool called Visual Studio, which is a great place to write programs. It comprises the compiler, along with an integrated editor, and debugger. It is provided in a number of versions with different feature sets. There is a free version, called Visual Studio Community edition, which is a great place to get started. Another free resource is the Microsoft .NET Framework. This provides a bunch of command line tools, i.e. things that you type to the command prompt, which can be used to compile and run C# programs. How you create and run your programs is up to you.

I'm not going to go into details of how to download and install the .NET framework; that is for other documents, I am going to assume that you are using a computer which has a text editor (usually Notepad) and the .NET framework installed.

The Human Computer

Of course, initially it is best if we just work through your programs on paper. I reckon that you write programs best when you are not sitting at the computer, i.e. the best approach is to write (or at least map out) your solution on paper a long way away from the machine. Once you are sitting in front of the keyboard there is a great temptation to start pressing keys and typing something in which might work. This is not good technique. You will almost certainly end up with something which almost works, which you will then spend hours fiddling with to get it going.

If you had sat down with a pencil and worked out the solution first you would probably get to a working system in around half the time.

Programmer's Point: Great Programmers debug less

I am not impressed by hacking programmers who spend whole days at terminals fighting with enormous programs and debugging them into shape. I am impressed by someone who turns up, types in the program and makes it work first time!

1.4.6 What Comprises a C# Program?

If your mum wanted to tell you how to make your favourite fruitcake she'd write the recipe down on a piece of paper. The recipe would be a list of ingredients followed by a sequence of actions to perform on them.

A program can be regarded as a recipe, but written for a computer to follow, not a cook. The ingredients will be values (called *variables*) that you want your program to work with. The program itself will be a sequence of actions (called *statements*) that are to be followed by the computer. Rather than writing the program down on a piece of paper you instead put it into a file on the computer, often called a *source file*.

This is what the compiler acts on. A source file contains three things:

- instructions to the compiler
- information about the structures which will hold the data to be stored and manipulated.
- instructions which manipulate the data.

To take these in turn:

Controlling the Compiler

The C# compiler needs to know certain things about your program. It needs to know which external resources your program is going to use. It also can be told about any options for the construction of your program which are important. Some parts of your program will simply provide this information to tell the compiler what to do

Storing the Data

Programs work by processing data. The data has to be stored within the computer whilst the program processes it. All computer languages support *variables* of one form or another. A variable is simply a named location in which a value is held whilst the program runs. C# also lets you build up *structures* which can hold more than one item, for example a single structure could hold all the information about a particular bank customer. As part of the program design process you will need to decide what items of data need to be stored. You must also decide on sensible names that you will use to identify these items.

Describing the Solution

The actual instructions which describe your solution to the problem must also be part of your program. A single, simple, instruction to do something in a C# program is called a *statement*. A statement is an instruction to perform one particular operation, for example add two numbers together and store the result.

The really gripping thing about programs is that some statements can change which statement is performed next, so that your program can look at things and decide what to do. In the case of C# you can lump statements together to form a lump of program which does one particular task. Such a lump is called a *method*.

A method can be very small, or very large. It can return a value which may or may not be of interest. It can have any name you like, and your program can contain as many methods as you see fit. One method may refer to others. The C# language also has a huge number of *libraries* available which you can use. These save you from "re-inventing the wheel" each time you write a program. We will look at methods in detail later in these notes.

Seasoned programmers break down a problem into a number of smaller ones and make a method for each.

Identifiers and Keywords

You give a name to each method that you create, and you try to make the name of the function fit what it does, for example `ShowMenu` or `SaveToFile`. The C# language actually runs your program by looking for a method with a special name, `Main`. This method is called when your program starts running, and when `Main` finishes, your program ends. The names that you invent to identify things are called *identifiers*. You also create identifiers when you make things to hold values; `woodLength` might be a good choice when we want to hold the length of wood required. Later on, we will look at the rules and conventions which you must observe when you create identifiers.

The words which are part of the C# language itself are called *keywords*. In a recipe a keyword would be something like "mix" or "heat" or "until". They would let you say things like *"**heat** sugar **until** molten"* or *"**mix until** smooth"*. In fact, you'll find that programs look a lot like recipes.

Objects

Some of the things in the programs that we write are objects that are part of the framework we are using. To continue our cooking analogy, these are things like mixing bowls and ovens, which are used during the cooking process.

Text in a Computer Program

There are two kinds of text in your program. There are the instructions that you want the computer to perform and there are the messages that you want the program to actually display in front of the user. Your mum might add the following instruction to her cake recipe:

Now write the words "Happy Christmas" on top of the cake in pink icing.

She is using double quote characters to mark the text that is to be drawn on the cake, and C# works in exactly the same way. "Happy Christmas" is not part of the instructions; it is what needs to be written.

2 Simple Data Processing

In this chapter we are going to create a genuinely useful program (particularly if you are in the double-glazing business). We will start by creating a very simple solution and investigating the C# statements that perform basic data processing. Then we will use additional features of the C# language to improve the quality of the solution we are producing.

2.1 A First C# Program

The first program that we are going to look at will read in the width and height of a window and then print out the amount of wood and glass required to make a window that will fit in a hole of that size. This is the problem we set out to solve as described in section1.2.2

2.1.1 The Program Example

Perhaps the best way to start looking at C# is to jump straight in with our first ever C# program. Here it is:

```csharp
using System;

class GlazerCalc
{
    static void Main()
    {
        double width, height, woodLength, glassArea;
        string widthString, heightString;

        widthString = Console.ReadLine();
        width = double.Parse(widthString);

        heightString = Console.ReadLine();
        height = double.Parse(heightString);

        woodLength = 2 * ( width + height ) * 3.25 ;

        glassArea = 2 * ( width * height ) ;

        Console.WriteLine ( "The length of the wood is " +
                woodLength + " feet" ) ;
        Console.WriteLine( "The area of the glass is " +
                glassArea + " square metres" ) ;
    }
}
```

Code Sample 01 GlazerCalc Program

This is a valid program. If you gave it to a C# compiler it would compile, and you could run it. The actual work is done by the two lines that I have highlighted. Broadly speaking the stuff before these two lines is concerned with setting things up and getting the values in to be processed. The stuff after the two lines is concerned with displaying the answer to the user.

We can now go through each line in turn and try to see how it fits into our program.

using System;

This is an instruction to the C# compiler to tell it that we want to use things from the `System` *namespace*. A namespace is a place where particular names have meaning. We have namespaces in our conversations too, if I am using the "Football" namespace and I say *"That team is really on fire"* I'm saying something good. If I am using the "Firefighter" namespace I'm saying something less good. A big part of learning to program is learning how to use all the additional features of the system which support your programs.

In the case of C# the `System` namespace is where lots of useful things are described. One of these useful things provided with C# is the `Console` class which will let me write things which will appear on the screen in front of the user. If I want to just refer to this as `Console` I have to tell the compiler I'm using the `System` namespace. This means that if I refer to something by a particular name the compiler will look in `System` to see if there is anything matching that name. We will use other namespaces later on.

class GlazerCalc

A C# program is made up of one or more *classes*. A class is a container which holds data and program code to do a particular job. In the case of our double glazing calculator the class just contains a single method which will work out our wood lengths and glass area, but a class can contain much more than that if it needs to. Classes are the basis of object oriented programming, as we shall see later.

You need to invent an identifier for every class that you create. I've called ours `GlazerCalc` since this reflects what it does. For now, don't worry too much about classes; just make sure that you pick sensible names for the classes that you create.

Oh, and one other thing. There is a convention that the name of the file which contains a particular class should match the class itself, in other words the program above should be held in a file called `GlazerCalc.cs`.

static

This keyword makes sure that the method which follows is always present, i.e. the word `static` in this context means "is part of the enclosing class and is always here". When we get to consider objects, we will find that this little keyword has all kinds of interesting ramifications. But for now, I'd be grateful if you'd just make sure that you put it here in order to make your programs work properly.

void

A `void` is nothing. In programming terms, the `void` keyword means that the method we are about to describe does not return anything of interest to us. The method will just do a job and then finish. In some cases, we write methods which return a result (in fact we will use such a method later in the program).

However, in order to stop someone else accidentally making use of the value returned by our `Main` method, we are explicitly stating that it returns nothing. This makes our programs safer, in that the compiler now knows that if someone tries to use the value returned by this method, this must be a mistake.

Main

You choose the names of your methods to reflect what they are going to do for you. Except for `Main`. This method (and there must be one, and only one such method) is where your program starts running.

When your program is loaded and run the first method given control is the one called `Main`. If you miss out the `Main` method the system quite literally does not know where to start.

()

This is a pair of brackets enclosing nothing. This may sound stupid, but actually tells the compiler that the method `Main` has no parameters. A parameter to a method gives the method something to work on. When you define a method, you can tell C# that it works on one or more things, for example `sin(x)` could work on a floating point value of angle `x`. We will cover methods in very great detail later in this document.

{

This is a *brace*. As the name implies, braces come in packs of two, i.e. for every open brace there must be a matching close. Braces allow programmers to lump pieces of program together. Such a lump of program is often called a *block*. A block can contain the declaration of variables used within it, followed by a sequence of program statements which are executed in order. In this case the braces enclose the working parts of the method `Main`.

When the compiler sees the matching close brace at the end it knows that it has reached the end of the method and can look for another (if any). The effects of an un-paired brace are invariably fatal....

double

By now you probably feel that you need a drink. But that is not what `double` means in this context. What it means is *"double precision floating point number"*.

Our program needs to remember certain values as it runs. Notably it will read in values for the width and height of the windows and then calculate and print values for the glass area and wood length. C# calls the places where values are put *variables*. At the beginning of any block you can tell C# that you want to reserve some space to hold some data values. Each item can hold a particular kind of value. Essentially, C# can handle three types of data, floating point numbers, integer numbers and text (i.e. letters, digits and punctuation). The process of creating a variable is called *declaring* the variable.

You declare some variables of a particular type by giving the type of the data, followed by a list of the names you want the variables to have. We are using the type double for now. Later we will use other types. A *double* variable can hold a very wide range of values to a very high precision.

width, height, woodLength, glassArea

This is a list. A list of items in C# is separated by `,` (comma) characters. In this case it is a list of variable names. Once the compiler has seen the word `double` (see above) it is expecting to find the name of at least one variable to be created. The compiler works its way through the list, creating boxes which can hold values of type `double` and giving them the appropriate names. From this point on we can refer to the above names, and the compiler will know that we are using that particular variable.

> ## Programmer's Point: Know where your data comes from
> In fact, given the limitations in the accuracy to which people can read tape measures, and the fact that we are not going to make any windows as wide as the universe, a double precision floating point number is overkill for this application. You would instead ask the customer if it is OK to just express the dimensions in millimetres instead. We will look at the considerations driving the choice of particular variable types a bit later on. All these decisions are driven by the metadata (data about data) that you gather when you are finding out about the system you are creating.

`;`

The semicolon marks the end of the list of variable names, and also the end of that declaration statement. All statements in C# programs are separated by the `;` character, this helps to keep the compiler on the right track.

The `;` character is actually very important. It tells the compiler where a given statement ends. If the compiler does not find one of these where it expects to see one it will produce an error. You can equate these characters with the sprocket holes in film, they keep everything synchronised.

`string widthString, heightString;`

We have made some variables which can hold numbers. Now we are going to make some which can contain strings. This is because when we read the numbers from our user we first read them in as strings of text. We then convert the text into a number. The variables `widthString` and `heightString` (note the sensible names) will contain text versions of the numbers.

`widthString =`

This is an *assignment* statement. In this C# statement we are going to change the value in a variable. Our program is going to read a line of text from the user and place the result in the variable we have called `widthString`. Remember that a variable is simply a named box of a particular size, which can hold a single data item (in this case a string of text).

A good proportion of your programs will be instructions to assign new values to variables, as the various results are calculated. C# uses the = character to make assignments happen. The first part of this statement is the name of a previously defined variable. This is followed by the = character which I call the *gozzinta*. I call it that because the value on the right gozzinta (goes into) the variable on the left. Sorry.

`Console.`

On the right of the equals we have the thing which is going to be assigned to `widthString`. In this case the result is going to be the string returned by the method `ReadLine`. This method is part of an object called `Console` which looks after the user input and output. The full stop (.) separates the object identifier from the method identifier.

`ReadLine`

This indicates that the `ReadLine` method is to be invoked. This asks the running program to dash off, do whatever statements there are in this method, and then come back. Methods are a way in which you can break up your program into a number of chunks, each of which has a particular job. They also mean that you only have to write a particular piece of code once, put it in a method, and then call that method whenever you want that particular job done. The C# system contains a number of built in methods to do things for our programs. `ReadLine` is one of these.

When this program runs the `ReadLine` method is invoked (or called). It will wait for the user to enter a line of text and press the Enter key. Whatever is typed in is then returned as a string by the `ReadLine` method. The result of the method call is placed in the `widthString` variable.

()

A method call is followed by the *parameters* to the method. A parameter is something that is passed into a method for it to work on. Think of it as raw materials for a process of some kind. In the case of `ReadLine` it has no raw materials; it is going to fetch the information from the user who will type it in. However, we **still** have to provide the list of parameters even if it is empty.

;

We have seen the semi-colon before. It marks the end of a statement in our program.

width =

This is another assignment (Mr. Phelps/Hawke[1]). The variable `width` is being given a value. Many statements in your programs will simply be moving data around and performing actions on it.

double.

But the rest of the statement looks a bit scary. In fact, it is not too tricky. We are asking Mr. `double` (the thing responsible holding for double precision floating point numbers) to do a little job for us. In this case the little job is "take the string held by `widthString` and convert it into a double precision floating point number". Mr. `double` provides this ability by exposing a method called `Parse`.

Note that there is nothing wrong or naughty about something in C# exposing its methods. It is how we get things done for us. When you come to design larger programs you will find that the best way to do this is to create *components* which expose methods to get the job done. The whole of the C# library set is provided as a series of methods and one of the things that you will have to get to grips with is where the methods are and how to use them. As with many things in life, the trick is knowing who to ask…

Parse

The Parse method has the job of converting the string it has been given into a double precision floating point number. To do this it must look along the string, pull out each digit in turn and then calculate the actual value, as in "12" means a ten and two units. This process of looking along things is often called *parsing*. Hence the name of the method we are using. The method is given the string that is to be parsed and returns the number that it has found.

Note that this gives significant potential for evil, in that if the user doesn't type in a value or types something like "Twenty Five" the `Parse` method call will not be able to resolve a number and will fail as a result. How it fails, and how you can resolve this failure, will be left for a future section in order to add more excitement to this text.

---

[1] Obscure movie/TV show reference for you there folks.

```
(widthString);
```

We have seen that a call of a method must be followed by the raw materials (*parameters*) for that method. In the case of `ReadLine` there are no parameters, but we still need to supply an empty list to indicate this. In the case of `Parse` the method needs to be given the string that it is to work on. We do this by putting the name of the string variable containing the text (`widthString`) into the brackets as above. The value of the information in `widthString` (i.e. the text that the user has typed in) is passed into the `Parse` method for it to work on and extract the number from.

```
heightString = Console.ReadLine();
height = double.Parse(heightString);
```

These two statements simply repeat the process of reading in the text of the height value and then converting it into a double precision value holding the height of the window.

```
woodLength = 2*(width + height)*3.25 ;
```

This is the actual nub of the program itself. This is the bit that does the work. It takes the height and width values and uses them to calculate the length of wood required.

The calculation is an expression much like above, this time it is important that you notice the use of parenthesis to modify the order in which values are calculated in the expression. Normally C# will work out expressions in the way you would expect, i.e. all multiplication and division will be done first, followed by addition and subtraction. In the above expression I wanted to do some parts first, so I did what you would do in mathematics, I put brackets around the parts to be done first. When I write programs I use brackets even when the compiler does not need them. This makes the program clearer.

Note that I use a factor of `3.25` to allow for the fact that the customer wants the length of wood in feet. There are around `3.25` feet in a meter, so I multiply the result in meters by this factor.

The + and * characters in the expression are called *operators* in that they cause an operation to take place. The other items in the expression are called *operands*. These are what the operators work on.

```
glassArea = 2 * ( width * height ) ;
```

This line repeats the calculation for the area of the glass. Note that the area is given in square meters, so no conversion is required. I've put one multiplication in brackets to allow me to indicate that I am working out two times the area (i.e. for two panes of glass). There is no need to do this particularly, but I think it makes it slightly clearer.

Console.WriteLine

This is a call of a method, just like the `ReadLine` method, except that this one takes what it is given and then prints it out on the console.

```
(
```

This is the start of the *parameters* for this method call. We have seen these used in the calls of `Parse` and also `ReadLine`

"The length of the wood is "

This is a *string literal*. It is a string of text which is literally just in the program. The string of text is enclosed in double quote characters to tell the compiler that this is part of a value in the program, not instructions to the compiler itself.

+

Plus is an addition operator. We have seen it applied to add two integers together. However, the plus here means something completely different[2]. In this case it means "add two strings together".

You will have to get used to the idea of *context* in your programs. We have seen this with namespaces. Here it is with operators. The C# system uses the context of an operation to decide what to do. In the case of the previous +, between two double precision floating point numbers it means "do a sum". Here it has a string on the left-hand side. This means that it is going to perform string concatenation rather than mathematical addition.

woodLength

This is another example of context at work. Previously we have used woodLength as a numeric representation of a value, in this program the length of the wood required. However, in the context it is being used at the moment (added to the end of a string) it cannot work like that.

The C# compiler must therefore ask the woodLength data item to convert itself into a string so it can be used correctly in this position. Fortunately, it can do this, and so the program works as you would expect.

It is very important that you understand precisely what is going on here. Consider:

```
Console.WriteLine ( 2.0 + 3.0 );
```

This would perform a numeric calculation (2.0 + 3.0) and produce a double precision floating point value. This result value would then be asked to provide a string version of itself to be printed, giving the output:

```
5
```

But the line of code:

```
Console.WriteLine ( "2.0" + 3.0 );
```

Would regard the + as concatenating two strings. It would ask the value 3 to convert itself into a string (sounds strange – but this is what happens). It would then produce the output:

```
2.03
```

The string "2.0" has the text of the value 3.0 added on the end. This difference in behaviour is all because of the context of the operation that is being performed.

You can think of all of the variables in our program being tagged with *metadata* (there is that word again) which the compiler uses to decide what to do with them. The variable heightString is tagged with information that says "this is a string, use a plus with this and you concatenate". The variable woodLength is tagged with metadata which says "this is a double precision floating point value, use a plus with this and you perform arithmetic".

---

[2] Another TV show reference

+ " feet"

Another concatenation here. We are adding the word feet on the end. Whenever I print a value out I **always** put the units on the end. This makes it much easier to ensure that the value makes sense.

)

The bracket marks the end of the parameter being constructed for the `WriteLine` method call. When the method is called the program first assembles a completed string out of all the components, adding (or concatenating) them to produce a single result. It then passes the resulting string value into the method which will print it out on the console.

;

The semi-colon marks the end of this statement.

}

Now for some really important stuff. The program is essentially complete. We have added all the behaviours that we need. However, the compiler still needs to be told that we have reached the end of the program. This first close brace marks the end of the block of code which is the body of the Main method. A block of code starts with a { and ends with a }. When the compiler sees this, it says to itself "that is the end of the Main method".

}

The second closing brace has an equally important job to the first. It marks the end of the class `GlazerCalc`. In C# everything exists inside a class. A class is a container for a whole bunch of things, including methods. If we want to (and we will do this later) we may put a number of methods into a class. For now however, we only want the one method in the class. And so, we use the second closing brace to mark the end of the class itself.

Punctuation

That marks the end of our program. One of the things that you will have noticed is that there is an awful lot of punctuation in there. This is vital and must be supplied exactly as C# wants it, otherwise you will get what is called a compilation error. This simply indicates that the compiler is too stupid to make sense of what you have given it!

You will quickly get used to hunting for and spotting compilation errors. One of the things you will find is that the compiler does not always detect the error where it takes place; consider the effect of missing out a "(" character. However, note that just because the compiler reckons your program is OK is no guarantee of it doing what you want!

Another thing to remember is that the layout of the program does not bother the compiler, the following is just as valid:

```
using System;class GlazerCalc{static void Main(){double width, height,
woodLength, glassArea;string widthString, heightString;widthString =
Console.ReadLine();width = double.Parse(widthString);heightString =
Console.ReadLine();height = double.Parse(heightString);woodLength = 2 * ( width
+ height ) * 3.25 ;glassArea = 2 * ( width * height ) ;Console.WriteLine (
```

```
"The length of the wood is " + woodLength + " feet" ) ;Console.WriteLine(
"The area of the glass is " + glassArea + " square metres" ) ;}}
```

- although if anyone writes a program which is laid out this way they will get a smart rap on the knuckles from me!

Programmer's Point: Program layout is very important

You may have noticed the rather attractive layout that I have used when I wrote the program. Items inside braces are indented so that it is very clear where they belong. I do not do this because I find such listings artistically pleasing. I do it because otherwise I am just about unable to read the program and make sense of what it does. JustlikeIfindithardtoreadenglishwithouttheproperspacing I find it hard to read a program if it has not been laid out correctly.

2.2 Manipulating Data

In this section we are going to take a look at how we can write programs that manipulate data, how values can be stored, retrieved and generally fiddled with. This provides us with the ability to perform the data processing part of programs.

2.2.1 Variables and Data

In the glazing program above, we decided to hold the width and the height of the windows that we are working on in variables that we described as `double`. Before we can go much further in our programming career we need to consider just what this means, and what other types of data we can store in programs that we write.

Programs operate on data. A programming language must give you a way of storing the data you are processing, otherwise it is useless. What the data actually means is something that you as a programmer decide (see the above digression on data).

A variable is a named location where you can store something. You can think of it as a box of a particular size with a name painted on the box. You chose the name to reflect what is going to be stored there (we used sensible names like `woodLength` in the above program). You also need to choose the *type* of the variable (particular size and shape of box) from the range of storage types which C# provides. The type of the variable is part of the *metadata* about that variable.

Programs also contain *literal values*. A literal value is just a value in your program which you use for some purpose. For each type of variable, the C# language has a way in which literal values of that type are expressed.

2.2.2 Storing Numbers

When considering numeric values there are two kinds of data:

- Nice chunky individual values, for example the number of sheep in a field, teeth on a cog, apples in a basket. These are referred to as *integers*.
- Nasty real world type things, for example the current temperature, the length of a piece of string, the speed of a car. These are referred to as *reals*.

In the first case we can hold the value exactly; you always have an exact number of these items, they are *integral*.

In the second case we can never hold what we are looking at exactly. Even if you measure a piece of string to 100 decimal places it is still not going to give you its exact length - you could always get the value more accurately. These are *real*. A computer is digital, i.e. it operates entirely on patterns of bits which can be regarded as numbers. Because we know that it works in terms of ons and offs it has problems holding real values. To handle real values the computer actually stores them to a limited accuracy, which we hope is adequate (and usually is).

This means that when we want to store something we have to tell the computer whether it is an integer or a real. We also need to consider the range of possible values that we need to hold so that we can choose the appropriate type to store the data. When you are writing a specification, you should worry about the precision to which values are to be held. Too much accuracy may slow the machine down - too little may result in the wrong values being used.

You tell C# about a variable you want to create by declaring it. The declaration also identifies the type of the thing we want to store. Think of this as C# creating a box of a particular size, specifically designed to hold items of the given type. The box is tagged with some *metadata* (there is that word again) so that the system knows what can be put into it and how that box can be used

Storing integer values

Integers are the easiest type of value for the computer to store. Each value will map onto a particular pattern of bits. The only issue is one of range. The bigger the value the larger the number of bits that you need to represent it.

C# provides a variety of integer types, depending on the range of values you would like to store:

sbyte	8 bits	-128 to 127
byte	8 bits	0 to 255
short	16 bits	-32,768 to 32,767
ushort	16 bits	0 to 65,535
int	32 bits	-2,147,483,648 to 2,147,483,647
uint	32 bits	0 to 4,294,967,295
long	64 bits	-9,223,372,036,854,775,808 to 9,223,372,036,854,775,807
ulong	64 bits	0 to 18,446,744,073,709,551,615
char	16 bits	0 to 65,535

The standard integer type, `int`, can hold frighteningly large numbers in C#, in the range -2,147,483,648 to 2,147,483,647. If you want to hold even larger integers than this (although I've no idea why you'd want this) there is a `long` version.

Note that we can go one further negative than positive. This is because the numbers are stored using "2's complement" notation.

An example of an integer variable would be something which kept track of the number of sheep in a field:

```
int numberOfSheep;
```

This creates a variable which could keep track of over two thousand million sheep! It also lets a program manipulate "negative sheep" which is probably not meaningful (unless you run a sheep bank of course and let people borrow them). Remember that the language itself is unaware of any such considerations. If you want to make sure that we never have more than 1,000 sheep and the number of sheep never goes negative you must add this behaviour yourself.

When you edit your program source using Visual Studio (or another code editor that supports *syntax highlighting*) you will find that the names of types that are built into the C# language (such as `int` and `float`) are displayed in blue, as shown above.

Programmer's Point: Check your own maths

Something else which you should bear in mind is that a program will not always detect when you exceed the range of a variable. If I put the value 255 into a variable of type byte this is OK, because 255 is the biggest possible value of the type can hold. However, if I add one to the value in this variable the system may not detect this as an error. In fact this may cause the value to "wrap round" to 0. Which could cause my program big problems.

---

integer literal values

An integer literal is expressed as a sequence of digits with no decimal point:

```
23
```

This is the integer value 23. I could use it in my program as follows:

```
numberOfSheep = 23;
```

If I am using one of the "shorter" types the literal value is regarded by the compiler as being of that type:

```
sbyte tinyVal = 127;
```

In this statement the 127 is regarded as an `sbyte` literal, not an integer. This means that if I do something stupid:

```
sbyte tinyVal = 128;
```

(the maximum value that an `sbyte` can hold is 127) the compiler will detect that I have made a mistake and the program will not compile.

2.2.3 Storing real values

"Real" is a generic term for numbers which are not integers. They have a decimal point and a fractional part. Depending on the value the decimal point floats around in the number, hence the name `float`.

C# provides a type of box which can hold a real number. A standard `float` value has a range of $1.5E-45$ to $3.4E48$ with a precision of only 7 digits (i.e. not as good as most pocket calculators).

If you want more precision (although of course your programs will use up more computer memory and run more slowly) you can use a `double` box instead (double is an abbreviation for double precision). This takes up more computer memory but it has a range of $5.0E-324$ to $1.7E308$ and a precision of 15 digits.

An example of a `float` variable could be something which held the average price of ice cream:

```
float averageIceCreamPriceInPence;
```

An example of a `double` variable could be something which held the width of the universe in inches:

```
double univWidthInInches;
```

Finally, if you want the ultimate in precision but require a slightly smaller range you can use the `decimal` type. This uses twice the storage space of a `double` and holds values to a precision of 28-29 digits. It is used in financial calculations where the numbers are not so large but they need to be held to very high accuracy.

```
decimal robsOverdraft;
```

real literal values

There are two ways in which you can store floating point numbers; as float or as double. When it comes to putting literal values into the program itself the compiler likes to know if you are writing a floating-point value (smaller sized box) or double precision (larger sized box).

A `float` literal can be expressed as a real number with an `f` after it:

```
2.5f
```

A `double` literal is expressed as a real number without the `f`:

```
3.5
```

You can also use exponents to express double and float values:

```
9.4605284E15
```

This is a double precision literal value which is actually the number of meters in a light year. If you put an `f` on the end it becomes a floating-point literal value.

Unlike the way that integers work, with real numbers the compiler is quite fussy about how they can and can't be combined. This is because when you move a value from a double precision variable into an ordinary floating-point variable some of the precision is lost. This means that you have to take special steps to make sure that you as a programmer make clear that you want this to happen and that you can live with the consequences. This process is known as *casting* and we will consider it in detail a bit later.

Programmer's Point: Simple variables are probably best

You will find that I, and most programmers, tend to use just integers (`int`) and floating point (`float`) variable types. This may seem wasteful (it is most unlikely I'll ever need to keep track of two thousand million sheep) but it makes the programs easier to understand.

2.2.4 Storing Text

Sometimes the information we want to store is text. This can be in the form of a single character; at other times it will be a string. C# provides variables for looking after both of these types of information:

char variables

A char is a type of variable which can hold a single character. A character is what you get when you press a key on a keyboard or display a single character on the screen. C# uses a character set called UNICODE which can handle over 65,000 different character designs including a wide range of foreign characters.

An example of a character variable could be something which held the command key that the user has just pressed:

```
char commandKey;
```

char literal values

You express a character by enclosing it in single quotes:

```
'A'
```

This means "the character A". It is what your program would get if you asked it to read a character off the keyboard and the user held down shift and pressed A. If you are editing your program using an editor that supports *syntax highlighting* a character literal is shown in red.

Character Escape Sequences

This leads to the question "How do we express the ' (single quote) character". This is achieved by the use of an escape sequence. This is a sequence of characters which starts with a special escape character. Escape in this context means "escape from the normal hum-drum conventions of just meaning what you are and let's do something special". The escape character is the \ (backslash) character. Possible escape sequences are:

Character	Escape Sequence name
\'	Single quote
\"	Double quote
\\	Backslash
\0	Null
\a	Alert
\b	Backspace
\f	Form feed
\n	New line
\r	Carriage return
\t	Horizontal tab
\v	Vertical quote

The effect of these escape sequences depends on the device you send them to. Some systems will make a beep when you send the Alert character to them. Some clear the screen when you send the Form feed character.

You can use them as follows:

```
char beep = '\a';
```

Note that the a must be in lower case.

Character code values

We have already established that the computer actually manipulates numbers rather than actual letters. C# uses the Unicode standard to map characters onto numbers that represent them. If you wish, you can express a character literal as a value from the Unicode character set. The good news is that this gives you access to a huge range of characters (as long as you know the codes for them). The bad news is that you must express this value in *hexadecimal* which is a little bit harder to use than decimal. The best news of all is that you probably don't need to do this kind of thing very often, if at all.

As an example however, I happen to know that the Unicode value for capital a (A) is 65. This is represented in hexadecimal (base 16) as four sixteens and a single one (i.e. 41). I can therefore put this in my program as:

```
char capitalA = '\x0041';
```

Note that I have to put leading zeroes in front of the two hex digits.

string variables

A type of box which can hold a string of text. In C# a string can be very short, for example "Rob", or it can be very long, for example "War and Peace" (that is the book not the three words). A string variable can hold a line of text. However, because there are special characters which mean "take a new line" (see above) it is perfectly possible for a single string to hold a large number of lines of text.

An example of a string variable could be something which holds the line that the user has just typed in:

```
string commandLine;
```

string literal values

A string literal value is expressed enclosed in double quotes:

```
"this is a string"
```

The string can contain the escape sequences above:

```
"\x0041BCDE\a"
```

If we print this string it would print out:

```
ABCDE
```

- and try to ring the bell.

If I am just expressing text with no escape characters or anything strange I can tell the compiler that this is a *verbatim* string. I do this by putting an @ in front of the literal:

```
@"\x0041BCDE\a"
```

If I print this string I get:

```
\x0041BCDE\a
```

This can be useful when you are expressing things like file paths. The verbatim character has another trick, which is that you can use it to get string literals to extend over several lines:

```
@"The quick
brown fox
jumps over the lazy dog"
```

This expresses a string which extends over three lines. The line breaks in the string are preserved when it is stored.

2.2.5 Storing State using Booleans

A `bool` (short for boolean) variable is a type of box which can hold whether or not something is true. Sometimes that is all you want. If you are storing whether or not a subscription has been paid or not there is no need to waste space by using a type which can hold a large number of possible values. Instead you just need to hold the states `true` or `false`. These are the only two values which the `bool` type allows.

An example of a `bool` variable could be one which holds the state of a network connection:

```
bool networkOK;
```

bool literal values

These are easily expressed as either `true` or `false`:

```
networkOK = true ;
```

Programmer's Point: Think about the type of your variables

Choosing the right type for a variable is something of a skill. I tend to use floating point storage only as a last resort. They introduce a lack of precision that I am not too keen on. I find that with a little bit of ingenuity I can work in integers quite comfortably. For example, rather than store the price of an item as 1.5 pounds (needing the use of float) I will store the price as 150 pence.

Also, when considering how to store data it is important to remember where it comes from. In the example above, I've used the double type to hold the width and height of a window. This is **really stupid**. It does not consider the precision required or indeed how accurately the window can be measured. I would suspect that my glazing salesman will not be able to measure to accuracy greater than 1 mm and so it would make sense to only store the data to that precision.

This illustrates another metadata consideration, when you are given the prospect of storing floating point information; find out how it is being produced before you decide how it will be stored. As an example, you might think that being asked to work with the speed of a car you would have to store a floating-point value. However, when you find out that the speed sensor only gives answers to an accuracy of 1 mile per hour, this makes the job much simpler.

2.2.6 Identifiers

In C# an *identifier* is a name that the programmer chooses for something in the program. The name of a variable is more properly called an identifier. We will see other places where we create identifiers. C# has some rules about what constitutes a valid identifier:

- All identifiers names must start with a letter.
- After the letter you can have either letters or numbers or the underscore "_" character.

Upper and lower case letters are different, i.e. `Fred` and `fred` are different identifiers.

Here are a few example declarations, one of which are not valid (see if you can guess which one and why):

```
int fred ;
float jim ;
char 29yesitsme ;
```

One of the golden rules of programming, along with *"always use the keyboard with the keys uppermost"* is:

Always give your variables meaningful names.

According to the Mills and Boon romances that I have read, the best relationships are meaningful ones.

The convention in C# for the kind of variables that we are creating at the moment is to mix upper and lower case letters so that each word in the identifier starts with a capital:

```
float averageIceCreamPriceInPence;
```

This is sometimes called *camel case*, presumably because of the "humps" in the identifier which are caused by the capitals.

Programmer's Point: Think about the names of your variables

Choosing variable names is another skill you should work at. They should be long enough to be expressive but not so long that your program lines get too complicated. Perhaps the name averageIceCreamPriceInPence is a bit over the top in this respect. But I could live with it. Remember that you can always do sensible things with your layout to make the program look OK:

```
averageIceCreamPriceInPence =
            computedTotalPriceInPence / numberOfIceCreams;
```

2.2.7 Giving Values to Variables

Once we have got ourselves a variable we now need to know how to put something into it, and get the value out. C# does this by means of an assignment statement. There are two parts to an assignment, the thing you want to assign and the place you want to put it, for example consider the following:

```
class Assignment
{
    static void Main ()
    {
        int first, second, third ;
        first = 1 ;
        second = 2 ;
        third = second + first ;
    }
}
```

Code Sample 02 Silly Assignment Example

The first part of the program should be pretty familiar by now. Within the `Main` function we have declared three variables, `first`, `second` and `third`. These are each of integer type.

The last three statements are the ones which actually do the work. These are assignment statements. An assignment gives a value to a specified variable, which must be of a sensible type (note that you must be sensible about this because the compiler, as we already know, does not know or care what you are doing). The value which is assigned is an expression. The equals in the middle is there mainly to confuse us, it does not mean equals in the numeric sense; I like to think of it as a gozzinta (see above). Gozzintas take the result on the right hand side of the assignment and drop it into the box on the left, which means that:

```
2 = second + 1;
```

- is a piece of programming naughtiness which would cause all manner of nasty errors to appear.

Expressions

An expression is something which can be evaluated to produce a result. We can then use the result as we like in our program. Expressions can be as simple as a single value and as complex as a large calculation. They are made up of two things, *operators* and *operands*.

Operands

Operands are things the operators work on. They are usually *literal* values or the identifiers of variables. In the program above `first`, `second`, `third` are identifiers and 2 is a literal value. A literal value is something which is literally there in the code. A literal value has a type associated with it by the compiler.

Operators

Operators are the things which do the work: They specify the operation to be performed on the operands. Most operators work on two operands, one each side. In the program above + is the only operator.

Here are a few example expressions:

```
2 + 3 * 4
-1 + 3
(2 + 3) * 4
```

These expressions are worked out (evaluated) by C# moving from left to right, just as you would yourself. Again, just as in traditional maths all the multiplication and division is performed first in an expression, followed by the addition and subtraction.

C# does this by giving each operator a priority. When C# works out an expression it looks along it for all the operators with the highest priority and does them first. It then looks for the next ones down and so on until the final result is obtained. Note that this means that the first expression above will therefore return 14 and not 20.

If you want to force the order in which things are worked out you can put brackets around the things you want done first, as in the final example. You can put brackets inside brackets if you want, provided you make sure that you have as many open ones as close ones. Being a simple soul I tend to make things very clear by putting brackets around everything.

It is probably not worth getting too worked up about this expression evaluation as posh people call it; generally speaking things tend to be worked out how you would expect them.

For completeness here is a list of all operators, what they do and their precedence (priority). I am listing the operators with the highest priority first.

-	unary minus, the minus that C# finds in negative numbers, e.g. -1. Unary means applying to only one item.
*	multiplication, note the use of the * rather than the more mathematically correct but confusing x.
/	division, because of the difficulty of drawing one number above another on a screen we use this character instead
+	Addition.
-	subtraction. Note that we use exactly the same character as for unary minus.

This is not a complete list of all the operators available, but it will do for now. Because these operators work on numbers they are often called the numeric operators. But of course you should remember that some of them (for example +) can be used between other types of data as well. It is also possible to use operators in a way which causes values to be moved from one type to another. This can cause problems as we shall see now.

2.2.8 Changing the Type of Data

Whenever I move a value from one type to another the C# compiler gets very interested in what I am doing. It worries about whether or not the operation I'm about to perform will cause data to be lost from the program. It considers every operation in terms of "widening and narrowing" values.

Widening and Narrowing

The general principle which C# uses is that if you are "narrowing" a value it will always ask you to explicitly tell it that this is what you want to do. If you are widening there is no problem.

To understand what we mean by these terms we could consider suitcases. If I am packing for a trip I will take a case. If I decide to switch to a smaller case I will have to take everything out of the large case and put it into the smaller one. But it might not have room, so I have to leave behind one of my shirts. This is "narrowing".

However, if I change to a bigger case there is no problem. The bigger case will take everything that was in the smaller case and have room for more.

In C# terms the "size" of a type is the range of values (the biggest and smallest) and the precision (the number of decimal places). This means that if I write:

```
int i = 1 ;
float x = i;
```

This works fine because the floating-point type can hold all the values supported by the integer type. However:

```
float x = 1;
int i = x;
```

- would cause the compiler to complain (even though at the moment the variable x only holds an integer value). The compiler is concerned that you may be discarding information by such an assignment and treats it as an error.

Note that this applies within floating point values as well, for example:

```
double d = 1.5;
float f = d;
```

- would cause an error as well, since the compiler knows that a double is wider than a float.

Casting

We can force C# to regard a value as being of a certain type by the use of *casting*. A cast takes the form of an additional instruction to the compiler to force it to regard a value in a particular way. You cast a value by putting the type you want to see there in brackets before it. For example:

```
double d = 1.5;
float f = (float) d;
```

In the above code the message to the compiler is "I don't care that this assignment could cause the loss of information. I, as the writer of the program, will take the responsibility of making sure that the program works correctly". You can regard casting as the compiler's way of washing its hands of the problem. If a program fails because data is lost it is not because the compiler did something silly.

As we saw above, each type of variable has a particular range of possible values, and the range of floating point values is much greater than that for integers. This means that if you do things like this:

```
int i ;
i = (int) 1234567812345678901.999 ;
```

- the cast is doomed to fail. The value which gets placed in i will be invalid. Nothing in C# checks for mistakes like this. It is up to you when you write your program to make sure that you never exceed the range of the data types you are using - the program will not notice but the user certainly will! I do not think of this as a failing in C#. It gives you great flexibility, at the cost of assuming you know what you are doing....

A cast can also lose information in other ways:

```
int i ;
i = (int) 1.999 ;
```

The code above takes 1.999 (which would be compiled as a value of type double) and casts it to int. This process discards the fractional part, which means that the variable i will end up with the value 1 in it, even though the original number **was much closer to** 2. You should remember that this truncation takes place whenever you cast from a value with a fractional part (float, double, decimal) into one without.

Casting and Literal Values

We have seen that you can put "literal" values into your program. These are just values you want to use in your calculations. For example, in our double glazing program we had to multiply the wood length in meters by 3.25 to convert the length value from meters to feet (there are about 3.25 feet in a meter).

C# keeps careful track of the things that it is combining, and this includes how it allows literal values to be used. This is so that statements like:

```
int i ;
i = 3.4 / "stupid" ;
```

- will be treated with the contempt they richly deserve. The C# compiler knows that it is daft to divide the value 3.4 by the string "stupid". However, consider this:

```
float x ;
x = 3.4 ;
```

This code looks perfectly legal. However, it is not. This is because the literal value 3.4 is a double precision value when expressed as a literal, and the variable x has been declared as a floating point. If I want to put a floating point literal value into a floating point variable I can use casting:

```
float x ;
x = (float) 3.4 ;
```

This casts the double precision literal into a floating-point value, so that the assignment works.

To make life easier the creators of C# have added a different way we can express a floating-point literal value in a program. If you put an f after the value this is regarded as a floating-point value. This means that:

```
float x ;
x = 3.4f ;
```

- would compile correctly.

2.2.9 Types of Data in Expressions

When C# uses an operator, it decides as to the type of the result that is to be produced. Essentially, if the two operands are integer it says that the result should be integer. If the two are floating point it says that the result should be floating point. This can lead to problems, consider the following:

```
1/2
1/2.0
```

You might think that these would give the same result. Not so. The compiler thinks that the first expression, which involves only integers, should give an integer result. It therefore would calculate this to be the integer value `0` (the fractional part is always truncated). The second expression, because it involves a floating-point value would however be evaluated to give a double precision floating point result, the more accurate answer of `0.5`.

The way that an operator behaves depends on the context of its use. Later on, we will see that the `+` operator, which normally performs a numeric calculation, can be used between strings to concatenate them together, i.e. `"Ro" + "b"` would give the result `"Rob"`.

If you want complete control over the particular kind of operator the compiler will generate for you the program must contain explicit casts to set the correct context for the operator.

```
using System;
class CastDemo
{
    static void Main ()
    {
        int i = 3, j = 2 ;
        float fraction ;
        fraction = (float) i / (float) j ;
        Console.WriteLine ( "fraction : " + fraction ) ;
    }
}
```

Code Sample 03 Casting Demo

The `(float)` cast in the above tells the compiler to regard the values in the integer variables as floating-point ones, so that we get `1.5` printed out rather than `1`.

Programmer's Point: Casts can add clarity

I tend to put the casts in even if they are not needed, this can make the program clearer. It may not affect the result of the calculation but it will inform the reader of what I am trying to do.

2.2.10 Programs and Patterns

At this point we can revisit our double-glazing program and look at the way that it works. The code that actually does the work boils down to just a few lines which read in the data, store it in an appropriate type of location and then uses the stored values to calculate the result that the user requires:

```
string widthString = Console.ReadLine();
double width = double.Parse(widthString);

string heightString = Console.ReadLine();
int height = double.Parse(heightString);

woodLength = 2 * ( width + height ) * 3.25 ;

glassArea = 2 * ( width * height ) ;

Console.WriteLine ( "The length of the wood is " +
    woodLength + " feet" ) ;
Console.WriteLine("The area of the glass is " +
    glassArea + " square metres" ) ;
```

The interesting thing about this is that it is a *pattern* of behaviour which can be reused time and time again.

As an example, consider another friend of yours, who runs a chemist shop. He wants a program that will work out the total cost of tablets that he buys, and the number of bottles that he needs. He enters the cost of the tablets and the number he wants. The tablets are always sold in bottles that can contain up to 100 tablets.

You can very easily modify your program to do this job, the only hard part is figuring out how many bottles that are needed for a particular number of tablets. If you just divide the number of tablets by 100 an integer division will give you the wrong answer (for any number of tablets less than 100 your program will tell you that 0 bottles are needed). One way to solve this is to add 99 to the number of tablets before you perform the division, forcing the number of bottles required to "round up" any number of tablets greater than 0. This makes the active part of the program as follows:

```csharp
int bottleCount = ((tabletCount + 99) / 100) ;

int salePrice = bottleCount * pricePerBottle ;
```

We can then put the rest of the code around this to make a finished solution:

```csharp
string pricePerBottleString = Console.ReadLine();
int pricePerBottle = int.Parse(pricePerBottleString);

string tabletCountString = Console.ReadLine();
int tabletCount = int.Parse(tabletCountString);

int bottleCount = ((tabletCount + 99) / 100) ;

int salePrice = bottleCount * pricePerBottle ;

Console.WriteLine ( "The number of bottles is " +
    bottleCount ) ;
Console.WriteLine( "The total price is " +
    salePrice ) ;
```

Remember that if you divide two integers the result is always rounded down and the fractional part discarded.

The interesting thing here is that the program for the chemist is actually just a variation on the program for the double-glazing salesman. Both conform to a pattern of behaviour (read data in, process it, print it out) which is common to many applications. Any time that you are asked to write a program that reads in some data, works out some answers and then prints out the result you can make use of this pattern.

Part of the skill of a programmer is identifying the nature of a problem in terms of the best pattern to be used to solve it.

2.3 Writing a Program

The programs that we have created up until now have been very simple. They just read data in, do something with it and then print out the result. However, we will need to create programs which do things which are more complex than this. They may have to decide based on the data which they are given. They may need to repeat things until something is true. They may need to read in a large amount of data and then process that in a number of different ways.

In this section we are going to consider how we can give our programs that extra level of complexity, and look at the general business of writing programs.

2.3.1 Software as a story

Some people say that writing a program is a bit like writing a story. I'm not completely convinced that this is true. I have found that some computer manuals are works of fiction, but programs are something else. I think that while it is not a story as such, a good program text does have some of the characteristics of good literature:

- It should be easy to read. At no point should the hapless reader be forced to backtrack or brush up on knowledge that the writer assumes is there. All the names in the text should impart meaning and be distinct from each other.
- It should have good punctuation and grammar. The various components should be organised in a clear and consistent way.
- It should look good on the page. A good program is well laid out. The different blocks should be indented and the statements spread over the page in a well-formed manner.
- It should be clear who wrote it, and when it was last changed. If you write something good you should put your name on it. If you change what you wrote you should add information about the changes that you made and why.

A big part of a well written program is the comments that the programmer puts there. A program without comments is a bit like an aeroplane which has an autopilot but no windows. There is a chance that it might take you to the right place, but it will be very hard to tell where it is going from the inside.

Block Comments

When the C# compiler sees the "/*" sequence which means the start of a comment it says to itself:

"Aha! Here is a piece of information for greater minds than mine to ponder. I will ignore everything following until I see a */ which closes the comment."

As an example:

```
/* This program works out glass and wood required for
   a double glazing salesman. */
```

Be generous with your comments. They help to make your program much easier to understand. You will be very surprised to find that you quickly forget how you got your program to work. You can also use comments to keep people informed of the particular version of the program, when it was last modified and why, and the name of the programmer who wrote it – even if it was you.

If you are using an editor that supports *syntax highlighting* you will find that comments are usually displayed in green.

Line Comments

Another form of comment makes use of the // sequence. This marks the start of a comment which extends to the end of that particular line of code. It is useful for putting a quick note on the end of a statement:

```
position = position + 1 ; // move on to the next customer
```

I've annotated the statement to give the reader extra information about what it actually does.

Programmer's Point: Don't add too much detail

Writing comments is a very sensible thing to do. But don't go mad. Remember that the person who is reading your program can be expected to know the C# language and doesn't need things explained to them in too much detail:

```
goatCount = goatCount + 1 ; // add one to goatCount
```

This is plain insulting to the reader I reckon. If you chose sensible identifiers you should find that your program will express most of what it does directly from the code itself.

2.3.2 Controlling Program Flow

Our first double glazing program is very simple, it runs straight through from the first statement to the last, and then stops. Often you will come across situations where your program must change what it does according to the data which is given to it. Basically, there are three types of program flow:

1. straight line
2. chosen depending on a given condition
3. repeated according to a given condition

Every program ever written is composed of the three elements above, and very little else! You can use this to good effect when designing an overall view of how your program is going to work. At the moment we have only considered programs which run in a straight line and then stop. The path which a program follows is sometimes called its "thread of execution". When you call a method the thread of execution is transferred into the method until it is complete.

Conditional Execution - if

The program above to work out the wood and glass for our glazing man is nice; in fact our customer will probably be quite pleased with it. However, it is not perfect. The problem is not with the program, but with the user.

If you give the program a window width of `-1` it goes ahead and works out a stupid result. Our program does not have any checking for invalid widths and heights. The user might have grounds for complaint if the program fails to recognise that he has given a stupid value, in fact a number of cases are currently being fought in the United States courts where a program has failed to recognise invalid data, produced garbage and caused a lot of damage.

What we want to do is notice the really stupid replies and tell the user that he has done something dubious. In our program specification, which we give the customer, we have said something like (this is our metadata):

The program will reject window dimensions outside the following ranges:

```
width less than 0.5 metres
width greater than 5.0 metres
height less than 0.75 metres
height greater than 3.0 metres
```

This means that we have done all we can; If the program gets `1` rather than `10` for the width then that is the users' problem, the important thing from our point of view is that the above specification stops us from being sued!

In order to allow us to do this the program must notice naughty values and reject them. To do this we can use the construction:

```
if (condition)
    statement or block we do if the condition is true
else
    statement or block we do if the condition is false
```

The condition determines what happens in the program. So, what do we mean by a condition? C# has a way in which true and false can be explicitly stated in a program. We have already seen that the `bool` type is used to store this *logical* state.

We can create conditions which return a logical result. These are called "logical conditions". Which is logical. The simplest condition is simply the value true or false, for example:

```
if (true)
    Console.WriteLine ( "hello mum" );
```

This is valid, although rather useless as the condition is always true, so `"hello mum"` is always printed (note that we left the else portion off - this is OK because it is optional).

Conditions and Relational Operators

To make conditions work for us we need a set of additional relational operators which we can use in logical expressions. Relational operators work on operands, just like numeric ones. However, any expression involving them can only produce one of two values, `true` or `false`. Relational operators available are as follows:

==

equals. If the left hand side and the right hand side are equal the expression has the value `true`. If they are not equal the value is `false`.

```
4 == 5
```

- would evaluate to `false`. Note that it is not particularly meaningful to compare floating point variables to see if they hold exactly the same values. Because of the fact that they are held to limited precision you might find that conditions fail when they should not for example the following equation:

```
x = 3.0 * (1.0 / 3.0) ;
```

- may well result in x containing `0.99999999`, which would mean that:

```
x == 1.0
```

- would be `false` - even though mathematically the test should evaluate to `true`.

!=

not equal. The reverse of equals. If the operands are not equal the expression has the value `true`, if they are equal it has the value `false`. Again, this test is not advisable for use with floating point numbers.

If you want to compare floating point values subtract them and see if the difference is very small.

<

less than. If the operand on the left is less than the one on the right the value of the expression is `true`. If the left hand operand is larger than or equal to the right hand one the expression gives `false`. It is quite valid to compare floating point numbers in this way.

>

greater than. If the operand on the left is greater than the one on the right the result is `true`. If the operand on the left is less than or equal to the one on the right the result is `false`.

<=

less than or equal to. If the operand on the left is less than or equal to the one on the right you get `true`, otherwise you get `false`.

>=

greater than or equal to. If the operand on the left is greater than or equal to the one on the right you get `true`, otherwise it is `false`.

!

not. This can be used to invert a particular value or expression, for example you can say `!true`, which is `false`, or you could say: `!(x==y)` - which means the same as `(x!=y)`. You use not when you want to invert the sense of an expression.

Combining Logical Operators

Sometimes we want to combine logical expressions, to make more complicated choices, for example to test for a window width being valid we have to test that it is greater than the minimum and less than the maximum. C# provides additional operators to combine logical values:

&&

and. If the operands on each side of the && are true the result of the && is true. If one of them is false the result is false, for example

    (width >= 0.5) && (width <= 5.0)

- this would be true if the width was **valid** according to our above description. I've put brackets around each of the conditions in this example, so that it is easier to see what is going on. However, the compiler is able to work out that the && needs to be applied between the result of the two logical expressions, so they are not actually required.

||

or. If either of the operands each side of the || are true the result of the expression is true. The expression is only false if both operands are false, for example:

    width < 0.5 || width > 5.0

- this would be true if the width was **invalid**. We are saying that the width is invalid if it is less than the minimum or larger than the maximum. Note that to reverse the sense of the condition (i.e. true when the value is invalid) we not only have to change the > into <= in each expression, but also change the && into an ||.

De Morgan's theorem is the basis of this. Using these operators in conjunction with the `if` construction we can make decisions and change what our program will do in response to the data we get.

Programmer's Point: Break down your conditions

If you find that you are making huge and complicated conditions to get a statement obeyed you might find that you can make things clearer by using more than one if statement, and indenting the code in an appropriate way. This will make the code easier to debug as well, because you can watch the program step through your conditions one at a time, instead of going off in a particular direction based on a huge condition you will then have to unpick.

Using Blocks to Combine Statements

We have decided that if the user gives a value outside our allowed range an error is generated and the value is then set to the appropriate maximum or minimum. To do this we have to do two statements which are selected on a particular condition, one to print out the message and the other to perform an assignment. You can do this by using the { and } characters. A number of statements lumped together between { and } characters is regarded as a single statement, so we do the following:

```
if ( width > 5.0 )
{
    Console.WriteLine ("Width too big, using maximum\n") ;
    width = 5.0 ;
}
```

The two statements are now a block, which is performed only if width is greater than 5.0. You can lump many hundreds of statements together in this way, the compiler does not mind. You can also put such blocks of code inside other blocks, this is called nesting.

The number of { and } characters must agree in your program, otherwise you will get strange and incomprehensible errors when the compiler hits the end of the file in the middle of a block or reaches the end of your program half way down your file!

Programmer's Point: Use Layout to Inform the Reader

I make things much easier to understand by indenting a particular block by a number of spaces, i.e. each time I open a block with the { character I move my left margin in a little way. I can then see at a glance whereabouts I am in the levels at any time. This is what proper programmers do.

Metadata, Magic Numbers and const

A magic number is a value with a special meaning. It will never be changed within the program; it is instead a constant which is used within it. When I write my glazing program I will include some magic numbers which give the maximum and minimum values for heights and widths. These come from the *metadata* I was so careful to gather when I wrote the specification for the program.

Now I could just use the values 0.5, 5.0, 0.75 and 3.0 - but these are not packed with meaning and make the program hard to change. If, for some reason, my maximum glass size becomes 4.5 metres I have to look all through the program and change only the appropriate values. I do not like the idea of "magic numbers" in programs, what I would like to do is replace each number with something a bit more meaningful.

We can do this by making a variable which is constant, i.e. it can never be changed.

```
const double PI=3.141592654;
```

This means that you can do things like:

```
circ = rad * 2 * PI ;
```

This is both more meaningful (we are using PI not some anonymous value) and makes the program quicker to write. Anywhere you use a magic number you should use a constant of this form, for example:

```
const double MAX_WIDTH = 5.0 ;
```

This makes your programs much easier to read, and also much easier to change. There is a convention that you always give constant variables names which are expressed in CAPITAL LETTERS. This is so that when you read your program you can tell which things have been defined.

We can therefore modify our double-glazing program as follows:

```csharp
using System;

class GlazerCalc
{
    static void Main()
    {
        double width, height, woodLength, glassArea;

        const double MAX_WIDTH = 5.0 ;
        const double MIN_WIDTH = 0.5 ;
        const double MAX_HEIGHT = 3.0 ;
        const double MIN_HEIGHT = 0.75 ;

        string widthString, heightString;

        Console.Write ( "Give the width of the window : " );
        widthString = Console.ReadLine();
        width = double.Parse(widthString);

        if (width < MIN_WIDTH) {
            Console.WriteLine ( "Width is too small.\n\n " ) ;
            Console.WriteLine ( "Using minimum" ) ;
            width = MIN_WIDTH ;
        }

        if (width > MAX_WIDTH) {
            Console.WriteLine ( "Width is too large.\n\n" ) ;
            Console.WriteLine ( "Using maximum" ) ;
            width = MAX_WIDTH ;
        }

        Console.Write ( "Give the height of the window : " );
        heightString = Console.ReadLine();
        height = double.Parse(heightString);

        if (height < MIN_HEIGHT) {
            Console.WriteLine( "Height is too small.\n\n" ) ;
            Console.WriteLine ( "Using minimum" ) ;
            height = MIN_HEIGHT ;
        }
        if (height > MAX_HEIGHT) {
            Console.WriteLine( "Height is too large.\n\n" ) ;
            Console.WriteLine ( "Using maximum" ) ;
            height = MAX_HEIGHT ;
        }

        woodLength = 2 * ( width + height ) * 3.25 ;

        glassArea = 2 * ( width * height ) ;

        Console.WriteLine ( "The length of the wood is " +
                woodLength + " feet" ) ;
        Console.WriteLine( "The area of the glass is " +
                glassArea + " square metres" ) ;
    }
}
```

Code Sample 04 Complete GlazerCalc

This program fulfils our requirements. It will not use values incompatible with our specification. However, I would still not call it perfect. If our salesman gives a bad height the program simply limits the value and needs to be re-run, with the height having to be entered again.

What we would really like is a way that we can repeatedly fetch values for the width and height until we get one which fits. C# allows us to do this by providing looping constructions.

2.3.3 Loops

Conditional statements allow you to do something if a given condition is true. However often you want to repeat something while a particular condition is true, or a given number of times.

C# has three ways of doing this, depending on precisely what you are trying to do. Note that we get three methods not because we need three but because they make life easier when you write the program (a bit like an attachment to our chainsaw to allow it to perform a particular task more easily). Most of the skill of programming involves picking the right tool or attachment to do the job in hand. (the rest is finding out why the tool didn't do what you expected it to!).

In the case of our program we want to repeatedly get numbers in while we are getting invalid ones, i.e. giving a proper number should cause our loop to stop. This means that if we get the number correctly first time the loop will execute just once. You might think that I have pulled a fast one here; all I have done is change:

> Get values until you see one which is OK

into

> Get values while they are not OK

Part of the art of programming is changing the way that you think about the problem to suit the way that the programming language can be told to solve it.

do -- while loop

In the case of our little C# program we use the do -- while construction which looks like this:

```
do
    statement or block
while (condition) ;
```

This allows us to repeat a chunk of code until the condition at the end becomes false. Note that the test is performed after the statement or block, i.e. even if the test is bound to fail the statement is performed once.

A condition in this context is exactly the same as the condition in an if construction, raising the intriguing possibility of programs like:

```
using System;

class Forever
{
    public static void Main ()
    {
        do
                Console.WriteLine ( "Hello mum" ) ;
        while ( true );
    }
}
```

Code Sample 05 Infinite loop

This is a perfectly legal C# program. How long it will run for is an interesting question, the answer contains elements of human psychology, energy futures and cosmology, i.e. it will run until:

1. You get bored with it.
2. Your electricity runs out.
3. The universe implodes.

This is a chainsaw situation, not a powerful chainsaw situation. Just as it is possible with any old chainsaw to cut off your leg if you try really hard so it is possible to use any programming language to write a program which will never stop. It reminds me of my favourite shampoo instructions:

1. Wet Your Hair
2. Add Shampoo and Rub vigorously.
3. Rinse with warm water.
4. Repeat.

I often wonder how many people are still washing their hair at the moment?

while loop

Sometimes you want to decide whether or not to repeat the loop before you perform it. If you think about how the loop above works the test is done after the code to be repeated has been performed once. For our program this is exactly what we want, we need to ask for a value before we can decide whether or not it is valid. In order to be as flexible as possible C# gives us another form of the loop construction which allows us to do the test first:

```
while (condition)
    statement or block
```

Note that C# tries to reduce the number of keys you need to press to run the program by leaving out the word do. (if you put the do in the compiler will take great delight in giving you an error message - but you had already guessed that of course!).

for loop

Often you will want to repeat something a given number of times. The loop constructions we have given can be used to do this quite easily:

```
using System;

class WhileLoopInsteadOfFor
{
    public static void Main ()
    {
        int i ;
        i = 1 ;
        while ( i < 11 )
        {
                Console.WriteLine ( "Hello mum" ) ;
                i = i + 1 ;
        }
    }
}
```

Code Sample 06 While Loop instead of For

This useless program prints out `hello mum` 10 times. It does this by using a variable to control the loop. The variable is given an initial value (1) and then tested each time we go around the loop. The control variable is then increased for each pass through the statements. Eventually it will reach **11**, at which point the loop terminates and our program stops.

The variable which controls things is called the control variable, and is frequently given the name i.

C# provides a construction to allow you to set up a loop of this form all in one:

```
for ( setup ; finish test ; update )
{
    things we want to do a given
    number of times
}
```

We could use this to re-write the above program as:

```
using System;

class ForLoop
{
    public static void Main ()
    {
        int i ;
        for ( i = 1 ; i < 11 ; i = i + 1 )
        {
                Console.WriteLine ( "Hello mum" ) ;
        }
    }
}
```

Code Sample 07 For loop

The setup puts a value into the control variable which it will start with. The test is a condition which must be true for the `for` -- loop to continue. The update is the statement which is performed to update the control variable at the end of each loop. Note that the three elements are separated by semicolons. The precise sequence of events is as follows:

1. Put the setup value into the control variable.
2. Test to see if we have finished the loop yet and exit to the statement after the for loop if we have.
3. Perform the statements to be repeated.
4. Perform the update.
5. Repeat from step 2.

Writing a loop in this way is quicker and simpler than using a form of `while` because it keeps all the elements of the loop in one place instead of leaving them spread about the program. This means that you are less likely to forget to do something like give the control variable an initial value, or update it.

If you are so stupid as to mess around with the value of the control variable in the loop you can expect your program to do stupid things, i.e. if you put `i` back to `0` within the loop it will run forever. And serve you right.

Programmer's Point: Don't be clever/stupid

Some people like to show how clever they are by doing cunning things with the setup, condition and update statements, which can do things other than simple assignment, increment and test. Some programmers think they are very clever if they can do all the work "inside" the for part at the top and have an empty statement after it.

I call these people "the stupid people". There is rarely need for such convoluted code. When you are writing programs the two things which you should be worrying about are "How do I prove this works?" and "How easy is this code to understand?" Complicated code does not help you do either of these things.

Breaking Out of Loops

Sometimes you may want to escape from a loop whilst you are in the middle of it, i.e. your program may decide that there is no need or point to go on and wishes to leap out of the loop and continue the program from the statement after it.

You can do this with the `break` statement. This is a command to leave the loop immediately. Your program would usually make some form of decision to quit in this way. I find it most useful so that I can provide a "get the heck out of here" option in the middle of something, for example in the following program snippet the variable `aborted`, normally `false` becomes `true` when the loop has to be abandoned and the variable `runningOK`, normally `true`, becomes `false` when it is time to finish normally.

```
while (runningOK)
{
    complex stuff
    ....
    if (aborted)
    {
        break ;
    }
    ....
    more complex stuff
    ....
}
....
bit we get to if aborted becomes true
....
```

Note that we are using two variables as switches, they do not hold values as such; they are actually used to represent states within the program as it runs. This is a standard programming trick that you will find very useful.

You can break out of any of the three kinds of loop. In every case the program continues running at the statement after the last statement of the loop.

Programmer's Point: Be careful with your breaks

The break keyword smells a little like the dreaded goto statement, which programmers are often scared of. The goto is a special one that lets execution jump from one part of the program to another. For this reason the goto is condemned as a potentially dangerous and confusing device. The break statement lets you jump from any point in a loop to the statement just outside the loop. This means that if my program is at the statement immediately following the loop, there are a number of ways it could have got there; one for every break in the loop above. This can make the code harder to understand. The break construction is less confusing than the goto, but can still lead to problems. In this respect we advise you to exercise caution when using it.

Going back to the top of a loop

Every now and then you will want to go back to the top of a loop and do it all again. This happens when you have gone as far down the statements as you need to. C# provides the `continue` keyword which says something along the lines of:

Please do not go any further down this time round the loop. Go back to the top of the loop, do all the updating and stuff and go around if you are supposed to.

In the following program the bool variable `Done_All_We_Need_This_Time` is set true when we have gone as far down the loop as we need to.

```
for ( item = 1 ; item < Total_Items ; item=item+1 )
{
    .....
    item processing stuff
    ....
    if (Done_All_We_Need_This_Time) continue ;
    ....
    additional item processing stuff
    ....
}
```

The `continue` causes the program to re-run the loop with the next value of item if it is OK to do so. You can regard it as a move to step 2 in the list above.

More Complicated Decisions

We can now think about using a loop to test for a valid width or height. Essentially, we want to keep asking the user for a value until we get one which is OK; i.e. if you get a value which is larger than the maximum or smaller than the minimum ask for another. To do this we have to combine two tests to see if the value is OK. Our loop should continue to run if:

```
width > MAX_WIDTH or width < MIN_WIDTH
```

To perform this test we use one of the logical operators described above to write a condition which will be true if the width is invalid:

```
if ( width < MIN_WIDTH || width > MAX_WIDTH ) ..
```

Programmer's Point: Get used to flipping conditions

One of the things that you will have to come to terms with is the way that you often have to reverse the way you look at things. Rather than saying "Read me a valid number" you will have to say "Read numbers while they are not valid". This means that you will often be checking to find the thing that you don't want, rather than the thing that you do. Remember the notes about reversing conditions above when you write the code.

Complete Glazing Program

This is a complete solution to the problem that uses all the tricks discussed above.

```
using System;

class GlazerCalc
{
    static void Main()
    {
```

```
        double width, height, woodLength, glassArea;
        const double MAX_WIDTH = 5.0 ;
        const double MIN_WIDTH = 0.5 ;
        const double MAX_HEIGHT = 3.0 ;
        const double MIN_HEIGHT = 0.75 ;
        string widthString, heightString;

        do {
            Console.Write ( "Give the width of the window between " +
                    MIN_WIDTH + " and " + MAX_WIDTH + " :" );
            widthString = Console.ReadLine();
            width = double.Parse(widthString);
        } while ( width < MIN_WIDTH ||  width > MAX_WIDTH ) ;

        do {
            Console.Write ( "Give the height of the window between " +
                    MIN_HEIGHT + " and " + MAX_HEIGHT + " :" );
            heightString = Console.ReadLine();
            height = double.Parse(heightString);
        } while ( height < MIN_HEIGHT || height > MAX_HEIGHT );

        woodLength = 2 * ( width + height ) * 3.25 ;

        glassArea = 2 * ( width * height ) ;

        Console.WriteLine ( "The length of the wood is " +
                woodLength + " feet" ) ;
        Console.WriteLine( "The area of the glass is " +
                glassArea + " square metres" ) ;
    }
}
```

Code Sample 08 GlazerCalc with Loops

2.3.4 Operator Shorthand

So far, we have looked at operators which appear in expressions and work on two operands, e.g.

`window_count = window_count + 1`

In this case the operator is + and is operating on the variable `window_count` and the value 1. The purpose of the above statement is to add 1 to the variable `window_count`. However, it is a rather long-winded way of expressing this, both in terms of what we have to type and what the computer will actually do when it runs the program. C# allows us to be terser if we wish, the line:

`window_count++`

- would do the same thing. We can express ourselves more succinctly and the compiler can generate more efficient code because it now knows that what we are doing is adding one to a particular variable. The ++ is called a unary operator, because it works on just one operand. It causes the value in that operand to be increased by one. There is a corresponding -- operator which can be used to decrease (decrement) variables. You can see examples of this construction in the for loop definition in the example above.

The other shorthand which we use is when we add a particular value to a variable. We could put:

`house_cost = house_cost + window_cost;`

This is perfectly OK, but again is rather long winded. C# has some additional operators which allow us to shorten this to:

```
house_cost += window_cost;
```

The `+=` operator combines addition and the assignment, so that the value in `house_cost` is increased by `window_cost`. Some other shorthand operators are:

a += b	the value in a is replaced by a + b
a -= b	the value in a is replaced by a - b
a /= b	the value in a is replaced by a / b
a *= b	the value in a is replaced by a * b

There are other combination operators; I will leave you to find them!

Statements and Values

One of the really funky things about C# is that all statements return a value, which you can use in another statement if you like. Most of the time you will ignore this value, which is OK, but sometimes it can be very useful, particularly when we get around to deciding things (see later). In order to show how this is done, consider the following:

```
i = (j=0);
```

This is perfectly legal (and perhaps even sensible) C#. It has the effect of setting both i and j to 0. An assignment statement always returns the value which is being assigned (i.e. the bit on the right of the gozzinta). This value can then be used as a value or operand. If you do this you are advised to put brackets around the statement which is being used as a value, this makes the whole thing much clearer for both you and the compiler!

When you consider operators like ++ there is possible ambiguity, in that you do not know if you get the value before or after the increment. C# provides a way of getting either value, depending on which effect you want. You determine whether you want to see the value before or after the sum by the position of the ++ :

    i++   means "Give me the value before the increment"

    ++i   means "Give me the value after the increment"

As an example:

```
int i = 2, j ;
j = ++i ;
```

- would make j equal to 3. The other special operators, += etc. all return the value after the operator has been performed.

Programmer's Point: Always strive for simplicity

Don't get carried away with this. The fact that you can produce code like:

```
height = width = speed = count = size = 0 ;
```

- does not mean that you should. Nowadays when I am writing a program my first consideration is whether or not the program is easy to understand. I don't think that the statement above is very easy to follow – so irrespective of how much more efficient it is, I still don't do it.

2.3.5 Neater Printing

If you have run any of the above programs you will by now have discovered that the way in which numbers are printed leaves much to be desired. Integers seem to come out OK, but floating point numbers seem to have a mind of their own. To get around this C# provides a slightly different way in which numbers can be printed. This provides more flexibility, and is also somewhat easier to use if you are printing a large number of values.

Note that the way that a number is printed does not affect how it is stored by the program, it just tells the printing method how it is supposed to be printed.

Using Placeholders in Print Strings

A placeholder just marks the place where the value is to be printed. Consider:

```
int i = 150 ;
double f = 1234.56789 ;
Console.WriteLine ( "i: {0} f: {1}", i, f ) ;
Console.WriteLine ( "i: {1} f: {0}", f, i ) ;
```

This would print out:

```
i: 150 f: 1234.56789
i: 150 f: 1234.56789
```

The {n} part of the string says "parameter number n, counting from 0". In the second write statement I have swapped the order of the numbers, but since I've swapped the order of the parameters too the output is the same.

If I do something mad, for example use {99} to try and get the 99th parameter, the `WriteLine` method will fail with an error. This error will **not** be picked up by the compiler however, the program will fail when it runs.

Adjusting real number precision

Placeholders can have formatting information added to them:

```
int i = 150 ;
double f = 1234.56789 ;
Console.WriteLine ( "i: {0:0} f: {1:0.00}", i, f ) ;
```

This would print out:

```
i: 150 f: 1234.57
```

The 0 characters stand for one or more digits. When placed after a decimal point they can be used to control the number of decimal places which are used to express a value. Note that doing this means that if the number is an integer it is printed out as `12.00`.

Specifying the number of printed digits

I can specify a particular number of digits by putting in a given number of zeroes:

```
int i = 150 ;
double f = 1234.56789 ;
Console.WriteLine ( "i: {0:0000} f: {1:00000.00}", i, f );
```

This would print out:

```
i: 0150 f: 01234.57
```

Note that if I do this I get leading zeroes printed out, which is useful if you are printing things like cheques.

Really Fancy Formatting

If you want really fancy levels of control you can use the # character. A # in the format string means "put a digit here if you have one":

```
int i = 150 ;
double f = 1234.56789 ;
Console.WriteLine ( "i: {0:#,##0} f: {1:##,##0.00}", i, f );
```

I have used the # character to get my thousands printed out with commas:

```
i: 150 f: 1,234.57
```

Note that the formatter only uses the # characters and commas that it needs. The value 150 does not have a thousands digit so it and the comma are left out. Note also though that I have included a 0 as the smallest digit. This is so that when I print the value 0 I actually get a value printed, otherwise when I print zero I get nothing on the page.

Printing in columns

Finally I can add a width value to the print layout information. This is very useful if you want to print material in columns:

```
int i = 150 ;
double f = 1234.56789 ;
Console.WriteLine ( "i: {0,10:0} f: {1,15:0.00}", i, f ) ;
Console.WriteLine ( "i: {0,10:0} f: {1,15:0.00}", 0, 0 ) ;
```

This would produce the output:

```
i:        150 f:         1234.57
i:          0 f:            0.00
```

The integer value is printed in a column 10 characters wide, and the double is printed in a 15 character wide column. At the moment the output is right justified, if I want the numbers left justified I make the width negative:

```
int i = 150 ;
double f = 1234.56789 ;
Console.WriteLine ( "i: {0,-10:0} f: {1,-15:0.00}", i, f ) ;
Console.WriteLine ( "i: {0,-10:0} f: {1,-15:0.00}", 0, 0 ) ;
```

This would produce the output:

```
i: 150        f: 1234.57
i: 0          f: 0.00
```

Note that this justification would work even if you were printing a string rather than a number, so if you want to print columns of words you can use this technique to do it.

You can specify the print width of any item, even a piece of text, which makes printing in columns very easy.

3 Creating Programs

In this chapter we will build on our programming abilities to make programs that are broken down into manageable chunks and find out how a program can store and manipulate large amounts of data using arrays.

3.1 Methods

We have already come across the methods `Main`, `WriteLine` and `ReadLine`. `Main` is the method we write which is where our program starts. `WriteLine` and `ReadLine` were provided by the creators of C# to give us a way of displaying text and reading information from the user.

This is what methods are all about. Your programs will contain methods that you create to solve parts of the problem and they will also use methods that have been provided by other people. In this section we are going to consider why methods are useful and how you can create your own.

3.1.1 The Need for Methods

In the glazing program above we spend a lot of time checking the values of inputs and making sure that they are in certain ranges. We have exactly the same piece of code to check widths and heights. If we added a third thing to read, for example frame thickness, we would have to copy the code a third time. This is not very efficient; it makes the program bigger and harder to write. What we would like to do is write the checking code once and then use it at each point in the program. To do this you need to define a method to do the work for you.

Method and Laziness

We have already established that a good programmer is creatively lazy. One of the tenets of this is that a programmer will try to do a given job once and once only.

Up until now all our programs have been in a single method. The method is the block of code which follows the main part in our program. However, C# lets us create other methods which are used when our program runs. Methods give us two new weapons:

- We can use methods to let us re-use a piece of code which we have written.
- We can also use methods to break down a large task into a number of smaller ones.

We will need both of these when we start to write larger programs. Again, as with lots of features of the C# language, methods don't actually make things possible, but they do help with the organisation of our programs.

Essentially you take a block of code and give it a name. Then you can refer to this block of code to do something for you. As a silly example:

```csharp
using System ;

class MethodDemo
{
    static void doit ()
    {
        Console.WriteLine ("Hello");
```

```
    }
    public static void Main ()
    {
        doit();
        doit();
    }
}
```

Code Sample 09 Simple Method

In the main method I make two calls of `doit`. Each time I call the method the code in the block which is the body of the method is executed. In this case it contains a single statement which prints `"Hello"` on the console. The result of running the above program would be:

```
Hello
Hello
```

So, we can use methods to save us from writing the same code twice. We simply put the code inside a method body and then call it when we need it.

3.1.2 Parameters

At this point methods are useful because they let us use the same block of statements at many points in the program. However, they become more useful if we allow them to have parameters.

A parameter is a means of passing a value into a method call. The method is given the data to work on. As an example, consider the code below:

```
using System ;

class MethodDemo
{
    static void silly ( int i )
    {
        Console.WriteLine ( "i is : " + i ) ;
    }

    public static void Main ()
    {
        silly ( 101 ) ;
        silly ( 500 ) ;
    }
}
```

Code Sample 10 Method with parameters

The method `silly` has a single integer parameter. Within the block of code which is the body of this method we can use the parameter `i` as an integer variable. When the method starts the value supplied for the parameter is copied into it. This means that when the program runs we get output like this:

```
i is : 101
i is : 500
```

3.1.3 Return values

A method can also return a value to the caller. You have already used this feature, the methods `ReadLine` and `Parse` both return results that we have used in our programs:

```
using System ;

class ReturnDemo
```

```
    {
        static int sillyReturnPlus ( int i )
        {
            i = i + 1;
            Console.WriteLine ( "i is : " + i ) ;
            return i;
        }

        public static void Main ()
        {
            int res;
            res = sillyReturnPlus (5);
            Console.WriteLine ( "res is : " + res ) ;
        }
    }
```

Code Sample 11 Method return with plus

The method `sillyReturnPlus` takes the value of the parameter and returns it plus one.

The value that a method returns can be used anywhere in a program where a variable of that type could be used, in other words a call of `sillyReturnPlus` can take the place of an integer. See if you can work out what this code would display:

```
res = sillyReturnPlus (5) + sillyReturnPlus (7) + 1;
Console.WriteLine ( "res is : " + res ) ;
```

It is actually OK to ignore the value returned by a method, but this is actually a rather pointless thing to do:

```
sillyReturnPlus (5); // will compile but do nothing useful
```

3.1.4 Arguments and Parameters

When you read about C# you will find the words parameter and argument used interchangeably. This is actually not quite right. Understanding the difference will make C# documentation and error messages seem more sensible and might even give you a feeling of superiority over lessor programmers who don't know the truth.

A **parameter** is the special kind of variable that is defined in the method header and used inside that method to represent the value that was fed into the method call.

```
static int sillyReturnPlus (int i)
{
    i = i + 1;
    Console.WriteLine ( "i is : " + i ) ;
    return i;
}
```

The method `sillyReturnPlus` above has a single parameter, which is of type integer and has the identifier `i`.

An **argument** is the value that is supplied to the method when it is called.

```
sillyReturnPlus(99);
```

In the statement above the argument is the value 99. So, if I do something stupid:

```
sillyReturnPlus("banjo");
```

- I get the following error message when I try to compile the code:

```
Error    2    Argument 1: cannot convert from 'string' to 'int'
```

This is telling me that the argument (the thing that was put between the brackets in the call of the method) does not agree with the definition of the parameter (which has been defined as an integer).

3.1.5 A Useful Method

Now we can start to write genuinely useful methods:

```
static double readValue (
    string prompt, // prompt for the user
    double low,    // lowest allowed value
    double high    // highest allowed value
    )
{
    double result = 0;
    do
    {
        Console.WriteLine (prompt +
            " between " + low +
            " and " + high );
        string resultString = Console.ReadLine ();
        result = double.Parse(resultString);
    } while ( (result < low) || (result > high) );
    return result ;
}
```

The `readValue` method is told the prompt to use and the lowest and the highest allowed values. It can then be used to read values and make sure that they are in range. We can use this method to read anything and make sure that value supplied is within a particular range.

```
double windowWidth = readValue (
    "Enter width of window: ", MIN_WIDTH, MAX_WIDTH) ;

double age = readValue ( "Enter your age: ", 0, 70) ;
```

The first call of `readValue` gets the width of a window. The second reads an age between 0 and 70.

```
using System;

class UsefulMethod
{
    static double readValue(
        string prompt, // prompt for the user
        double low,    // lowest allowed value
        double high    // highest allowed value
        )
    {
        double result = 0;
        do
        {
            Console.WriteLine(prompt +
                " between " + low +
                " and " + high);
            string resultString = Console.ReadLine();
            result = double.Parse(resultString);
        } while ((result < low) || (result > high));
        return result;
    }

    const double MAX_WIDTH = 5.0;
    const double MIN_WIDTH = 0.5;
```

```
        public static void Main()
        {
            double windowWidth = readValue(
                "Enter width of window: ", MIN_WIDTH, MAX_WIDTH);

            Console.WriteLine("Width: " + windowWidth);

            double age = readValue("Enter your age: ", 0, 70);

            Console.WriteLine("Age: " + age);
        }
    }
```

Code Sample 12 Using a Useful Method

Programmer's Point: Design with methods

Methods are a very useful part of the programmer's toolkit. They form an important part of the development process. Once you have worked out what the customer wants and gathered your metadata you can start thinking about how you are going to break the program down into methods. Often you find that as you write the code you are repeating a particular action. If you do this you should consider taking that action and moving it into a method. There are two reasons why this is a good idea:

1: It saves you writing the same code twice.

2: If a fault is found in the code you only have to fix it in one place.

Moving code around and creating methods is called *refactoring*. This will be an important part of the Software Engineering we do later.

3.1.6 Named and Optional Arguments

When you create a method which has parameters you tell the compiler the name and type of each parameter in turn:

```
static double readValue (
    string prompt, // prompt for the user
    double low,    // lowest allowed value
    double high    // highest allowed value
    )
{
    ...
}
```

The method `readValue` has been defined as having three parameters. A call of the method must have three argument values: a prompt, a low value and a high value.

This means that the following call of `readValue` would be rejected by the compiler:

```
x = readValue(25, 100, "Enter your age");
```

This is because the prompt string must go first, followed by the low and high limits for the value to be read.

If you want to make method calls and not have to worry about the order of the arguments you can name each one:

```
x = readValue(low:25, high:100, prompt: "Enter your age");
```

Now the compiler is using the name of each argument, rather than its positon in the list. This has the useful side effect of making it much clearer to someone reading your code the exact meaning of each argument value.

Programmer's Point: I love using named arguments

I love this feature of C#. It makes programs clearer and it also means you don't have to scratch your head and wonder if the low value is given before the high value when you create the method call.

Optional Arguments

Sometimes the value of an argument might have a sensible default value. For example, if we just wanted the `readValue` to fetch a value from the user and not display a prompt we could do this by providing an empty string:

```
x = readValue(low:25, high:100, prompt: "");
```

However, this is a bit messy. Instead we can change the definition of the method to give a default value for the prompt parameter:

```
static double readValue (
    double low,           // lowest allowed value
    double high,          // highest allowed value
    string prompt = "",   // optional prompt for the user
    )
{
    ...
}
```

We can now call the method and leave the prompt out if we like:

```
x = readValue(25, 100);
```

When the method runs the prompt will be set to an empty string if the user doesn't provide a value.

Note that I've had to rearrange the order of the parameters so that the prompt is the last parameter. Optional parameters must be provided after all the required ones.

There is a potential problem here however. Consider this method:

```
static double readValue(
    double low,      // lowest allowed value
    double high,     // highest allowed value
    string prompt = "", // optional prompt for the user
    string error = ""   // optional error message
)
{
    ...
}
```

This has two optional parameters, a prompt and an error message. The idea is that the user of the method can give a custom error message if the user gives an invalid age. I can now make a call of the method like this:

```
x = readValue(25, 100, "Enter your age", "Age out of range");
```

If I don't want a prompt or a custom error message I can leave them out. But if I just supply one argument it is mapped onto first one in the sequence of optional parameters. In other words, I can't supply a custom error message without providing a custom prompt.

The way to get round this (as I'm sure you have figured out) is to identify the optional parameters that you want to use by their name.

```
x = readValue(25, 100, error:"Age out of range");
```

This call of `readValue` would use the default prompt, but would have a custom error message.

Programmer's Point: I'm not so keen on default values for parameters

By now I hope you are thinking that programming is as much a craft as anything else. This means that we can look at certain behaviours and consider them in the context of the craft of writing code, in the same way as someone wanting to make a chess piece would worry about a suggestion that they might like to use a chainsaw to do it.

Default parameter values can hide information from users of your methods. They can provide "secret switches" that make things work in a particular way and which a user might need to know about to make something work properly. If you do use them, make good use of comments in both the method and the code that uses it, so that someone reading your code also understands what the default behaviours do and how these can be modified.

3.1.7 Parameter Passing by Value

A method is very good for getting work done, but it can be a bit limited because of the way that it works. For example, if I want to write a method which reads in the name and the age of a person I have a problem. From what we have seen of methods, they can only return one value. So I could write a method which returns the name of a person, or write one which returns an age. But I can't write a method that returns both values at the same time as a method can only return one value. As you will find out when you try, changing the value of a parameter does not change the value of the thing passed in. This is because, unless you specify otherwise, only the **value** of an argument is passed into a call to a method.

So, what do I mean by "passing parameters by value". Consider:

```
static void addOne ( int i )
{
    i = i + 1;
    Console.WriteLine ( "i is : " + i ) ;
}
```

The method `addOne` adds one to the parameter; prints the result out and then returns:

```
int test = 20 ;
addOne(test);
Console.WriteLine ( "test is : " + test ) ;
```

The piece of C# above calls the method with the variable `test` as the argument. When it runs it prints out the following:

```
i is : 21
test is : 20
```

It is **very important** that you understand what is happening here. The **value** of `test` is being used in the call of `addOne`. The program works out the result of the expression to be passed into the method call as an argument. It then passes this value into the call. This means that you can write calls like:

```
test = 20 ;
addOne(test + 99);
```

This would print out:

```
i is : 120
```

Pass by value is very safe, because nothing the method does can affect variables in the code which calls it. However, it is a limitation when we want to create a method which returns more than one value.

3.1.8 Parameter Passing By Reference

Fortunately, C# provides a way that, rather than sending the value of a variable into a method, a reference to that variable is supplied instead. Inside the method, rather than using the value of the variable the reference is used to get the actual variable itself. Effectively the thing that is passed into the method is the position or address of the variable in memory, rather than the content of the variable.

It is very important that you understand how references work. If you don't understand these you can't call yourself a proper programmer!

So, rather than passing in "20" in our above call the compiler will generate code which passes in "memory location 5023" instead (assuming that the variable test is actually stored at 5023). This memory location is used by the method, instead of the value. In other words:

"If you pass by reference, changes to the parameter change the variable whose reference you passed"

If you find references confusing you are not alone. However, we use them in real life all the time with no problems. If you say "Deliver the carpet to 23 High Street." you are giving the delivery man a reference. Using a reference in a program is just the same. The program will say "Get the value from location 5023" rather than "The value is 1".

Consider the code:

```
static void addOneToRefParam ( ref int i )
{
    i = i + 1;
    Console.WriteLine ( "i is : " + i ) ;
}
```

Note that the keyword `ref` has been added to the information about the parameter.

```
test = 20 ;
addOneToRefParam(ref test);
Console.WriteLine ( "test is : " + test ) ;
```

The code above makes a call to the new method, and also has the word `ref` in front of the parameter. In this case the output is as follows:

```
i is : 21
test is : 21
```

In this case the method call has made changes to the content of the variable. Note that C# is careful about when a parameter is a reference. You have to put the word `ref` in the method heading and also in the call of the method.

Programmer's Point: Document your side-effects

A change by a method to something around it is called a *side effect* of the method. In other words, when someone calls our addOneToRefParam method, it is going to have the "side effect" of changing something outside the method itself (namely the value of the parameter passed by reference). Generally speaking you have to be careful with side effects, as someone reading your program has to know that your method has made changes in this way.

3.1.9 Passing Parameter values as "out" references

When you pass a parameter as a reference you are giving the method complete control of it. Sometimes you don't want this. Instead you want to just allow the method to change the variable. This is the case when we want to read in the name and age of a user. The original value of the parameters is of no interest to the method. Instead it just wants to deliver results to them. In this case I can replace the `ref` with the keyword out:

```
static void readPerson ( out string name, out int age )
{
    name = readString ( "Enter your name : " ) ;
    age = readInt ( "Enter your age : ", 0, 100 ) ;
}
```

The method `readPerson` reads the name and the age of a person. Note that it uses two more methods that I have created, `readString` and `readInt`.

I can call `readPerson` as follows:

```
string name ;
int age ;
readPerson ( out name, out age ) ;
```

Note that I must use the out keyword in the call of the method as well.

The `readPerson` method will read the person and deliver the information into the two variables.

Programmer's Point: Languages can help programmers

The out keyword is a nice example of how the design of a programming language can make programs safer and easier to write. It makes sure that a programmer can't use the value of the parameter in the method. It also allows the compiler to make sure that somewhere in the method the output parameters are assigned values. This is very useful. It means that if I mark the parameters as out I **must** have given them a value for the program to compile. This makes it harder for me to get the program wrong, as I am protected against forgetting to do that part of the job.

3.1.10 Method Libraries

The first thing that a good programmer will do when they start writing code is to create a set of libraries which can be used to make their job easier. In the code above I have written a couple of library methods which I can use to read values of different types:

```
static string readString ( string prompt )
{
    string result ;
    do
    {
        Console.Write ( prompt ) ;
        result = Console.ReadLine ();
    } while ( result == "" ) ;
    return result ;
}

static int readInt ( string prompt, int low, int high )
{
    int result ;

    do
```

```csharp
    {   string intString = readString (prompt) ;
        result = int.Parse(intString);
    } while ( ( result < low ) || ( result > high ) );

    return result;
}
```

The `readString` method will read text and make sure that the user does not enter empty text. The `readInt` method reads a number within a particular range. Note how I have rather cleverly used my `readString` method in my `readInt` one, so that the user can't enter an empty string when a number is required. We can use the methods as follows:

```csharp
string name;
name = readString( "Enter your name : " );

int age;
age = readInt ( "Enter your age : ", 0, 100);
```

I could add methods to read floating point values as well. In fact one thing I tend to do when working on a project is create little library of useful methods like these which I can use.

```csharp
using System;

class MethodLibraries
{
    static string readString(string prompt)
    {
        string result;
        do
        {
            Console.Write(prompt);
            result = Console.ReadLine();
        } while (result == "");
        return result;
    }

    static int readInt(string prompt, int low, int high)
    {
        int result;

        do
        {
            string intString = readString(prompt);
            result = int.Parse(intString);
        } while ((result < low) || (result > high));

        return result;
    }

    public static void Main()
    {
        string name;
        name = readString("Enter your name : ");
        Console.WriteLine("Name: " + name);

        int age;
        age = readInt("Enter your age : ", 0, 100);
        Console.WriteLine("Age: " + age);
    }
}
```

Code Sample 13 Using Method Libraries

Programmer's Point: Always consider the failure behaviours

Whenever you write a method you should give some thought to the ways that it could fail. If the method involves talking to the user it is possible that the user may wish to abandon the method, or that the user does something that may cause it to fail. You need to consider whether or not the method should deal with the problem itself or pass the error onto the system which tried to use it.

If the method deals with the error itself this may lead to problems because the user may have no way of cancelling a command. If the method passes the error on to the code which called it you have to have a method by which an error condition can be delivered to the caller. I often solve this problem by having my methods return a code value. If the return value is 0 this means that the method returned correctly. If the return value is non-zero this means that the method did not work and the value being returned is an error which identifies what went wrong. This adds another dimension to program design, in that you also have to consider how the code that you write can fail, as well as making sure that it does the required job! We are going to discuss error management later

3.2 Variables and Scope

We have seen that when we want to store a quantity in our program we can create a variable to hold this information. The C# compiler makes sure that the correctly sized chunk of memory is used to hold the value and it also makes sure that we only ever use that value correctly. The C# compiler also looks after the part of a program within which a variable has an existence. This is called the *scope* of a variable.

3.2.1 Scope and blocks

We have already seen that a block is a number of statements which are enclosed in curly brackets. Any block can contain any number of *local* variables, i.e. variables which are local to that block.

The scope of a local variable is the block within which the variable is declared. As far as the C# language is concerned you can declare a variable at any point in the block, but you **must** declare it before you use it. When the execution of the program moves outside a block any local variables which are declared in the block are automatically discarded. The methods that we have created have often contained local variables; the variable `result` in the `readInt` method is local to the method block.

3.2.2 Nested Blocks

We have seen that in C# the programmer can create blocks inside blocks. Each of these *nested* blocks can have its own set of local variables:

```
{
    int i ;
    {
        int j ;
    }
}
```

The variable `j` has the scope of the inner block. This means that only statements in the inner block can use this variable. In other words the code:

```
{
    int i ;
    {
        int j ;
    }
```

```
        j = 99 ;
    }
```

- would cause an error, as the variable j does not exist at this point in the program.

In order to keep you from confusing yourself by creating two versions of a variable with the same name, C# has an additional rule about the variables in the inner blocks:

```
{
    int i ;
    {
        int i ;
    }
}
```

This is not a valid program because C# does not let a variable in an inner block have the same name as one in an outer block. This is because inside the inner block there is the possibility that you may use the "inner" version of i when you intend to use the outer one. In order to remove this possibility the compiler refuses to allow this. Note that this is in contrast to the situation in other languages, for example C++, where this behaviour is allowed.

It is however perfectly acceptable to reuse a variable name in successive blocks because in this situation there is no way that one variable can be confused with another.

```
{
    int i ;
}
{
    int i ;
    {
        int j ;
    }
}
```

The first incarnation of i has been destroyed before the second, so this code is OK.

For loop local variables

A special kind of variable can be used when you create a for loop construction. This allows you to declare a control variable which exists for the duration of the loop itself:

```
for ( int i = 0 ; i < 10 ; i = i + 1 )
{
    Console.WriteLine ( "Hello" ) ;
}
```

The variable i is declared and initialized at the start of the for loop and only exists for the duration of the block itself.

3.2.3 Data Member in classes

Local variables are all very well, but they disappear when the program execution leaves the block where they are declared. We often need to have variables that exist outside the methods in a class.

Variables Local to a Method

Consider the following code:

```
class LocalExample
{
```

```
        static void OtherMethod ()
        {
            local = 99; // this will not compile
        }

        static void Main ()
        {
            int local = 0;
            Console.WriteLine ("local is :" + local);
        }
    }
```

Code Sample 14 Non-compiling local variable

The variable `local` is declared and used within the `Main` method, and can't be used anywhere else. If a statement in `OtherMethod` tries to use `local` the program will fail to compile.

Variables which are Data Members of a Class

If I want to allow two methods in a class to share a variable I will have to make the variable a member of the class. This means declaring it outside the methods in the class:

```
class MemberExample
{

    // the variable member is part of the class
    static int member = 0 ;

    static void OtherMethod ()
    {
        member = 99;
    }

    static void Main ()
    {
        Console.WriteLine ("member is : " + member);
        OtherMethod();
        Console.WriteLine ("member is now : " + member);
    }
}
```

Code Sample 15 Using a member variable

The variable `member` is now part of the class `MemberExample`, and so the `Main` method and `OtherMethod` can both use this variable. The program above would print out:

```
member is : 0
member is now : 99
```

This is because the call of `OtherMethod` would change the value of `member` to 99 when it runs.

Class variables are very useful if you want to have a number of methods "sharing" a set of data. For example, if you were creating a program to play chess it would be sensible to make the variable that stores the board into a member of the class. Then the methods that read the player move, display the board, and calculate the computer move could all use the same board information.

Static class members

Note that I have made the data member of the class static, so that it is part of the class and not an instance of the class. This is not something to worry about just now; we will investigate the precise meaning of static later on. For now you just have to remember to put in the `static` keyword, otherwise your program will not compile.

One common programming mistake is to confuse `static` with `const`. Marking a variable as `const` means "the value cannot be changed". Marking a variable with `static` means "the variable is part of the class and is always present". If it helps you can think of static as something which is always with us, like the background static noise on your radio when you tune it off station. Alternatively you can think of it as stationary, and therefore not going anywhere.

Programmer's Point: Plan your variable use

You should plan your use of variables in your programs. You should decide which variables are only required for use in local blocks and which should be members of the class. Bear in mind that if you make a variable a member of the class it can be used by any method in that class (which increases the chances of something bad happening to it). I am very careful to keep the number of member variables in a class to the minimum possible and use local variables if I only need to store the value for a small part of the code.

3.3 Arrays

We now know how to create programs that can read values in, calculate results and print them. Our programs can also make decisions based on the values supplied by the user and also repeat actions a given number of times.

It turns out that you now know about nearly all the language features that are required to implement every program that has ever been written. Only one thing is missing, and that is the ability to create programs which store large amounts of data. Arrays are one way to do this, and we are going to find out about them next.

3.3.1 Why We Need Arrays

Your fame as a programmer is now beginning to spread far and wide. The next person to come and see you is the chap in charge of the local cricket team. He would like you to write a program for him to help him analyse the performance of his players. When a game of cricket is played each member of the team will score a particular number of runs. What the customer wants is quite simple; given a set of player scores from a game he wants a list of those scores in ascending order.

The next thing you do is refine the specification and add some metadata. You discuss sensible ranges (no player can score less than 0 or more than 1000 runs in a game). You draw out a rough version of what the program will accept, and what information it will print out. You decide how much money you are going to be paid, and when. Finally, to make this the perfect project, you agree on when the software must be finished and how you are going to demonstrate it to your new customer and you write all this down and get it signed. With all this sorted, all you have to do now is write the actual program itself. "This is easy" you think. The first thing to do is define how the data is to be stored:

```
int score1, score2, score3, score4, score5, score6, score7,
    score8, score9, score10, score11 ;
```

Now you can start putting the data into each variable. You can use your new number reading methods for this:

```
score1 = readInt ( "Player 1 score : ", 0,1000);
score2 = readInt ( "Player 2 score : ", 0,1000);
score3 = readInt ( "Player 3 score : ", 0,1000);
score4 = readInt ( "Player 4 score : ", 0,1000);
```

```
    score5 = readInt ( "Player 5 score : ", 0,1000);
    score6 = readInt ( "Player 6 score : ", 0,1000);
    score7 = readInt ( "Player 7 score : ", 0,1000);
    score8 = readInt ( "Player 9 score : ", 0,1000);
    score10 = readInt ( "Player 10 score : ", 0,1000);
    score11 = readInt ( "Player 11 score : ", 0,1000);
```

All we have to do next is sort them..... Hmmmm..... This is awful! There seems to be no way of doing it. Just deciding whether `score1` is the largest value would take an `if` construction with 10 comparisons! Clearly there has to be a better way of doing this, after all, we know that computers are very good at sorting this kind of thing.

C# provides us with a thing called an *array*. An array allows us to declare a whole row of a particular kind of box. We can then use things called *subscripts* to indicate which box in the row that we want to use. Consider the following:

```
using System;
class ArrayDemo
{
    public static void Main ()
    {
        int [] scores = new int [11] ;
        for ( int i=0; i<11; i=i+1)
        {
            scores [i] = readInt ( "Score : ", 0,1000);
        }
    }
}
```

The `int [] scores` part tells the compiler that we want to create an array variable. You can think of this as a tag which can be made to refer to a given array.

The bit which makes the array itself is the `new int [11]`. When C# sees this it says "Aha! What we need here is an array". It then gets some pieces of wood and makes a long thin box with 11 compartments in it, each large enough to hold a single integer. It then paints the whole box red - because boxes which can hold integers are red. It then gets a piece of rope and ties the tag scores to this box. If you follow the rope from the scores tag you reach the array box. Actually, it probably doesn't use wood or rope, but you should get a picture of what is going on here.

3.3.2 Array Elements

Each compartment in the box is called an element. In the program you identify which element you mean by putting its number in square brackets [ ] after the array name. This part is called the *subscript*. Note that the thing which makes arrays so wonderful is the fact that you can specify an element by using a variable. In fact you can use any expression which returns an integer result as a subscript, i.e.

```
    scores [i+1]
```

- is quite OK. (as long as you don't fall off the end of the array). When an array is created all the elements in the array are set to 0.

Array Element Numbering

C# numbers the boxes starting at 0. This means that you specify the element at the start of the array by giving the subscript 0. There is consequently no element `scores [11]`. If you look at the part of the program which reads the values into the array you will see that we only count from 0 to 10. This is very important. An attempt to go outside the array bounds of `scores` cause your program to fail as it runs. If you find this confusing; "The first element has the subscript 0" then the best way to regard the subscript is as the distance down the array you have to travel to get to the element that you need.

One thing adding to this confusion is the fact that this numbering scheme is not the same in other languages. Visual Basic numbers array elements starting at 1. I'm sorry about this; it just goes to show that not everything about programming is consistent.

3.3.3 Large Arrays

The real power of arrays comes from our being able to use a variable to specify the required element. By running the variable through a range of values we can then scan through an array with a very small program; indeed to change the program to read in 1000 scores we only have to make a couple of changes:

```
using System;
class ArrayDemo
{
    public static void Main ()
    {
        int [] scores = new int [1000] ;
        for ( int i=0; i<1000; i=i+1)
        {
            scores [i] = readInt ( "Score : ", 0,1000);
        }
    }
}
```

The variable i now ranges from 0 to 999, vastly increasing the amount of data we are storing.

Managing Array Sizes

A good trick when working with arrays is to make use of constant variables to hold the size of the array. This has two significant benefits:

- It makes the program easier to understand
- It makes the program easier to change

A constant variable is given a value when it is declared. This value can then only be read by the program, never updated. So, if I wanted to write a scores program that could be easily changed for any size of team I could write:

```
using System;
class ArrayDemo
{
    public static void Main ()
    {
        const int SCORE_SIZE = 1000;
        int [] scores = new int [SCORE_SIZE] ;
        for ( int i=0; i < SCORE_SIZE; i=i+1)
        {
            scores [i] = readInt ( "Score : ", 0,1000);
        }
    }
}
```

Code Sample 16 Using an Array

The variable SCORE_SIZE is an integer which has been marked with const. This means that it cannot be changed by statements within the program. It will never have a value other than 1000. There is a convention that constants of this kind are given in LARGE LETTERS with an underscore between words.

Everywhere I previously used a fixed value to represent the size of the array I now use my constant instead. This means that if the size of the team changes I just have to change the value assigned when the constant is declared and then re-compile the program. The other benefit of this is that the for loop now looks a lot more meaningful. Since the value of i is now going from 0 to SCORE_SIZE it is more obvious to the reader that it is working through the score array.

3.3.4 Creating a Two Dimensional Array

However, sometimes we want to hold more than just a row. Sometimes we want a grid. We can do this by creating a TWO DIMENSIONAL array. You can think of this as an "array of arrays" if you like (but only if this doesn't make your head hurt). For example, to hold the board for a game of noughts and crosses (tic tac toe) we could use:

```
int [,] board = new int [3,3];
board [1,1] = 1;
```

This looks very like our one dimensional array, but there are some important differences. The [,] now has a comma. The presence of a comma implies something each side of it. This means that the array now has two dimensions, rather than just one. So when we give the size of the board we must supply two dimensions rather than just one. Then, when we want to specify an element we have to give two subscript values. In the code above I've set the value in the middle square (the best one) to 1.

You can think of a 2D array as a grid:

	0	1	2
0	0	0	0
1	0	1	0
2	0	0	0

The first subscript could be used to specify which row and the second which column. The diagram above shows the board with the best move already taken.

In the example above the array is square (i.e. the same dimension across as up). We can change this if we like:

```
int [,] board = new int [3,10];
```

- but this would make it rather hard to play a sensible game on.

3.3.5 Arrays and Lookup Tables

Arrays make great lookup tables. They provide a neat way of going from a number to something else. For example, you might want to print out the name of the month, from the month value. You could do this by using tests:

```
int monthNo = 1;
string monthName;

if (monthNo == 1)
    monthName = "January";

if (monthNo == 2)
    monthName = "February";
```

However, this would be tedious to write. A neater way would be to use an array which you could call `monthNames`. Then we would could do something like this:

```
monthName = monthNames[monthNo];
```

For this to work we would have to make sure that each of the elements in the `monthNames` array would hold the name of the array.

```
string[] monthNames = new string[13];
```

So we would have to do some setting up before we use the lookup table:

```
monthNames[1] = "January";
monthNames[2] = "February";
```

Programmer's Point: Sometimes it is OK to "waste" array element 0

If you have followed the text carefully up to now you will have spotted something odd here. I have said that arrays are indexed starting at 0, in other words the element at the very start of the `monthNames` array will have the subscript of zero, which means I should really be putting the string "January" into `monthNames[0]`. This is true if I want to make the most efficient use of the storage, but it does make my program harder to understand, in that whenever I use the array to decode a month value (which of course goes from 1 to 12) I will have to subtract 1 from the value. In this case I reckon it is defensible to create an array which is one larger than required (so that the subscripts range from 0 to 12) and then ignore the element at the start.

A programming purist might point out that if a program tries to use the element at the base of the names array (the one with subscript 0) it is in danger of displaying an invalid month value. We can guard against this by making that element into a null reference.

```
monthNames[0] = null;
```

This means that if the code ever tries to use this element in the array it will throw an exception and stop. If the purist still continues to complain that this might lead to programs misbehaving we can ask them to consider the effect of a programmer leaving off the "month minus one" part when they decode a month value. In this case we would have the wrong month name printed and the program would continue to run. I'd much rather have a program explode in a shower of sparks and flames than silently do the wrong thing.

Of course, at the moment it looks like we have exchanged one piece of tediousness (doing lots of tests to get the month string) with another (initialising lots of array elements). However, it turns out that C# has a really neat way that you can set up the elements in an array.

```
string[] monthNames = new string[]
{
    null, // null element for non existent month 0
    "January", "February", "March", "April",
    "May", "June", "July", "August",
    "September", "October", "November", "December"
};
```

A program can contain a list of initialisation values which are then used to create an array with the required content. Note that the initialisation process will even work out the length of the array automatically if required. You can also initialise 2D arrays as well.

```
int [,] squareWeights = new int [3,3]
{
    {1,0,1},
    {0,2,0},
```

```
        {1,0,1}
};
```

The code above makes a 2D array that contains weighting values for a clever noughts and crosses (tic tac toe) playing program that I might write. It represents my belief that the centre and corner squares are the most valuable. When my program is making its first move it will look for a square that has the highest number, and try to play there.

3.3.6 More than Two Dimensions

Once in a blue moon you may need to use more than two dimensions. If you go to three dimensions you can think in terms of a pile of grids if you like, with the third dimension (which you could call z) giving you the particular grid. If we wanted to play three dimensional noughts and crosses in a board which is a cube we can declare the array to do it as follows:

```
int [,,] board = new int [3,3,3];
board [1,1,1] = 1;
```

This code creates a three-dimensional board and then gets the highly valuable location right in the middle of the game cube.

You can go to more than three dimensions if you like, in that C# does not have a problem with this. However, you might have big problems because this is very hard to understand and visualise.

Note that sometimes you might think that you need to add a second dimension, when what you really want to do is add another array. For example, to go back to our cricket scores program, if the team captain wants to store the names of the players you would not do this by adding another dimension to the scores array, instead you would declare a second array of strings to hold the name of each player:

```
int [] scores = new int [11] ;
string [] names = new string [11] ;
```

Your program would have to make sure that the name and score information for each player always lined, in other words the element at subscript 0 in the names array would contain the name of the player scoring the value at element 0 in the scores array.

Programmer's Point: Keep your dimensions low

In all my years of programming I've never had to use anything more than three dimensions. If you find yourself having lots of dimensions I would suggest that you are trying to do things the wrong way and should step back from the problem. It may be that you can get a much more efficient solution by creating a struct and then making an array of the structure items. We will talk about structures later.

3.4 Exceptions and Errors

I hate it when things go wrong with my program. If there is one thing I've learnt from programming it is that when someone makes your program crash they look clever, and you look stupid. Consider:

```
Enter your age: Twenty One
```

The program is asking the user to enter their age. The user is entering their age, but they are not using numbers. This causes your program to get rather upset:

```
Unhandled Exception: System.FormatException: Input string was not in a correct format.
    at System.Number.StringToNumber(String str, NumberStyles options, NumberBuffer&
number, NumberFormatInfo info, Boolean parseDecimal)
```

```
    at System.Number.ParseInt32(String s, NumberStyles style, NumberFormatInfo info)
    at RobsProgram.Main(String[] args)
```

This does seem very unfair. Someone daft enough to type their age as words is able to break the program. In this section we will find out how the C# language manages errors and how to make our programs much harder to break.

3.4.1 Exceptions and the Parse method

`Parse` is the method we use to convert strings of text into numeric values.

```
int age = int.Parse(ageString);
```

The above statement uses `int.Parse` to convert the string in `ageString` into an integer result which is then stored in the variable `age`.

This works well, but it is not without its limitations. The problem with `Parse` is that if you give it a string that contains invalid text it doesn't know what to do with it. At work if I ever get a problem that I can't deal with I solve the problem by passing it onto my boss. After all, the boss earns the big bucks and is paid to sort things out.

`Parse` solves its problems by throwing an *exception* for another part of the program to catch. This is the C# equivalent of a note to the boss that says "I don't know what to do with this. Any ideas?" If nothing catches the exception (in effect the boss is not around to deal with the problem) then the exception will finish the program. The C# runtime system will display the contents of the exception then stop, as it did above.

3.4.2 Catching Exceptions

We can make our programs deal with invalid text input to `Parse` by adding code that will *catch* the exceptions that `Parse` throws and try to fix the problem. In programming terms this is called "dynamic error handling" in that our program is responding to an error when it occurs. To do this we have to use a new C# construction, the try – catch clause. The `try` keyword is followed by a block of code. After the block of code comes the `catch` clause. If any of the statements following the `try` throws an exception the program runs the code in the `catch` clause to handle this error.

```
int age;
try
{
    age = int.Parse(ageString);
    Console.WriteLine("Thank you");
}
catch
{
    Console.WriteLine("Invalid age value");
}
```

Code Sample 17 Simple Exception Catching

The code above uses `Parse` to decode the age string. However, the parse action takes place inside the `try` block. If the call of `Parse` throws an exception the code in the `catch` block runs and will display a message to the user. Note that once the exception has been thrown there is no return to the code in the `try` block, i.e. if the parse fails the program will not display the message "Thank you".

3.4.3 The Exception Object

When I pass a problem up to my boss I will hand over a note that describes it. Exceptions work in the same way. An exception is a type of object that contains details of a problem that has occurred. When `Parse` fails it creates an exception object that describes the bad thing that has just happened (in this case input string not in the correct format). The program above ignores the exception object and just registers to the exception event but we can improve the diagnostics of our program by catching the exception if we wish:

```csharp
int age;
try
{
    age = int.Parse(ageString);
    Console.WriteLine("Thank you");
}
catch (Exception e)
{
    // Get the error message out of the exception
    Console.WriteLine(e.Message);
}
```

Code Sample 18 Using the Exception message

The `catch` now looks like a method call, with the `Exception` e being a parameter to the method. This is exactly how it works. Within the `catch` clause the value of e is set to the exception that was thrown by `Parse`. The `Exception` type has a property called `Message` which contains a string describing the error. If a user types in an invalid string the program above will write the text in the exception, which contains the message:

```
Input string was not in a correct format.
```

This message is obtained from the exception that was thrown. This is useful if the code inside the `try` block could throw several different kinds of exception, since it means that the message reflects what has actually happened. The `Exception` object also contains other properties that can be useful.

3.4.4 Exception Nesting

When an exception is thrown the run time system, which is managing the execution of your program inside the computer, will look for the enclosing catch clause. If your program does not contain a catch for the exception it will be caught by a catch which is part of the run time system. The code in this catch clause will display the exception details and then stop the program. Programs can have multiple levels of `try – catch`, and the program will use the `catch` which matches the level of the code in the `try` block.

```csharp
try
{
    // Exceptions at this level will be caught by the
    // "outer" catch clause

    try
    {
        // Exceptions at this level will be caught by the
        // "inner" catch clause
    }
    catch (Exception inner)
    {
        // This is the "inner" catch clause
    }

    // Exceptions at this level will be caught by the
```

```
        // "outer" catch clause
    }
    catch (Exception outer)
    {
        // This is the "outer" catch clause
    }
```

The code above shows how this works. If code in the innermost block throws an exception the run time system will find the inner catch clause. However, once execution leaves that inner block the outer catch is the one which will be run in the event of an exception being thrown.

Programmer's Point: Don't Catch Everything

Ben calls this Pokemon® syndrome: "Gotta catch'em all". Don't feel obliged to catch every exception that your code might throw. If someone asks your Load method to fetch a file that doesn't exist the best thing it can do is throw a "file not found" exception, not try and handle things by returning a null reference or empty item. Returning a placeholder will just cause bigger problems later when something tries to use the empty item that was returned. The faster you can get a fault to manifest itself the easier it is to identify the cause.

3.4.5 Adding a Finally Clause

Sometimes there are things that your program must do irrespective of whether or not an exception is thrown. These actions include things like closing files, releasing resources and generally tidying up. However, we know that when an exception is thrown the statements in the catch clause are called, and the program never returns to the try part of the program. The code in the catch clause could return from the method it is running within or even throw an exception itself. In these situations any code following your try – catch construction would not get the chance to run.

Fortunately C# provides a solution to this problem by allowing you to add a finally clause to your try-catch construction. Statements inside the finally clause will run irrespective of whether or not the program in the try block throws an exception.

```
    try
    {
        // Code that might throw an exception
    }
    catch (Exception outer)
    {
        // Code that catches the exception
    }
    finally
    {
        // Code that is obeyed whether an exception
        // is thrown or not
    }
```

In the above code the statements in the finally part are guaranteed to run, either when the statements in the try part have finished, or just before execution leaves the catch part of your program.

3.4.6 Throwing an Exception

Now that we know how to catch exceptions, the next thing we need to consider is how to throw them. This turns out to be very easy:

```
    throw new Exception("Boom");
```

The statement above makes a new exception and then throws it. When you make a new exception you can give it a string that contains the message the exception will deliver. In this case I have used the somewhat unhelpful message "Boom". Throwing an exception might cause your program to end if the code does not run inside a `try - catch` construction.

3.4.7 Exception Etiquette

Exceptions are best reserved for situations when your program really cannot go any further. If you are going to throw an exception this should be in a situation where your program really could not do anything else. For example if a user of the double glazing program enters a window height which is too large the program can simply print the message "Height too large" and ask for another value. This means that errors at this level are not worthy of exception throwing. I reserve my exceptions for catastrophic events that my program really cannot deal with and must pass on to something else, and you should too.

Programmer's Point: Plan your Exception Handling

When you design a program you should consider what events count as "showstoppers" and how you are going to deal with them. You can even create your own custom exception types based on the one provided by the System and use these in your error handling.

3.5 The Switch Construction

We now know nearly everything you need to know about constructing a program in the C# language. You may find it rather surprising, but there is really very little left to know about programming itself. Most of the rest of C# is concerned with making the business of programming simpler. A good example of this is the `switch` construction.

3.5.1 Making Multiple Decisions

Suppose you are refining your double-glazing program to allow your customer to select from a pre-defined range of windows. You ask something like

```
Enter the type of window:

1 = casement
2 = standard
3 = patio door
```

Your program can then calculate the cost of the appropriate window by selecting type and giving the size. Each method asks the relevant questions and works out the price of that kind of item.

When you come to write the program you will probably end up with something like:

```
static void handleCasement ()
{
    Console.WriteLine("Handle Casement");
}

static void handleStandard ()
{
    Console.WriteLine("Handle Standard");
}

static void handlePatio ()
{
```

```
        Console.WriteLine("Handle patio");
    }
```

These methods are the ones which will eventually deal with each type of window. At the moment they just print out that they have been called. Later you will go on and fill the code in (this is actually quite a good way to construct your programs). Once you have the methods in place, the next thing you need to do is write the code that will call the one that the user has selected.

We already have a method that we can use to get a number from the user (it is called `readInt` and is given a prompt string and high and low limits). Our program can use this method to get the selection value and then pick the method that needs to be used.

3.5.2 Selecting using the `if` construction

When you come to perform the actual selection you end up with code which looks a bit like this:

```
int selection ;
selection = readInt ( "Window Type : ", 1, 3 ) ;

if ( selection == 1 )
{
    handleCasement();
}
else
{
    if ( selection == 2 )
    {
        handleStandard();
    }
    else
    {
        if ( selection == 3 )
        {
            handlePatio() ;
        }
        else
        {
            Console.WriteLine ( "Invalid number" );
        }
    }
}
```

This would work OK, but is rather clumsy. You have to write a large number of `if` constructions to activate each option.

3.5.3 The `switch` construction

Because you have to do this a lot C# contains a special construction to allow you to select one option from a number of them based on a particular value. This is called the *switch* construction. If you write the above using it your program would look like this.

```
switch (selection)
{
    case 1 :
        handleCasement ();
        break ;
    case 2 :
        handleStandard () ;
        break ;
```

```
        case 3 :
            handlePatio () ;
            break ;
        default :
            Console.WriteLine ( "Invalid number" ) ;
            break ;
    }
```

Code Sample 19 Using a Switch

The `switch` construction takes a value which it uses to decide which option to perform. It executes the `case` which matches the value of the `switch` variable. Of course this means that the type of the cases that you use must match the switch selection value although, in true C# tradition, the compiler will give you an error if you make a mistake. The `break` statement after the call of the relevant method is to stop the program running on and performing the code which follows. In the same way as you break out of a loop, when the `break` is reached the `switch` is finished and the program continues running at the statement after the switch.

Another useful feature is the `default` option. This gives the `switch` somewhere to go if the switch value doesn't match any of the cases available; in our case (sorry!) we put out an appropriate message.

You can use the `switch` construction with types other than numbers if you wish:

```
    switch (command)
    {
        case "casement" :
            handleCasement ();
            break ;
        case "standard" :
            handleStandard () ;
            break ;
        case "patio" :
            handlePatio () ;
            break ;
        default :
            Console.WriteLine ( "Invalid command" ) ;
            break ;
    }
```

This switch uses a string to control the selection of the cases. However, your users would not thank you for doing this, since it means that they have to type in the complete name of the option, and of course if they type a character wrong the command is not recognised.

Multiple cases

You can use multiple case items so that your program can execute a particular switch element if the command matches one of several options:

```
    switch (command)
    {
        case "casement" :
        case "c" :
            handleCasement ();
            break ;
        case "standard" :
        case "s" :
            handleStandard () ;
            break ;
        case "patio" :
        case "p" :
            handlePatio () ;
```

```
        break ;
    default :
        Console.WriteLine ( "Invalid command" ) ;
        break ;
}
```

The above switch will select a particular option if the user types the full part of the name or just the initial letter. If you want to perform selection based on strings of text like this I'd advise you to take a look at the `ToUpper` and `ToLower` methods provided by the `string` type. These can be used to obtain a version of a string which is all in upper or lower case, which can make the testing of the commands much easier:

```
switch (command.ToUpper())
{
    case "CASEMENT" :
    case "C" :
    ....
```

Programmer's Point: switches are a good idea

Switches make a program easier to understand as well as quicker to write. It is also easier to add extra commands if you use a switch since it is just a matter of putting in another case. However, I'd advise against putting large amounts of program code into a switch case. Instead you should put a call to a method as I have above.

3.6 Using Files

If you want your program to be properly useful you have to give it a way of storing data when it is not running. We know that you can store data in this way; that is how we have kept all the programs we have created so far, in files.

Files are looked after by the operating system of the computer. What we want to do is use C# to tell the operating system to create files and let us access them. The good news is that although different operating systems use different ways to look after their files, the way in which you manipulate files in C# is the same for any computer. We can write a C# program which creates a file on a Windows PC and then use the same program to create a file on a UNIX system with no problems.

3.6.1 Streams and Files

C# makes use of a thing called a stream to allow programs to work with files. A stream is a link between your program and a data resource. Data can flow up or down your stream, so that streams can be used to read and write to files. The stream is the thing that links your program with the operating system of the computer you are using. The operating system actually does the work, and the C# library you are using will convert your request to use streams into instructions for the operating system you are using at the time:

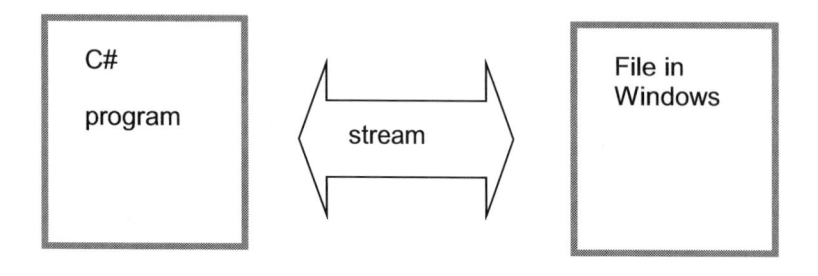

A C# program can contain an object representing a particular stream that a programmer has created and connected to a file. The program performs operations on the file by calling methods on the stream object to tell it what to do.

C# has a range of different stream types which you use depending on what you want to do. All of the streams are used in exactly the same way. In fact you are already familiar with how streams are used, since the Console class, which connects a C# program to the user, is implemented as a stream. The ReadLine and WriteLine methods are commands you can give any stream that will ask it to read and write data.

We are going to consider two stream types which let programs use files; these are the StreamWriter and StreamReader types.

3.6.2 Creating an Output Stream

You create a stream object just like you would create any other one, by using new. When the stream is created it can be passed the name of the file that is to be opened.

```
StreamWriter writer ;
writer = new StreamWriter("test.txt");
```

The variable writer will be made to refer to the stream that you want to write into. When the new StreamWriter is created the program will open a file called test.txt for output and connect the stream to it. If this process fails for any reason, perhaps your operating system is not able/allowed to write to the file or the name is invalid, then the action will fail with an appropriate exception.

Note however that this code does not have a problem if the file test.txt already exists. All that happens is that a brand new, empty, file is created in place of what was there. This is potentially dangerous. It means that you could use the two statements above to completely destroy the contents of an existing file, which would be bad. Most useful programs ask the user whether or not an existing file should be overwritten, you will find out later how to do this.

3.6.3 Writing to a Stream

Once the stream has been created it can be written to by calling the write methods it provides.

```
writer.WriteLine("hello world");
```

The above statement calls the WriteLine method on the stream to make it write the text "hello world" into the file test.txt. This is exactly the same technique that is used to write information to the console for the user to read. In fact you can use all the writing features including those we explored in the neater printing section to format your output.

Each time you write a line to the file it is added onto the end of the lines that have already been written. If your program got stuck writing in an infinite loop it is possible that it might fill up the storage device. If this happens, and the write cannot be performed successfully, the call of WriteLine will throw an exception. A properly written program should probably make sure that any exceptions like this (they can also be thrown when you open a file) are caught and handled correctly.

3.6.4 Closing a Stream

When your program has finished writing to a stream it is very important that the stream is explicitly closed using the Close method:

```
writer.Close();
```

When the `Close` method is called the stream will write out any text to the file that is waiting to be written and disconnect the program from the file. Any further attempts to write to the stream will fail with an exception. Once a file has been closed it can then be accessed by other programs on the computer, i.e. once the close has been performed you can use the Notepad program to open `test.txt` and take a look at what is inside it. Forgetting to close a file is bad for a number of reasons:

- It is possible that the program may finish without the file being properly closed. In this situation some of the data that you wrote into the file will not be there.

- If your program has a stream connected to a file other programs may not be able to use that file. It will also be impossible to move or rename the file.

- An open stream consumes a small, but significant, part of operating resource. If your program creates lots of streams but does not close them this might lead to problems opening other files later on.

So, close the file or suffer the consequences.

3.6.5 Streams and Namespaces

If you rush out and try the above bits of code you will find that they don't work. Sorry about that. There is something else that you need to know before you can use the `StreamWriter` type. Like lots of the objects that deal with input and output, this object is defined in the `System.IO` *namespace*. We have touched on namespaces before, when we reflected on the need to have the statement `using System;` at the start of our C# programs. Now we need to find out more about them.

Namespaces are all to do with finding resources. The C# language provides the keywords and constructions that allow us to write programs, but on top of this there are a whole lot of extra resources supplied with a C# installation. These resources are things like the `Console` object that lets us read and write text to the user. A C# installation actually contains many thousands of resources, each of which must be uniquely identified. If you were in charge of cataloguing a huge number of items you would find it very helpful to lump items into groups. Museum curators do this all the time. They put all the Roman artefacts in one room, and the Greek ones in another. The designers of the C# language created a namespace facility where programmers can do the same kind of thing with their resources.

A namespace is, quite literally, a "space where names have meaning". The full name of the `Console` class that you have been using to write text to the user is `System.Console`. That is, the `Console` class in the `System` namespace. In fact it is quite OK to use this full form in your programs:

```
System.Console.WriteLine("Hello World");
```

The above uses the *fully qualified name* of the console resource and calls the method `WriteLine` provided by that resource. However, we've not had to use this form because at the start of our programs we have told the compiler to use the `System` namespace to find any names it hasn't seen before. The `using` keyword allows us to tell the compiler where to look for resources.

```
using System;
```

This statement tells the compiler to look in the `System` namespace for resources. Once we have specified a namespace in a program file we no longer need to use the fully qualified name for resources from that namespace. Whenever the compiler finds an item it hasn't seen before it will automatically look in the namespaces it has been told to use. In other words, when the compiler sees the statement:

```
Console.WriteLine("Hello World");
```

- it knows to look in the `System` namespace for that object so that it can use the `WriteLine` method on it. If the programmer miss-types the class name:

```
Consle.WriteLine("Hello World");
```

- the compiler will look in the `System` namespace, fail to find an object called `Console` and generate a compilation error.

This is the same error that you will get if you try to use the `StreamWriter` class without telling the compiler to look in the `System.IO` namespace. In other words, to use the file handing classes you will need to add the following statement at the very top of your program:

```
using System.IO;
```

It is possible to put one namespace inside another (just like a librarian would put a cabinet of Vases in the Roman room which he could refer to as Roman.Vases) and so the IO namespace is actually held within the System namespace. However, just because you use a namespace, this does not imply that you use all the namespaces defined within it, and so you must include the above line for file handling objects to be available.

Namespaces are a great way to make sure that names of items that you create don't clash with those from other programmers. We will see how you can create your own namespaces later on.

```csharp
using System;
using System.IO;

class FileWriteDemo
{
    public static void Main()
    {
        StreamWriter writer;
        writer = new StreamWriter("test.txt");
        writer.WriteLine("hello world");
        writer.Close();
    }
}
```

Code Sample 20 Complete File Write

3.6.6 Reading from a File

Reading from a file is very similar to writing, in that the program will create a stream to do the actual work. In this case the stream that is used is a `StreamReader`.

```csharp
StreamReader reader = new StreamReader("Test.txt");
string line = reader.ReadLine();
Console.WriteLine (line);
reader.Close();
```

The above program connects a stream to the file `Test.txt`, reads the first line from the file, displays it on the screen and then close the stream. If the file can't be found then the attempt to open it will fail and the program will throw an exception.

Detecting the End of an Input File

Repeated calls of `ReadLine` will return successive lines of a file. However, if your program reaches the end of the file the `ReadLine` method will return an empty string each time it is called. Fortunately the `StreamReader` object provides a property called `EndOfStream` that a program can use to determine when the end of the file has been reached. When the property becomes true the end of the file has been reached.

```csharp
StreamReader reader = new StreamReader("Test.txt");
while (reader.EndOfStream == false)
```

```csharp
{
    string line = reader.ReadLine();
    Console.WriteLine(line);
}
reader.Close();
```

The above code will open up the file test.txt and display every line in the file on the console. The while loop will stop the program when the end of the file is reached.

```csharp
using System;
using System.IO;

class FileWriteandReadDemo
{
    public static void Main()
    {
        StreamWriter writer;
        writer = new StreamWriter("test.txt");
        writer.WriteLine("hello world");
        writer.Close();

        StreamReader reader = new StreamReader("Test.txt");
        while (reader.EndOfStream == false)
        {
            string line = reader.ReadLine();
            Console.WriteLine(line);
        }
        reader.Close();
    }
}
```

Code Sample 21 File Write and Read

The above code sample first puts a line of text in a file and then opens the file and prints it back to the screen.

3.6.7 File Paths in C#

If you have used a computer for a while you will be familiar with the idea of folders (sometimes called directories). These are used to organise information we store on the computer. Each file you create is placed in a particular folder. If you use Windows you will find that there are several folders created for you automatically. One can be used for Documents, another for Pictures and another one for Music. You can create your own folders inside these (for example Documents\Stories).

The location of a file on a computer is often called the *path* to the file. The path to a file can be broken into two parts, the location of the folder and the name of the file itself. If you don't give a folder location when you open a file (as we have been doing with the file Test.txt) then the system assumes the file that is being used is stored in the same folder as the program which is running. In other words, if you are running the program FileRead.exe in the folder MyProgs then the above programs will assume that the file Test.txt is in the MyProgs folder too.

If you want to use a file in a different folder (which is a good idea, as data files are hardly ever held in the same place as programs run from) you can add path information to a filename:

```csharp
string path;
path = @"c:\data\2009\November\sales.txt";
```

The above statements create a string variable which contains the path to a file called sales.txt. This file is held in the folder November, which is in turn held in the folder 2009, which is held in the folder data which is on drive C.

The backslash (\) characters in the string serve to separate the folders along the path to the file. Note that I have specified a string literal that doesn't contain control characters (that is what the @ at the beginning of the literal means) as otherwise the \ characters in the string will get interpreted by C# as the start of a control sequence. If you have problems where your program is not finding files that you know are there, I'd advise you to make sure that your path separators are not getting used as control characters.

4 Creating Solutions

4.1 Our Case Study: Friendly Bank

The bulk of this section is based on a case study which will allow you to see the features of C# in a strong context. You are taking the role of a programmer who will be using the language to create a solution for a customer.

The program we are making is for a bank, the "United Friendly and Really Nice Bank of Lovely People ™", otherwise known as the Friendly Bank. We will be creating the entire bank application using C# and will be exploring the features of C# that make this easy.

It is unlikely that you will get to actually implement an entire banking system during your professional career as a programmer (although it might be quite fun – and probably rather lucrative). However, from a programming point of view it is an interesting problem and as we approach it we will uncover lots of techniques which will be useful in other programs that we might write.

Programmer's Point: Look for Patterns

The number of different programs in the world is actually quite small. A lot of the things that our bank is going to do (store a large amount of information about a large number of individuals, search for information for a particular person, implement transactions that change the content of one or more items in the system) are common to many other types of programs, from video games to robots.

4.1.1 Bank System Scope

The *scope* of a system is a description of the things that the system is going to do. This is also, by implication, a statement of what the system will **not** do. This is equally as important, as a customer will not usually have a clear idea of what you are doing and may well expect you to deliver things that you have no intention of providing. By setting out the scope at the beginning you can make sure that there are no unpleasant surprises later on.

At the moment we are simply concerned with managing the account information in the bank. The bank manager has told us that the bank stores information about each customer. This information includes their name, address, account number, balance and overdraft value. Other data items might be added later.

There are many thousands of customers and the manager has also told us that there are also a number of different types of accounts (and that new types of account are invented from time to time).

The system must also generate warning letters and statements as required.

BANK NOTES

At the end of some sections there will be a description of how this new piece of C# will affect how we create our bank system. These notes should put the feature into a useful context.

4.2 Enumerated Types

These sound really posh. If anyone asks you what you learnt today you can say "I learnt how to use enumerated types" and they will be really impressed. Of course if they know about programming they'll just say "Oh, you mean you've numbered some states".

4.2.1 Enumeration and states

Enumerated sounds posh. But if you think of "enumerated" as just meaning "numbered" things get a bit easier. To understand what we are doing here we need to consider the problem which these types are intended to solve.

We know that if we want to hold an integer value we can use an `int` type. If we want to hold something which is either true or false we can use a `bool`. However, sometimes we want to hold a range of particular values or states.

Sample states

Enumerated types are very useful when storing *state* information. States are not quite the same as other items such as the name of a customer or the balance of their account.

For example, if I am writing a program to play the game Battleships (where squares of the "sea" hold different types of craft which can be attacked) I may decide that a given square of the sea can have the following thing in it:

- Empty sea
- Attacked
- Battleship
- Cruiser
- Submarine
- Rowing boat

If you think about it, I am sort of assembling more metadata here, in that I have decided that I need to keep track of the sea and then I have worked out exactly what I can put in it. I could do something with numbers if I like:

- Empty sea = 1
- Attacked = 2
- Battleship = 3
- Cruiser = 4
- Submarine = 5
- Rowing boat = 6

However, this would mean that I have to keep track of the values myself and remember that if we get the value 7 in a sea location this is clearly wrong.

C# has a way in which we can create a type which has just a particular set of possible values. These types are called "enumerated types":

```
enum SeaState
{
    EmptySea,
    Attacked,
    Battleship,
    Cruiser,
```

```
    Submarine,
    RowingBoat
} ;
```

I have created a type called `SeaState` which can be used to hold the state of a particular part of the sea. It can only have the given values above, and must be managed solely in terms of these named enumerations. For example I must write:

```
SeaState openSea ;
openSea = SeaState.EmptySea;
```

My variable `openSea` is only able to hold values which represent the state of the sea contents. Of course C# itself will actually represent these states as particular numeric values, but how these are managed is not a problem for me.

Note that types I create (like `SeaState`) will be highlighted by the editor in a blue colour which is not quite the same as keywords.

This shows that these items are extra types I have created which can be used to create variables, but they are not actually part of the C# language, like keywords are. It is important that you understand what is happening here. Previously we have used types that are part of C#, for example `int` and `double`. Now we have reached the point where we are actually creating our own data types which can be used to hold data values that are required by our application.

4.2.2 Creating an enum type

The new `enum` type can be created outside any class and creates a new type for use in any of my programs:

```
using System;

enum TrafficLight
{
    Red,
    RedAmber,
    Green,
    Amber
} ;

class EnumDemonstration
{
    public static void Main ()
    {
        TrafficLight light ;
        light = TrafficLight.Red;
    }
}
```

Code Sample 22 Enum Traffic Light

Every time that you have to hold something which can take a limited number of possible values, or states (for example `OnSale`, `UnderOffer`, `Sold`, `OffTheMarket` etc) then you should think in terms of using enumerated types to hold the values.

Programmer's Point: Use enumerated types

Enumerated types are another occasion where everyone benefits if you use them. The program becomes simpler to write, easier to understand and safer. You should therefore use them a lot.

For the bank, you want to hold the state of an item as well as other information about the customer. For example, we could have the states "Frozen", "New", "Active", "Closed" and "Under Audit" as states for our bank account. If this is the case it is sensible to create an enumerated type which can hold these values and no others

```
enum AccountState
{
    New,
    Active,
    UnderAudit,
    Frozen,
    Closed
} ;
```

We now have a variable which can hold state information about an account in our bank. Every account will contain a variable of type `AccountState` which represents the state of that account.

4.3 Structures

Structures let us organise a set of individual values into a cohesive lump which we can map onto one of the items in the problem that we are working on. This is important in many applications.

4.3.1 What is a Structure?

Often when you are dealing with information you will want to hold a collection of different things about a particular item. The Friendly Bank has commissioned an account storage system and you can use structures to make this easier. Like any good programmer who has been on my course you would start by doing the following:

1. Establish precisely the specification, i.e. get in written form exactly what they expect your system to do.
2. Negotiate an extortionate fee.
3. Consider how you will go about storing the data.

A sample structure

From your specification you know that the program must hold the following:

- customer name - string
- customer address - string
- account number - integer value
- account balance - integer value
- overdraft limit - integer value

The Friendly Bank have told you that they will only be putting up to 50 people into your bank storage so, after a while you come up with the following:

```
const int MAX_CUST = 50;

AccountState [] states = new AccountState [MAX_CUST] ;
string [] names = new string [MAX_CUST] ;
string [] addresses = new string [MAX_CUST] ;
int [] accountNos = new int [MAX_CUST] ;
int [] balances = new int [MAX_CUST] ;
int [] overdraft = new int [MAX_CUST] ;
```

What we have is an array for each single piece of data we want to store about a particular customer. If we were talking about a database (which is actually what we are writing), the lump of data for each customer would be called a record and an individual part of that lump, for example the overdraft value, would be called a field. In our program we are working on the basis that `balance[0]` holds the balance of the first customer in our database, `overdraft [0]` holds the overdraft of the first customer, and so on. (Remember that array subscript values start at 0).

This is all very well, and you could get a database system working with this data structure. However it would be much nicer to be able to lump your record together in a more definite way.

4.3.2 Creating a Structure

C# lets you create data structures. A structure is a collection of C# variables which you want to treat as a single entity. In C# a lump of data would be called a structure and each part of it would be called a field. To help us with our bank database we could create a structure which could hold all the information about a customer:

```
struct Account
{
    public AccountState State;
    public string Name ;
    public string Address ;
    public int AccountNumber ;
    public int Balance ;
    public int Overdraft ;
} ;
```

This defines a structure, called `Account`, which contains all the required customer information. Having done this we can now define some variables:

```
Account RobsAccount;
```

This statement creates a single Account variable which is called `RobsAccount`. The program can put values into the member elements of this account.

We refer to individual members of a structure by putting their name after the `struct` variable we are using with a . (full stop) separating them, for example:

```
RobsAccount.Name="Rob";
```

- would refer to the string field `Name` in the structured variable `RobsAccount`. (i.e. the `Name` value in `RobsAccount`)

```
using System;

enum AccountState
{
    New,
    Active,
    UnderAudit,
    Frozen,
    Closed
} ;

struct Account
{
    public AccountState State;
    public string Name;
    public string Address;
    public int AccountNumber;
```

```
        public int Balance;
        public int Overdraft;
    } ;

    class BankProgram
    {

        public static void Main()
        {
            Account RobsAccount;
            RobsAccount.State = AccountState.Active;
            RobsAccount.Balance = 1000000;
        }
    }
```

Code Sample 23 Generous Account Structure

This very generous piece of code creates an `AccountStructure` variable called `RobsAccount`, sets the account state to `Active` and then gives it a million pounds (although it doesn't do anything with this money).

Note how the structure and enum are declared outside the `BankProgram` class. Once I have created my structure I can use it in the same way that I would use something like `int` or `float`.

Structures get really useful when we create arrays of them. As we saw with the scoring program, it is hard to manage individual items, but if we use an array, things become much easier.

```
        const int MAX_CUST = 100;
        Account [] Bank = new Account [MAX_CUST];
```

This declaration sets up an entire array of customers, called **Bank** which can hold all the customers. Note that I've rather cleverly set up a variable called MAX_CUST which is presently set at 100. This gives the maximum number of customers that our bank can hold.

We can assign one structure variable to another, just as we would any other variable type. When the assignment is performed all the values in the source structure are copied into the destination:

```
        Bank[0] = RobsAccount;
```

This would copy the information from the `RobsAccount` structure into the element at the start of the `Bank` array.

You can do this with elements of an array of structures too, so that:

```
        Bank [25].Name
```

- would be the string containing the name of the customer in the element with subscript 25.

4.3.3 Using a Structure

Once we have our structure we can use it to store details of our bank customers:

```
    class AccountStructureArray
    {
        public static void Main()
        {
            const int MAX_CUST = 100;
            Account[] Bank = new Account[MAX_CUST];
            Bank[0].Name = "Rob";
            Bank[0].State = AccountState.Active;
            Bank[0].Balance = 1000000;
            Bank[1].Name = "Jim";
```

```
            Bank[1].State = AccountState.Frozen;
            Bank[1].Balance = 0;
        }
    }
```

Code Sample 24 Putting account information into arrays

You can see how this would work in the above code sample, which creates an array of 100 customer records and then sets up the first two elements in the array. Which of the account holders has the most money?

This program doesn't read in the data for all 100 bank customers, but it does show you how to access the various fields in an array of structure values.

Initial values in structures

When a structure is created as a local variable (i.e. in a block) the values in it are undefined. This means that if you try to use them in your program you will get a compilation error. This is exactly the same as if you use a variable in a program before giving it a value. In other words:

```
Account RobsAccount ;
Console.WriteLine ( "Name is : " + RobsAccount.Name ) ;
```

- would produce a compilation error. It is your job as programmer to make sure that you always put a value into a variable before you try to get something out of it.

Using Structure Types in Method Calls

A method can have parameters of structure type:

```
public void PrintAccount ( Account a )
{
    Console.WriteLine ( "Name: " + a.Name );
    Console.WriteLine ( "Address: " + a.Address );
    Console.WriteLine ( "Balance: " + a.Balance );
}
```

This method provides a quick way of printing out the contents of an account variable:

```
PrintAccount (RobsAccount);
```

The value of the structure RobsAccount is passed into the method for it to work on, just as we passed integers into methods that we have used before. It is also possible to pass array elements into the method call (because an element which is part of an array of Account values is by definition an Account instance).

```
    class BankProgram
    {

        public static void PrintAccount(Account a)
        {
            Console.WriteLine("Name: " + a.Name);
            Console.WriteLine("Address: " + a.Address);
            Console.WriteLine("Balance: " + a.Balance);
        }

        public static void Main()
        {
            const int MAX_CUST = 100;
            Account[] Bank = new Account[MAX_CUST];
            Bank[0].Name = "Rob";
```

```
            Bank[0].Address = "Robs House";
            Bank[0].State = AccountState.Active;
            Bank[0].Balance = 1000000;
            PrintAccount(Bank[0]);
            Bank[1].Name = "Jim";
            Bank[1].Address = "Jim's House";
            Bank[1].State = AccountState.Frozen;
            Bank[1].Balance = 0;
            PrintAccount(Bank[1]);
        }
    }
```

Code Sample 25 Printing Account values from an array

It is also possible to create methods that return results which are of a structure type, for example we could create a `ReadAccount` method that reads an account and returns it.

Programmer's Point: Structures are crucial

In a commercial system it is common to spend a very long time designing the structures which make up the data storage. They are the fundamental building blocks of the program since they hold all the data upon which everything else is built. You can regard the design of the structures and the constraints on their content as another big chunk of metadata about a system that you create.

Designing with Types

You can see that we have added a `State` value to the `Account` structure. This makes it easy for the program to keep track of the particular state of an account. What we have done is created a type which can hold a number of values (our `AccountState` enumerated type) and put it into another type we have designed which is to hold information about a bank Account holder. This approach is how you attack more complicated problems. We can get all the details of what the types should hold from the metadata that comes from discussion with our customer.

For example, if we want to create a really impressive double glazing management program we could come up with something like this:

```
    enum WindowState
    {
        Quoted,
        Ordered,
        Manufactured,
        Shipped,
        Installed
    } ;

    struct Window
    {
        public WindowState state ;
        public double Width ;
        public double Height ;
        public string Description ;
    } ;
```

This would hold information about a particular window in a house, including the dimensions of the window, the state of the window order and a string describing the window itself. For a particular house, which contains a number of windows, we could create an array of `Window` structures.

Programmer's Point: You should give state to your objects

The Account class above is a good example of an object that will be used in different ways, depending on the state that it is occupying. For example, it will not be possible to withdraw funds from an account which is in the Frozen state. Just about every object in a system can be improved by the addition of state. Orders can be Empty, Pending, Dispatched and Received. Aliens can be Sleeping, Attacking or Destroyed. Whenever you invent a new object you should immediately start to consider the states that it can occupy in your system.

4.4 Objects, Structures and References

You have seen that if you want to store a block of information about a particular item you can bring all this together in a structure. Structures are useful, but we would like to be able to solve other problems when we write large programs:

- We want to make sure that a given item in our program cannot be placed into an invalid state, i.e. we don't want to have bank accounts with empty or incorrect account numbers.

- We want to be able to break a large system down into distinct and separate components which can be developed independently and interchanged with others which do the same task, i.e. we want to get one team of programmers working on accounts, another on cheques, another on credit cards etc.

- We want to make sure that the effort involved with making new types of bank account is as small as possible, i.e. if the bank decides to introduce a new high interest deposit account we want to be able to make use of existing deposit account

To do all these things we are going to have to start to consider programs from the point of view of object based design. This section should come with some kind of a health warning along the lines of "some of these ideas might hurt your head a bit at the start". But the following points are also very important:

- objects don't add any new behaviours to our programs – we know just about everything we need to know to write programs when we have learnt about statements, loops, conditions and arrays.

- objects are best regarded as a solution to the problem of design. They let us talk about systems in general terms. We can go back and refine how the objects actually do their tasks later.

You can write just about every program that has ever been written just by using the technologies that we have so far looked at. But objects allow us to work in a much nicer way. And so we are going to have to get the hang of them, like it or not...

4.4.1 Objects and Structures

In C# objects and structures have a lot in common. They can both hold data and contain methods. However, there is a crucial difference between the two. Structures are managed in terms of *value* whereas objects are managed in terms of *reference*.

It is very important that you understand the distinction between the two, for it has a big impact on the way that they are used.

Creating and Using a Structure

Consider the code:

```
struct AccountStruct
{
```

```
        public string Name ;
    } ;

    class StructsAndObjectsDemo
    {
        public static void Main ()
        {
            AccountStruct RobsAccountStruct ;
            RobsAccountStruct.Name = "Rob";
            Console.WriteLine ( RobsAccountStruct.Name );
        }
    }
```

Code Sample 26 Simple Account Stucture

This implements a very simple bank account, where we are only holding the name of the account holder. The `Main` method creates a structure variable called `RobsAccountStruct`.

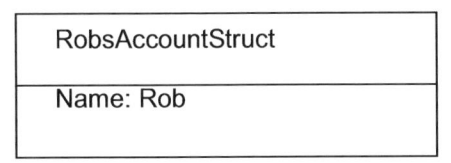

RobsAccountStruct
Name: Rob

It then sets the name property of the variable to the string "Rob". If we run this program it does exactly what you would expect, in that it prints out the name "Rob". If the structure contained other items about the bank account these would be stored in the structure as well, and I could use them in just the same way.

Creating and Using an Instance of a Class

We can make a tiny change to the program and convert the bank account to a class:

```
    class Account
    {
        public string Name ;
    } ;

    class StructsAndObjectsDemo
    {
        public static void Main ()
        {
            Account RobsAccount ;
            RobsAccount.Name = "Rob";
            Console.WriteLine (RobsAccount.Name );
        }
    }
```

Code Sample 27 Non-compiling Account class

The account information is now being held in a class, rather than a structure. The account class is called, quite simply, `Account`. The problem is that when we compile the program we get this:

```
ObjectDemo.cs(12,3): error CS0165: Use of unassigned local variable ' RobsAccount'
```

So, what is going on? To understand what is happening you need to know what is performed by the line:

```
Account RobsAccount;
```

This looks like a declaration of a variable called `RobsAccount`. But in the case of objects, this is not what it seems.

[luggage tag diagram labeled "RobsAccount"]

What you actually get when the program obeys that line is the creation of a *reference* called `RobsAccount`. Such references are allowed to *refer* to instances of the `Account`. You can think of them as a bit like a luggage tag, in that they can be tied to something with a piece of rope. If you have the tag you can then follow the rope to the object it is tied to.

But when we create a reference we don't actually get one of the things that it refers to. The compiler knows this, and so it gives me an error because the line:

```
RobsAccount.Name = "Rob";
```

- is an attempt to find the thing that is tied to this tag and set the name property to "Rob". Since the tag is presently not tied to anything our program would fail at this point. The compiler therefore says, in effect, "you are trying to follow a reference which does not refer to anything, therefore I am going to give you a 'variable undefined' error".

We solve the problem by creating an instance of the class and then connecting our tag to it. This is achieved by adding a line to our program:

```
class Account
{
    public string Name ;
} ;

class StructsAndObjectsDemo
{
    public static void Main ()
    {
        Account RobsAccount ;
        RobsAccount = new Account();
        RobsAccount.Name = "Rob";
        Console.WriteLine (RobsAccount.Name );
    }
}
```

Code Sample 28 Compiling Account Class

The line I have added creates a new `Account` object and sets the reference `RobsAccount` to refer to it.

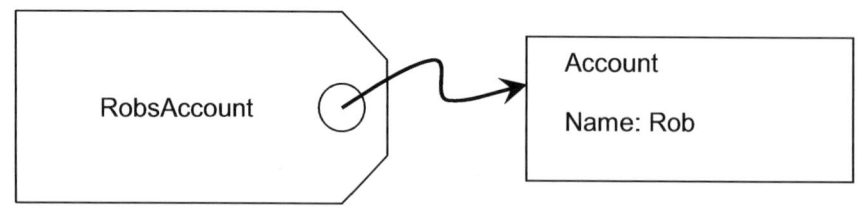

[diagram: luggage tag "RobsAccount" with arrow pointing to box labeled "Account, Name: Rob"]

We have seen this keyword `new` before. We use it to create arrays. This is because an array is actually implemented as an object, and so we use `new` to create it. The thing that new creates is an *object*. An object is an instance of a class. I'll repeat that in a posh font:

"An object is an instance of a class"

I have repeated this because it is very important that you understand this. A class provides the instructions to C# as to what is to be made, and what it can do. The new keyword causes C# to use the class information to actually make an instance. Note that in the above diagram I have called the object an `Account`, not `RobsAccount`. This is because the object instance does not have the identifier `RobsAccount`, it is simply the one which `RobsAccount` is connected to at the moment.

4.4.2 References

We now have to get used to the idea that if we want to use objects, we have to use references. The two come hand in hand and are inseparable. Structures are kind of useful, but for real object oriented satisfaction you have to have an object, and that means that we must manage our access to a particular object by making use of references to it. Actually this is not that painful in reality, in that you can treat a reference as if it really was the object just about all of the time, but you must remember that when you hold a reference you do not hold an instance, you hold a tag which is tied onto an instance...

Multiple References to an Instance

Perhaps another example of references would help at this point. Consider the following code:

```
Account RobsAccount ;
RobsAccount = new Account();
RobsAccount.Name = "Rob";
Console.WriteLine (RobsAccount.Name );
Account Temp ;
Temp = RobsAccount;
Temp.Name = "Jim";
Console.WriteLine (RobsAccount.Name );
```

Code Sample 29 Multiple References

The question is; what would the second call of `WriteLine` print out? If we draw a diagram the answer becomes clearer:

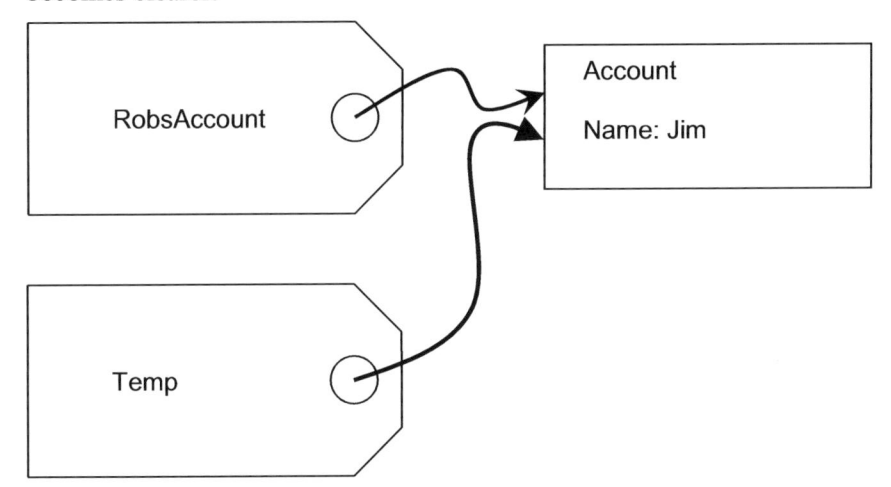

Both of the tags refer to the same instance of `Account`. This means that any changes which are made to the object that `Temp` refers to will also be reflected in the one that `RobsAccount` refers to, *because they are the same object*. This means that the program would print out Jim, since that is the name in the object that `RobsAccount` is referring to.

This indicates a trickiness with objects and references. There is no limit to the number of references that can be attached to a single instance, so you need to remember that changing the object that a reference refers to may well change that instance from the point of view of other objects.

No References to an Instance

Just to complete the confusion we need to consider what happens if an object has no references to it:

```
Account RobsAccount ;
RobsAccount = new Account();
RobsAccount.Name = "Rob";
Console.WriteLine (RobsAccount.Name );
RobsAccount = new Account();
RobsAccount.Name = "Jim";
Console.WriteLine (RobsAccount.Name );
```

Code Sample 30 No references to an instance

This code makes an account instance, sets the name property of it to Rob and then makes another account instance. The reference `RobsAccount` is made to refer to the new item, which has the name set to Jim. The question is: What happens to the first instance? Again, this can be made clearer with a diagram:

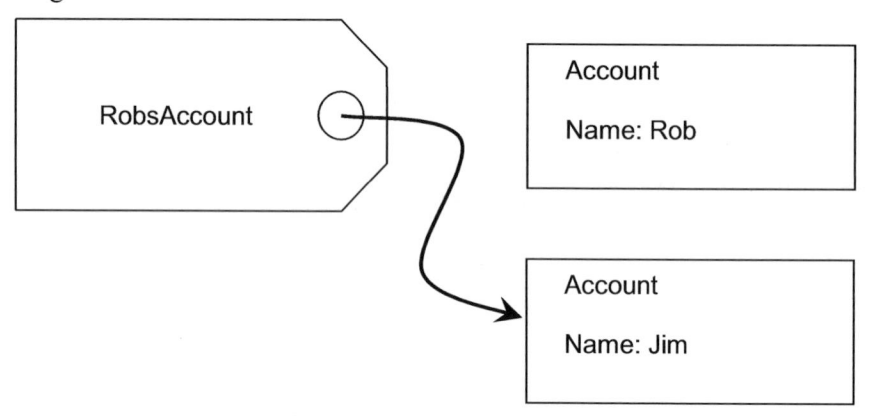

The first instance is shown "hanging" in space, with nothing referring to it. As far as making use of data in the instance is concerned, it might as well not be there. Indeed the C# language implementation has a special process, called the "Garbage Collector" which is given the job of finding such useless items and disposing of them. Note that the compiler will not stop us from "letting go" of items like this.

You should also remember that you can get a similar effect when a reference to an instance goes out of scope:

```
{
    Account localVar ;
    localVar = new Account();
}
```

The variable `localVar` is local to the block. This means that when the program execution leaves the block the local variable is discarded. This means that the only reference to the account is also removed, meaning another job for the garbage collector.

Programmer's Point: Try to avoid the Garbage Collector

While it is sometimes reasonable to release items you have no further use for, you must remember that creating and disposing of objects will take up computing power. When I work with objects I worry about how much creating and destroying I am doing. Just because the objects are disposed of automatically doesn't mean that you should abuse the facility.

4.4.3 Why Bother with References?

References don't sound much fun at the moment. They seem to make it harder to create and use objects and may be the source of much confusion. So why do we bother with them?

To answer this, we can consider the Pacific Island of Yap. The currency in use on this island is based around 12 feet tall stones which weigh several hundred pounds each. The value of a "coin" in the Yap currency is directly related to the number of men who died in the boat bringing the rock to the island. When you pay someone with one of these coins you don't actually pick it up and give it to them. Instead you just say "The coin in the road on top of the hill is now yours". In other words, they use references to manage objects that they don't want to have to move around.

That is why we use references in our programs. Consider a bank which contains many accounts. If we wanted to sort them into alphabetical order of customer name we have to move them all around.

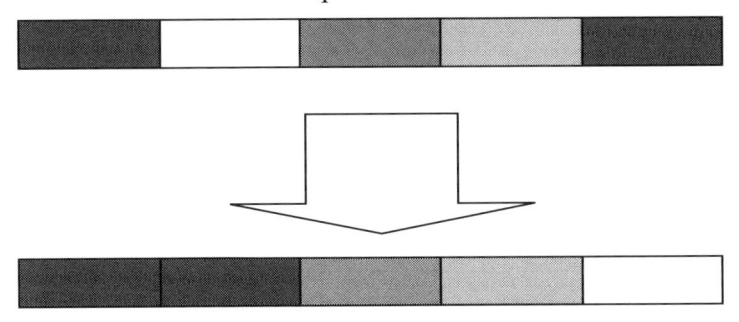

Sorting by moving objects around

If we held the accounts as an array of structure items we would have to do a lot of work just to keep the list in order. The bank may well want to order the information in more than one way too, for example they might want to order it on both customer surname and also on account number. Without references this would be impossible. With references we just need to keep a number of arrays of references, each of which is ordered in a particular way:

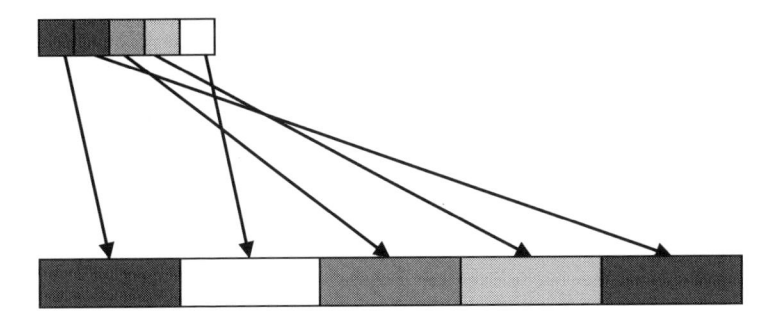

Sorting by using references

If we just sort the references we don't have to move the large data items at all. New objects can be added without having to move any objects, instead the references can be moved around.

References and Data Structures

Our list of sorted references is all very good, but if we want to add something to our sorted list we still have to move the references around. We can get over this, and also speed up searching, by structuring our data into a tree form.

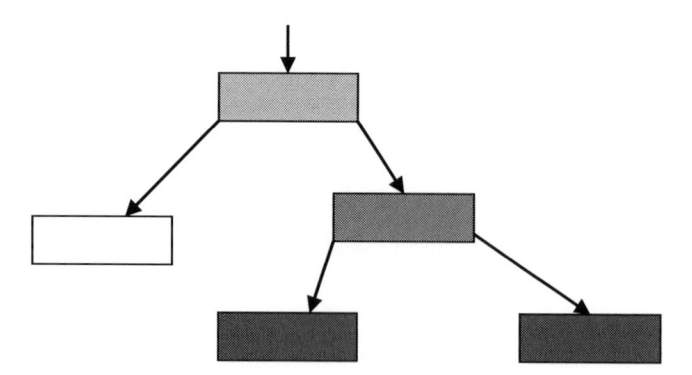

Sorting by use of a tree

In the tree above each node has two references; one can refer to a node which is "lighter", the other to a node which is "darker". If I want a sorted list of the items I just have to go as far down the "lighter" side as I can and I will end up at the lightest. Then I go up to the one above that (which must be the next lightest). Then I go down the dark side (Luke) and repeat the process. The neat thing about this approach is also that adding new items is very easy; I just find the place on the tree that they need to be hung on and attach the reference there.

Searching is also very quick, in that I can look at each node and decide which way to look next until I either find what I am looking for or I find there is no reference in the required direction, in which case the item is not in the structure.

Programmer's Point: Data Structures are Important

This is not a data structures document, it is a programming document. If you don't get all the stuff about trees just yet, don't worry. Just remember that references are an important mechanism for building up structures of data and leave it at that. But sometime in the future you are going to have to get your head around how to build structures using these things.

Reference Importance

The key to this way of working is that an object can contain references to other objects, as well as the data payload. We will consider this aspect of object use later; for now we just need to remember that the reference and the object are distinct and separate.

BANK NOTES: REFERENCES AND ACCOUNTS

For a bank with many thousands of customers the use of references is crucial to the management of the data that they hold. The accounts will be held in the memory of the computer and, because of the size of each account and the number of accounts being stored, it will not be possible to move them around memory if we want to sort them.

This means that the only way to manipulate them is to leave them in the same place and have lists of references to them. The references are very small "tags" which can be used to locate the actual item in memory. Sorting a list of references is very easy, and it would also be possible to have several such lists. This means that we can offer the manager a view of his bank sorted by customer name and another view sorted in order of balance. And if the manager comes along with a need for a new structure or view we can create that in terms of references as well.

4.5 Designing with Objects

We are now going to start thinking in terms of objects. The reason that we do this is that we would like a way of making the design of our systems as easy as possible. This all comes back to the "creative laziness" that programmers are so famous for. The thing that we are trying to do here is best expressed as:

"Put off all the hard work for as long as we can, and if possible get someone else to do it."

Objects let us do this. If we return to our bank account we can see that there are a number of things that we need to be able to do with it:

- pay money into the account
- draw money out of the account
- find the balance
- print out a statement
- change the address of the account holder
- print out the address of the account holder
- change the state of the account
- find the state of the account
- change the overdraft limit
- find the overdraft limit

Rather than saying "We need to do these operations on a bank account", object-based design turns this on its head, a bit like President Kennedy did all those years ago:

"And so, my fellow Americans: ask not what your country can do for you—ask what you can do for your country" (huge cheers)

We don't do things to the bank account. Instead we ask it to do these things for us. The design of our banking application can be thought of in terms of identifying the objects that we are going to use to represent the information and then specifying what things they should be able to do. The really clever bit is that once we have decided what the bank account should do, we then might be able to get somebody else to make it do these things.

If our specification is correct and they implement it properly, we don't have to worry precisely how they made it work – we just have to sit back and take the credit for a job well done.

This brings us back to a couple of recurring themes in this document; *metadata* and *testing*. What a bank account object should be able to do is part of the metadata for this object. And once we have decided on the actions that the account must perform, the next thing we need to do is devise a way in which each of the actions can be tested.

In this section we are going to implement an object which has some of the behaviours of a proper bank account.

Programmer's Point: Not Everything Should Be Possible

Note that there are also some things that we should **not** be able to do with our bank account objects. The account number of an account is something which is unique to that account and should never change. We can get this behaviour by simply not providing a means by which it can be changed. It is important at design time that we identify what should not be possible, along with what should be done. We might even identify some things as being audited, in that an object will keep track of what has been done to it. That way we can easily find out if bad things are being done.

4.5.1 Data in Objects

So, we can consider our bank account in terms of what we want it to do for us. The first thing is to identify all the data items that we want to store in it. For the sake of simplicity, for now I'm just going to consider how I keep track of the balance of the accounts. This will let me describe all the techniques that are required without getting bogged down too much.

```
class Account
{
    public decimal Balance;
}
```

The `Account` class above holds the member that we need to store about the balance of our bank accounts. Members of a class which hold a value which describes some data which the class is holding are often called *properties*. I've used the decimal type for the account balance, since this is specially designed to hold financial values.

We have seen that each of the data items in a class is a *member* of it and stored as part of it. Each time I create an instance of the class I get all the members as well. We have already seen that it is very easy to create an instance of a class and set the value of a member:

```
Account RobsAccount ;
RobsAccount = new Account();
RobsAccount.Balance = 99;
```

The reason that this works is that the members of the object are all *public* and this means that anybody has direct access to them. This means that any programmer writing the application can do things like:

```
RobsAccount.Balance = 0;
```

- and take away all my money. If we are going to provide a way of stopping this from happening we need to protect the data inside our objects.

4.5.2 Member Protection inside objects

If objects are going to be useful we have to have a way of protecting the data within them. Ideally I want to get control when someone tries to change a value in my objects, and stop the change from being made if I don't like it. The posh word for this is *encapsulation*. I want all the important data hidden inside my object so that I have complete control over what is done with it. This technology is the key to my *defensive programming* approach which is geared to making sure that, whatever else happens, my part of the program does not go wrong.

For example, in our bank program we want to make sure that the balance is never changed in a manner that we can't control. The first thing we need to do is stop the outside world from playing with our balance value:

```
class Account
{
    private decimal balance;
}
```

The property is no longer marked as `public`. Instead it is now `private`. This means that the outside world no longer has direct access to it. If I write the code:

```
RobsAccount.balance = 0;
```

- I will get an error when I try to compile the program:

```
PrivateDemo.cs(13,3): error CS0122: 'PrivateMembers.Account.balance' is inaccessible due to its protection level
```

The balance value is now held inside the object and is not visible to the outside world.

Changing private members

I can tell what you are thinking at this point. You are thinking "What is the point of making it private, now you can't change it at all". Well, thanks for the vote of confidence folks. It turns out that I can change the value, but only using code actually running in the class. Consider the program:

```csharp
class Account
{
  private decimal balance = 0;

  public bool WithdrawFunds ( decimal amount )
  {
    if ( balance < amount )
    {
      return false ;
    }
    balance = balance - amount ;
    return true;
  }
}

class Bank
{
  public static void Main ()
  {
    Account RobsAccount;
    RobsAccount = new Account();
    if ( RobsAccount.WithdrawFunds (5) )
    {
      Console.WriteLine ( "Cash Withdrawn" ) ;
    }
    else
    {
      Console.WriteLine ( "Insufficient Funds" ) ;
    }
  }
}
```

Code Sample 31 Withdraw insufficient funds

This creates an account and then tries to draw five pounds out of it. This will of course fail, since the initial balance on my account is zero, but it shows how I go about providing access to members in an account. The method `WithdrawFunds` is a member of the `Account` class and can therefore access private members of the class.

Programmer's Point: Metadata makes Members and Methods

I haven't mentioned metadata for at least five minutes. So perhaps now is a good time. The metadata that I gather about my bank system will drive how I provide access to the members of my classes. In the code above the way that I am protecting the balance value reflects how the customer wants me to make sure that this value is managed properly.

public Methods

You may have noticed that I made the `WithdrawFunds` method `public`. This means that code running outside the class can make calls to that method. This has got to be the case, since we want people to interact with our objects by calling methods in them. In general the rules are:

- if it is a data member (i.e. it holds data) of the class, make it `private`
- if it is a method member (i.e. it does something) make it `public`

Of course, the rules can be broken on special occasions. If you don't care about possible corruption of the member and you want your program to run as quickly as possible you can make a data member `public`. If you want to write a method which is only used inside a class and performs some special, secret, task you can make it `private`.

Programmer's Point: Use coding conventions to show which things are private

If you look closely at the code I write (and I would advise you to do this, it's good stuff) you will find that when I write the name of a public item I use a capital letter to start the name (as in the case of `WithdrawFunds` to withdraw from our bank account). But I make the first letter of private members lower case (as in the case of the balance data member of our bank account). This makes it easy for someone reading my code, because they can see from the name of a class member whether or not it is public or private. The convention also extends to variables which are local to a block. These (for example the ubiquitous i) always start with a lower-case letter.

Some people go further and do things like put the characters m_ in front of variables which are members of a class. They would call their `balance` value `m_balance` so that class members are easy to spot. I don't usually go that far, because I reckon that the name of the member is usually enough, but opinions differ on this one. The most important thing in this situation is that the whole programming team adopts the same conventions on matters like these. In fact, most development companies have documents that set out the coding conventions they use, and expect developers to adhere to these.

4.5.3 A Complete Account Class

We can now create a bank account class which controls access to the balance value:

```
public class Account
{
    private decimal balance = 0;

    public bool WithdrawFunds ( decimal amount )
    {
        if ( balance < amount )
        {
                return false ;
        }
        balance = balance - amount ;
        return true;
    }

    public void PayInFunds ( decimal amount )
    {
        balance = balance + amount ;
    }
```

```csharp
        public decimal GetBalance ()
        {
            return balance;
        }
    }
```

The bank account class that I have created above is quite well behaved. I have created three methods which I can use to interact with an account object. I can pay money in, find out how much is there and withdraw cash, for example:

```csharp
Account test = new Account();
test.PayInFunds(50);
```

At the end of this set of statements the test account should have 50 pounds in it. If it does not my program is faulty. The method `GetBalance` is called an *accessor* since it allows access to data in my business object. I could write a little bit of code to test these methods:

```csharp
Account test = new Account();
test.PayInFunds(50);
if ( test.GetBalance() != 50 )
{
    Console.WriteLine ( "Pay In test failed" );
}
else
{
    Console.WriteLine ( "Pay In test succeeded" );
}
```

Code Sample 32 Testing the Account Class

My program now tests itself, in that it does something and then makes sure that the effect of that action is correct. Of course I must still read the output from all the tests, which is tedious. Later we will consider the use of *unit tests* which make this much easier.

Programmer's Point: Make a Siren go off when your tests fail

The above test is good but not great. It just produces a little message if the test fails. You have to read that message, and if you don't notice it then you might think your code is OK. My tests count the number of errors that they have found. If the error count is greater than zero they print out a huge message in flashing red text to indicate that something bad has happened. Some development teams actually connect sirens and flashing red lights to their test systems, so that it is impossible to ignore a failing test. They then search out the programmer who caused the failure and make him or her pay for coffee for the next week.

4.5.4 Test Driven Development

I love test driven development. If I ever write anything new you can bet your boots that I will write it using a test driven approach. This solves three problems that I can see:

1. You don't do the testing at the end of the project. This is usually the worst time to test, since you might be using code that you wrote some time back. If the bugs are in an old piece of code you have to go through the effort of remembering how it works. Far better to test the code as you write it, when you have the best possible understanding of what it is supposed to do.

2. You can write code early in the project which will probably be useful later on. Many projects are doomed because people start programming before they have a proper understanding of the problem. Writing the tests first is actually a really good way of refining your understanding. And there is a good chance that the tests that you write will be useful at some point too.

3. When you fix bugs in your program you need to be able to convince yourself that the fixes have not broken some other part (about the most common way of introducing new faults into a program is to mend a bug). If you have a set of automatic tests that run after every bug fix you have a way of stopping this from happening.

So, please develop using tests. You will thank me later.

Programmer's Point: Some things are hard to test

Test development is a good way to travel, but it does not solve all your problems. Some types of programs are really hard to test in this way. Anything with a front end where users type in commands and get responses is very hard to test like this, because although it is easy to send things into a program it is often much harder to see what the program does in response. My approach in these situations is to make the user interface part a very thin layer which sits on top of requests to objects to do the work. In the case of our bank account above, the code that provides the user interface where the customer enters how much they want to withdraw will be very simple and connect directly to the methods provided by my objects. As long as my object tests are passed, I can be fairly confident that the user interface will be OK too.

The other kind of program that is very hard to test in this way is any kind of game. This is mainly because the quality of gameplay is not something you can design tests for. Only when someone comes back and says "The game is too hard because you can't kill the end of level boss without dying" can you actually do something about it. The only solution in this situation is to set out very clearly what your tests are trying to prove (so that the human testers know what to look for) and make it very easy to change the values that will affect the gameplay. For example it should be easy to adjust how much damage a hit from an alien causes to your spacecraft, and the speed of all the game objects.

4.6 Static Items

At the moment all the members that we have created in our class have been part of an instance of the class. This means that whenever we create an instance of the `Account` class we get a `balance` member. However, we can also create members which are held as part of the class, i.e. they exist outside of any particular instance.

4.6.1 Static class members

The `static` keyword lets us create members which are not held in an instance, but in the class itself.

It is very important that you learn what `static` means in the context of C# programs. We have used it lots in just about every program that we have ever written:

```
class AccountTest
{
  public static void Main ()
  {
    Account test = new Account();
    test.PayInFunds (50);
    Console.WriteLine ("Balance:" + test.GetBalance());
  }
}
```

The `AccountTest` class has a `static` member method called `Main`. We know that this is the method which is called to run the program. It is part of the **class** `AccountTest`. If I made fifty `AccountTest` instances, they would all share the same `Main` method. In terms of C# the keyword `static` flags a member as being part of the class, **not** part of an instance of the class. I will write that down again in a posh font, for it is important:

> *"A static member is a member of the class, not a member of an instance of the class"*

I don't have to make an instance of the `AccountTest` class to be able to use the `Main` method. This is how my program actually gets to work, in that when it starts it has not made any instances of anything, and so this method **must** be there already, otherwise it cannot run.

Static does not mean "cannot be changed". I think this is time for more posh font stuff:

> *Static does not mean "cannot be changed".*

Members of a class which have been made `static` can be used just like any other member of a class. Either a data member or a method can be made `static`.

4.6.2 Using a static data member of a class

Perhaps an example of `static` data would help at this point. Consider the interest rates of our bank accounts. The customer has told us that one of the members of the account class will need to be the interest rate on accounts. In the program we can implement this by adding another member to the class which holds the current interest rate:

```
public class Account
{
  public decimal Balance ;
  public decimal InterestRateCharged ;
}
```

Now I can create accounts and set balances and interest rates on them. (of course if I was doing this properly I'd make this stuff private and provide methods etc, but I'm keeping things simple just now).

```
Account RobsAccount = new Account();
RobsAccount.Balance = 100;
RobsAccount.InterestRateCharged = 10;
```

The snag is; I've been told that the interest rate is held for all the accounts. If the interest rate changes it must change for **all** accounts. This means that to implement the change I'd have to go through all the accounts and update the rate. This would be tedious, and if I missed one account, possibly expensive.

I solve the problem by making the interest rate member `static`:

```
public class Account
{
  public decimal Balance ;
  public static decimal InterestRateCharged ;
}
```

The interest rate is now part of the class, not part of any instance. This means that I have to change the way that I get hold of it:

```
Account RobsAccount = new Account();
RobsAccount.Balance = 100;
Account.InterestRateCharged = 10;
```

Since it is a member of the class I now have to use the class name to get hold of it instead of the name of the instance reference.

Programmer's Point: Static Data Members are Useful and Dangerous

When you are collecting metadata about your project you should look for things which can be made static. Things like the limits of values (the largest age that you are going to permit a person to have) can be made static. There might be a time where the age limit changes, and you don't want to have to update all the objects in your program.

But of course, as Spiderman's uncle said, "With great power comes great responsibility". You should be careful about how you provide access to static data items. A change to a single static value will affect your entire system. So they should always be made private and updated by means of method calls.

4.6.3 Using a `static` method in a class

We can make methods `static` too. We have been doing this for ages with the `Main` method. But you can also use them when designing your system. For example, we might have a method which decides whether or not someone is allowed to have a bank account. It would take in their age and income. It would then return true or false depending on whether these are acceptable or not:

```
public bool AccountAllowed ( decimal income, int age )
{
  if ( ( income >= 10000 ) && ( age >= 18 ) )
  {
      return true;
  }
  else {
      return false;
  }
}
```

The method above checks the age and income values for a prospective account; you must be over 17 and have at least 10000 pounds' income to be allowed an account. The snag is that, at the moment, we can't call the method until we have an `Account` instance. We can solve this by making the method `static`:

```
public static bool AccountAllowed ( decimal income, int age )
{
  if ( ( income >= 10000 ) && ( age >= 18 ) )
  {
      return true;
  }
  else
  {
      return false;
  }
}
```

Now the method is part of the class, not an instance of the class. I can now call the method by using the class name:

```
if ( Account.AccountAllowed ( 25000, 21 ) )
{
   Console.WriteLine ( "Allowed Account" );
}
```

This is nice because I have not had to make an instance of the account to find out if one is allowed.

Using member data in static methods

The `Allowed` method is OK, but of course I have fixed the age and income methods into it. I might decide to make the method more flexible:

```csharp
public class Account
{
  private decimal minIncome = 10000;
  private int minAge = 18;

  public static bool AccountAllowed(decimal income, int age)
  {
    if ( ( income >= minIncome) && ( age >= minAge) )
    {
      return true;
    }
    else
    {
      return false;
    }
  }
}
```

This is a better design, in that I now have members of the class which set out the upper limits of the age and income. However it is a bad program, since the class above will not compile:

```
AccountManagement.cs(19,21): error CS0120: An object reference is required for the
nonstatic field, method, or property 'Account.minIncome'

AccountManagement.cs(19,43): error CS0120: An object reference is required for the
nonstatic field, method, or property 'Account.minAge'
```

As usual, the compiler is telling us exactly what is wrong; using language which makes our heads spin. What the compiler really means is that *"a static method is using a member of the class which is not static"*.

If that doesn't help, how about this: The members `minIncome` and `minAge` are held within *instances* of the `Account` class. However, a static method can run without an instance (since it is part of the class). The compiler is unhappy because in this situation the method would not have any members to play with. We can fix this (and get our program completely correct) by making the income and age limits `static` as well:

```csharp
public class Account
{
  private static decimal minIncome ;
  private static int minAge ;

  public static bool AccountAllowed(decimal income, int age)
  {
    if ( ( income >= minIncome) && ( age >= minAge) )
    {
      return true;
    }
    else
    {
      return false;
    }
  }
}
```

Code Sample 33 Using AccountAllowed

If you think about it, this makes perfect sense. The limit values should not be stored in each class instance since we want the limits to be the same for all instances of the class, therefore, making them `static` is what we should have done in the first place.

Programmer's Point: Static Method Members can be used to make Libraries

Sometimes in a development you need to provide a library of methods to do stuff. In the C# system itself there are a huge number of methods to perform maths functions, for example sin and cos. It makes sense to make these methods static, in that in this situation all we want is the method itself, not an instance of a class. Again, when you are building your system you should think about how you are going to make such methods available for your own use.

BANK NOTES: STATIC BANK INFORMATION

The kind of problems that we can use `static` to solve in our bank are:

static member variable: the manager would like us to be able to set the interest rate for all the customer accounts at once. A single static member of the Account class will provide a variable which can be used inside all instances of the class. But because there is only a single copy of this value this can be changed and thereby adjust the interest rate for all the accounts. Any value which is held once for all classes (limits on values are another example of this) is best managed as a static value. The time it becomes impossible to use static is when the manager says "Oh, accounts for five year olds have a different interest rate from normal ones". At this point we know we can't use static because we need to hold different values for some of the instances.

static member method: the manager tells us that we need a method to determine whether or not a given person is allowed to have an account. I can't make this part of any Account instance because at the time we would want to use the method an account instance would not have been generated. I must make it `static`, so that it can execute without an instance.

4.7 The Construction of Objects

We have seen that our objects are created when we use new to bring one into being:

```
test = new Account();
```

If you look closely at what is happening you might decide that what is happening looks quite a bit like a method call.

This is actually exactly what is happening. When an instance of a class is created the C# system makes a call to a *constructor* method in that class. The constructor method is a member of the class and it is there to let the programmer get control and set up the contents of the shiny new object. One of the rules of the C# game is that every single class **must** have a constructor method to be called when a new instance is created.

"But wait a minute", you say, "We've been making objects for a while and I've never had to provide a constructor method". This is because the C# compiler is, for a change, being friendly here. Rather than shout at you for not providing a constructor method, the compiler instead quietly creates a *default* one for you and uses that.

You might think this is strange, in that normally the compiler loses no time in telling you off when you don't do something, but in this case it is simply solving the problem without telling you. There are two ways to look at this:

nice compiler: the compiler is trying to make life easier for you

evil compiler: the compiler knows that if it does this automatically now you will suffer more later when you try to understand why you don't need to add one

How you regard the action of the compiler is up to you.

4.7.1 The Default Constructor

A constructor method has the same name as the class, but it does not return anything. It is called when we perform new. If you don't supply a constructor (and we haven't so far) the compiler creates one for us.

```
public class Account
{
    public Account ()
    {
    }
}
```

This is what the default constructor looks like. It is `public` so that it can be accessed from external classes who might want to make instances of the class. It accepts no parameters. If I create my own constructor the compiler assumes that I know what I'm doing and stops providing the default one. This can cause problems, which we will discuss later.

4.7.2 Our Own Constructor

For fun, we could make a constructor which just prints out that it has been called:

```
public class Account
{
    public Account ()
    {
      Console.WriteLine ( "We just made an account" );
    }
}
```

This constructor is not very constructive (ho ho) but it does let us know when it has been called. This means that when my program executes the line:

```
robsAccount = new Account();
```

- the program will print out the message:

```
We just made an account
```

Note that this is not very sensible, in that it will result in a lot of printing out which the user of the program might not appreciate, but it does show how the process works.

Feeding the Constructor Information

It is useful to be able to get control when an `Account` is created, but it would be even nicer to be able to feed information into the `Account` when I create it. As an example, I might want to set the name, address, and initial balance of an account holder when the account is created. In other words I want to do:

```
robsAccount = new Account( "Rob Miles", "Hull", 0 );
```

This could create a new account and set the name property to `Rob Miles`, the address to `Hull` and the initial balance to zero. It turns out that I can do this very easily, all I have to do is make the constructor method to accept these parameters and use them to set up the members of the class:

```
class Account
{
  // private member data
  private string name;
  private string address;
  private decimal balance;

  // constructor
  public Account (string inName, string inAddress,
    decimal inBalance)
  {
    name = inName;
    address = inAddress;
    balance = inBalance;
  }
}
```

The constructor takes the values supplied in the parameters and uses them to set up the members of the `Account` instance that is being created. In this respect it behaves exactly as any other method call.

```
class Bank
{
    public static void Main()
    {
        Account robsAccount;
        robsAccount = new Account("Rob", "Robs House",
                                  1000000);
    }
}
```

Code Sample 34 Using a custom constructor

The code above would create an account for Rob which has 1000000 pounds in it. I wish.

Note that adding a constructor like this has one very powerful ramification:

You **must** use the new constructor to make an instance of a class, i.e. the only way I can now make an `Account` object is by supplying a name, address and starting balance. If I try to do this:

```
robsAccount = new Account();
```

- the compiler will stop being nice to me and produce the error:

```
AccountTest.cs(9,27): error CS1501: No overload for method 'Account' takes '0' arguments
```

What the compiler is telling me is that there is no constructor in the class which does not have any parameters. In other words, the compiler only provides a default constructor if the programmer doesn't provide a constructor.

This can cause confusion if we have made use of the default constructor in our program and we then add one of our own. The default constructor is no longer supplied by the compiler and our program now fails to compile correctly. In that situation you have to either find all the calls to the default one and update them, or create a default constructor of your own for these calls to use. Of course you don't have to do this because your design of the program was so good that you never have this problem. Just like me, hem hem.

4.7.3 Overloading Constructors

Overload is an interesting word. In the context of the "Star Trek" science fiction series it is what they did to the warp engines in every other episode. In the context of a C# program it means:

"A method has the same name as another, but has a different set of parameters"

The compiler is quite happy for you to overload methods, because it can tell from the parameters given at the call of the method which one to use. In the context of the constructor of a class, what this means is that you can provide several different ways of constructing an instance of a class. For example, many (but not all) of your accounts will be created with a balance value of zero, i.e. nothing in the account. This means that we would like to be able to write

```
robsAccount = new Account("Rob Miles", "Hull");
```

I've missed off the balance value, since I want to use the "default" one of zero. If your code does this the compiler simply looks for a constructor method which has two strings as parameters, and nothing else. Something a bit like this:

```
public Account (string inName, string inAddress)
{
  name = inName;
  address = inAddress;
  balance = 0;
}
```

Overloading a method name

In fact, you can overload any method name in your classes. This can be useful if you have a particular action which can be driven by a number of different items of data, for example you could provide several ways of setting the date of a transaction:

```
SetDate ( int year, int month, int day )

SetDate ( int year, int julianDate )

SetDate ( string dateInMMDDYY )
```

A call of:

```
SetDate (2005, 7, 23);
```

- would be matched up with the method which accepts three integer parameters and that code would be executed.

4.7.4 Constructor Management

If the Account class is going to have lots of constructor methods this can get very confusing for the programmer:

```
public Account (string inName, string inAddress,
   decimal inBalance)
{
  name = inName;
  address = inAddress;
  balance = inBalance;
}

public Account (string inName, string inAddress)
{
  name = inName;
```

```csharp
    address = inAddress;
    balance = 0;
}

public Account (string inName)
{
    name = inName;
    address = "Not Supplied";
    balance = 0;
}
```

I've made three constructors for an `Account` instance. The first is supplied with all the information, the second is not given a balance and sets the value to 0. The third is not given the address either, and sets the address to `"Not Supplied"`.

To do this I have had to duplicate code. Good programmers **hate** duplicating code. It is regarded as "dangerous extra work". The scary thing is that it is quite easy to do, just use the block copy command in the text editor and you can take the same piece of program and use it all over the place. But you should not do this. Because it is bad. If you need to change this piece of code you have to find every copy of the code and change it.

This happens more often than you'd think, even if you don't put a bug in your code, you still might find yourself having to change it because the specification changes. So, C# provides a way in which you can call one constructor from another. Consider:

```csharp
public Account (string inName, string inAddress,
    decimal inBalance)
{
    name = inName;
    address = inAddress;
    balance = inBalance;
}
public Account ( string inName, string inAddress ) :
    this (inName, inAddress, 0 )
{
}

public Account ( string inName ) :
    this (inName, "Not Supplied", 0 )
{
}
```

The keyword `this` means "another constructor in this class". As you can see in the code sample above, the highlighted bits of the code are calls to the first constructor. They simply pass the parameters which are supplied, along with any default values that we have created, on to the "proper" constructor to deal with. This means that the actual transfer of the values from the constructor into the object itself only happens in one method, and the other constructor methods just make calls to it.

The syntax of these calls is rather interesting, in that the call to the constructor takes place before the body of the constructor method. In fact it is outside the block completely. This is sensible, because it reflects exactly what is happening. The "`this`" constructor runs before the body of the other constructor is entered. In fact, in the code above, since the call of `this` does all the work, the body of the constructor can be empty.

```csharp
class Bank
{
    public static void Main()
    {
        const int MAX_CUST = 100;
        Account[] Accounts = new Account[MAX_CUST];
```

```
        Accounts[0] = new Account("Rob", "Robs House",
                                 1000000);
        Accounts[1] = new Account("Jim", "Jims House");
        Accounts[2] = new Account("Fred");
    }
}
```

Code Sample 35 Overloaded Constructors

The sample code above shows constructor overloading being used properly. The code creates an array of Account references (called Accounts) and then sets the first three elements to point to Account instances. The first element points to an Account for Rob with a full address and 1000000 pounds. The second element (element 1) refers to an account for Jim with his address and the default balance of 0. The third element (element 0) refers to an account for Fred which has the default address ("Not Supplied") and a default balance of 0.

Programmer's Point: Object Construction Should Be Planned

The way in which objects are constructed is something that you should plan carefully when you write your program. You should create one "master" constructor which handles the most comprehensive method of constructing the object. Then you should make all the other constructor methods use **this** to get hold of that method.

4.7.5 A constructor cannot fail

If you watch a James Bond movie there is usually a point at which agent 007 is told that the fate of the world is in his hands. Failure is not an option. Constructors are a bit like this. Constructors cannot fail. And this is a problem:

Whenever we have written methods in the past we have made sure that their behaviour is error checked so that the method cannot upset the state of our object. For example, attempts to withdraw negative amounts of money from a bank account should be rejected.

The whole basis of the way that we have allowed our objects to be manipulated is to make sure that they cannot be broken by the people using them. If you try to do something stupid with a method call it should refuse to perform the action and return something which indicates that it could not do the job.

So we know that when we create a method which changes the data in an object we have to make sure that the change is always valid. For example, we would not let the following call succeed:

```
RobsAccount.PayInFunds (1234567890);
```

There will be an upper limit to the amount of cash you can pay in at once, so the `PayInFunds` method will refuse to pay the money in. But what is to stop the following:

```
RobsAccount = new Account ("Rob", "Hull", 1234567890);
```

Like James Bond, constructors are not allowed to fail. Whatever happens during the constructor call, it will complete and a new instance will be created.

This poses a problem. It looks as if we can veto stupid values at every point except the one which is most important, i.e. when the object is first created.

Programmer's Point: Managing Failure is Hard Work

This brings us on to a kind of recurring theme in our quest to become great programmers. Writing code to do a job is usually very easy. Writing code which will handle all the possible failure conditions in a useful way is much trickier. It is a fact of programming life that you will (or at least should) spend more time worrying about how things fail than you ever do about how they work correctly.

Constructors and Exceptions

The only way round this at the moment is to have the constructor throw an exception if it is unhappy. This means that the user of the constructor must make sure that they catch exceptions when creating objects, which is not a bad thing. The really clever way to do this is to make the constructor call the set methods for each of the properties that it has been given, and if any of them returns with an error the constructor should throw the exception at that Point:

```
public Account (string inName, string inAddress)
{
  if ( SetName ( inName ) == false ) {
    throw new Exception ( "Bad name " + inName) ;
  }
  if ( SetAddress ( inAddress ) == false ) {
    throw new Exception ( "Bad address" + inAddress) ;
  }
}
```

If we try to create an account with a bad name it will throw an exception, which is what we want. The only problem here is that if the address is wrong too, the user of the method will not know this until they have fixed the name and then called the constructor again.

I hate it when I'm using a program and this happens. It is normally when I'm filling in a form on the web. I type in my name wrong and it complains about that. Then I put my name right, and it complains about my address. What I want is a way in which I can get a report of all the invalid parts of the item at once. This can be done, at the expense of a little bit of complication:

```
public Account(string inName, string inAddress,
    decimal inBalance)
{
    string errorMessage = "";

    if (SetBalance(inBalance)==false)
        errorMessage = errorMessage + "Bad Balance: " +
                    inBalance;

    if (SetName(inName) == false)
    {
        errorMessage = errorMessage + "Bad name: " + inName;
    }

    if (SetAddress(inAddress) == false)
    {
        errorMessage = errorMessage + " Bad addr: " +
                    inAddress;
    }

    if (errorMessage != "")
    {
        throw new Exception("Account construction failed "
            + errorMessage);
```

```
        }
    }
```
Code Sample 36 Constructor Failing

This version of the constructor assembles an error message which describes everything which is wrong with the account. Each new thing which is wrong is added to the message and then the whole thing is put into an exception and thrown back to the caller.

Programmer's Point: Consider the International Issues

The code above assembles a text message and sends it to the user when something bad happens. This is a good thing. However, if you write the program as above this might cause a problem when you install the code in a French branch of the bank. During the specification process you need to establish if the code is ever going to be created in multiple language versions. If it is you will need to manage the storage and selection of appropriate messages. Fortunately there are some C# libraries which are designed to make this easier.

BANK NOTES: CONSTRUCTING AN ACCOUNT

The issues revolving around the constructor of a class are not directly relevant to the bank account specification as such, since they really relate to how the specification is implemented, and not what the system itself actually does.

That said; if the manager says something like "The customer fills in a form, enters their name and address and this is used to create the new account" this gives you a good idea of what parameters should be supplied to the constructor.

4.8 From Object to Component

I take the view that as you develop as a software writer you go through a process of "stepping back" from problems and thinking at higher and higher levels. Posh people call this "abstraction". This is the progress that we have made so far:

- representing values by named locations (variables)
- creating actions which work on the variables (statements and blocks)
- putting behaviours into lumps of code which we can give names to. We can reuse these behaviours and also use them in the design process (methods)
- creating things which contain member variables as properties and member methods as actions (objects)

Rather than spend a lot of time at the start of a project worrying just how we are going represent an account and precisely what it should do, we just say "We need an account here" and then move on to other things. Later we will come back and revisit the problem in a greater level of detail, and from the point of view of what the `Account` class needs to do.

The next thing to do is consider how we take a further step back and consider expressing a solution using *components* and *interfaces*. In this section you will find out the difference between an object and a component, and how to design systems using them.

4.8.1 Components and Hardware

Before we start on things from a software point of view it is probably worth considering things from a hardware point of view. You should be familiar with the way that, in a typical home computer, some parts are not "hard wired" to the system. For example, the graphics adapter is usually a separate device which is plugged into the main board. This is good; because it means that I can buy a new graphics adapter at any time and fit it into the machine to improve the performance.

For this to work properly the people who make main boards and the people who make graphics adapters have had to agree on an *interface* between two devices. This takes the form of a large document which describes exactly how the two components interact, for example which signals are inputs, which signals are outputs and so on. Any main board which contains a socket built to the standard can accept a graphics card.

So, from the point of view of hardware, components are possible because we have created standard *interfaces* which describe exactly how they fit together.

Software components are **exactly the same**.

Why we Need Software Components?

At the moment you might not see a need for software components. When we are creating a system we work out what each of the parts of it need to do, and then we create those parts. It is not obvious at this stage why components are required.

Well, a system designed without components is exactly like a computer with a graphics adapter which is part of the main board. It is not possible for me to improve the graphics adapter because it is "hard wired" into the system.

However, it is unfortunately the case that with our bank system we may have a need to create different forms of bank account class. For example, we might be asked to create a "BabyAccount" class which only lets the account holder draw out up to ten pounds each time. This might happen even after we have installed the system and it is being used.

If everything has been hard wired into place this will be impossible. By describing objects in terms of their interfaces however, we can use anything which behaves like an Account in this position.

4.8.2 Components and Interfaces

One point I should make here is that we are **not** talking about the *user interface* to our program. The user interface is the way a person using our program would make it work for them. These are usually either text based (the user types in commands and gets responses) or graphical (the user clicks on "buttons" on a screen using the mouse).

An *interface* on the other hand just specifies how a software component could be used by another software component. Please don't be tempted to answer an exam question about the C# interface mechanism with a long description of how windows and buttons work. This will earn you zero marks.

Interfaces and Design

So, instead of starting off by designing classes we should instead be thinking about describing their interfaces, i.e. what it is they have to do. In C# we express this information in a thing called an *interface*. An interface is simply a set of method definitions which are lumped together.

Our first pass at a bank account interface could be as follows:

```csharp
public interface IAccount
{
   void PayInFunds ( decimal amount );
   bool WithdrawFunds ( decimal amount );
   decimal GetBalance ();
}
```

This says that the `IAccount` interface is comprised of three methods, one to pay money in; another to withdraw it and a third which returns the balance on the account. From the balance management point of view this is all we need. Note that at the interface level I am not saying how it should be done, I am instead just saying what should be done. An interface is placed in a source file just like a class, and compiled in the same way. It sets out a number of methods which relate to a particular task or role, in this case what a class must do to be considered a bank account.

Programmer's Point: Interface names start with I

We have seen that there are things called coding conventions, which set down standards for naming variables. Another convention is that the name of an interface should start with the letter I. If you don't do this your programs will compile fine, since the compiler has no opinions on variable names, but you may have trouble sleeping at night. And quite right too.

4.8.3 Implementing an Interface in C#

Interfaces become interesting when we make a class *implement* them. Implementing an interface is a bit like setting up a contract between the supplier of resources and the consumer. If a class implements an interface it is saying that for every method described in the interface, it has a corresponding implementation.

In the case of the bank account, I am going to create a class which implements the interface, so that it can be thought of as an account component, irrespective of what it really is:

```csharp
public class CustomerAccount : IAccount
{

   private decimal balance = 0;

   public bool WithdrawFunds ( decimal amount )
   {
      if ( balance < amount )
      {
         return false ;
      }
      balance = balance - amount ;
      return true;
   }

   public void PayInFunds ( decimal amount )
   {
      balance = balance + amount ;
   }

   public decimal GetBalance ()
   {
      return balance;
   }
}
```

The code above does not look that different from the previous account class. The only difference is the top line:

```
public class CustomerAccount : IAccount
{
...
```

The highlighted part of the line above is where the programmer tells the compiler that this class implements the `IAccount` interface. This means that the class contains concrete versions of all the methods described in the interface. If the class does not contain a method that the interface needs you will get a compilation error:

```
error CS0535: 'AccountManagement.CustomerAccount' does not implement interface member
'AccountManagement.IAccount.PayInFunds(decimal)'
```

In this case I missed out the `PayInFunds` method and the compiler complained accordingly.

4.8.4 References to Interfaces

Once we have made the `CustomerAccount` class compile, we have now got something which can be regarded in two ways:

- as a `CustomerAccount` (because that is what it is)
- as an `IAccount` (because that is what it can do)

People do this all the time. You can think of me in a whole variety of ways, here are two:

- Rob Miles the individual (because that is who I am)
- A writer (because that is what I can do)

If you think of me as a writer you would be using the interface that contains methods like `WriteBook`. And you can use the same methods with any other writer (i.e. person who implements that interface). From the point of view of a publisher, which has to manage a large number of interchangeable writer, it is much more useful for it to think of me as a writer, rather than Rob Miles the individual.

So, with interfaces we are moving away from considering classes in terms of what they are, and starting to think about them in terms of what they can do. In the case of our bank, this means that we want to deal with objects in terms of `IAccount`,(the set of account abilities) rather than `CustomerAccount` (a particular account class).

In C# terms this means that we need to be able to create reference variables which refer to objects in terms of interfaces they implement, rather than the particular type that they are. It turns out that this is quite easy:

```
IAccount account = new CustomerAccount();
account.PayInFunds(50);
Console.WriteLine("Balance: " + account.GetBalance());
```

Code Sample 37 Simple Interface

The `account` variable is allowed to refer to objects which implement the `IAccount` interface. The compiler will check to make sure that `CustomerAccount` does this, and if it does, the compilation is successful.

Note that there will never be an instance of `IAccount` interface. It is simply a way that we can refer to something which has that ability (i.e. contains the required methods).

This is the same in real life. There is no such physical thing as a "lecturer", merely a large number of people who can be referred to as having that particular ability or role.

4.8.5 Using interfaces

Now that we have our system designed with interfaces it is much easier to extend it. I can create a `BabyAccount` class which implements the `IAccount` interface. This implements all the required methods, but they behave slightly differently because we want all withdrawals of over ten pounds to fail:

```csharp
public class BabyAccount : IAccount
{
    private decimal balance = 0;

    public bool WithdrawFunds ( decimal amount )
    {
        if (amount > 10)
        {
            return false ;
        }
        if (balance < amount)
        {
            return false ;
        }
        balance = balance - amount ;
        return true;
    }

    public void PayInFunds ( decimal amount )
    {
        balance = balance + amount ;
    }

    public decimal GetBalance ()
    {
        return balance;
    }
}
```

The nice thing about this is that as it is a component we don't have to change all the classes which use it. When we create the account objects we just have to ask if a standard account or a baby account is required. The rest of the system can then pick up this object and use it without caring exactly what it is. We will of course have to create some tests especially for it, so that we can make sure that withdrawals of more than ten pounds do fail, but using the new kind of account in our existing system is very easy.

This means that we can create components that are used in the same way, but have different behaviours which are appropriate to the type of item they are representing.

```csharp
class Bank
{
    const int MAX_CUST = 100;

    public static void Main()
    {
        IAccount [] accounts = new IAccount[MAX_CUST];

        accounts[0] = new CustomerAccount();
        accounts[0].PayInFunds(50);
        Console.WriteLine("Balance: " +
                          accounts[0].GetBalance());

        accounts[1] = new BabyAccount();
        accounts[1].PayInFunds(20);
        Console.WriteLine("Balance: " +
```

```
                accounts[1].GetBalance());
        if (accounts[0].WithdrawFunds(20))
        {
            Console.WriteLine("Withdraw OK");
        }
        if (accounts[1].WithdrawFunds(20))
        {
            Console.WriteLine("Withdraw OK");
        }
    }
}
```

Code Sample 38 Using Components

The code above shows how this would really be used. The accounts array can hold references to any object that implements the `IAccount` interface. This includes `CustomerAccount` and `BabyAccount` objects. The first element in the array (element 0) is assigned to a `CustomerAccount` object and the second element (element 1) assigned to a `BabyAccount`. When methods are called on these objects the one in the particular type is used. This means that the final call of WithDrawFunds will fail because, although the baby has enough money in the bank they are not allowed to draw out more than 10 pounds.

4.8.6 Implementing Multiple Interfaces

A component can implement as many interfaces as are required. The `IAccount` interface lets me regard a component purely in terms of its ability to behave as a bank account. However, I may want to regard a component in a variety of ways. For example, the bank will want the account to be able to print itself out on paper.

You might think that all I have to do is add a print method to the `IAccount` interface. This would be reasonable if all I ever wanted to print was bank accounts. However, there will be lots of things which need to be printed, for example warning letters, special offers and the like. Each of these items will be implemented in terms of a component which provides a particular interface (`IWarning`, `ISpecialOffer` for example). I don't want to have to provide a print method in each of these, what I really want is a way that I can regard an object in terms of its ability to print.

This is actually very easy. I create the interface:

```
public interface IPrintToPaper
{
    void DoPrint ();
}
```

Now anything which implements the `IPrintToPaper` interface will contain the `DoPrint` method and can be thought of in terms of its ability to print.

A class can implement as many interfaces as it needs. Each interface is a new way in which it can be referred to and accessed.

```
public class BabyAccount : IAccount, IPrintToPaper
{
...
```

This means that a `BabyAccount` instance behaves like an account and it also contains a `DoPrint` method which can be used to make it print out.

4.8.7 Designing with Interfaces

If you apply the "abstraction" technique properly you should end up with a system creation process which goes along the lines of:

- gather as much *metadata* as you can about the problem; what is important to the customer, what values need to be represented and manipulated and the range of those values
- identify classes that you will have to create to represent the components in the problem
- identify the actions (methods) and the values (properties) that the components must provide
- put these into interfaces for each of the components
- decide how these values and actions are to be tested
- implement the components and test them as you go

You can/should do much of this on paper, before you write any code at all. There are also graphical tools that you can use to draw formal diagrams to represent this information. The field of Software Engineering is entirely based on this process.

You should also have spotted that interfaces are good things to hang tests on. If you have a set of fundamental behaviours that all bank accounts must have (for example paying in money must always make the account balance go up) then you can write tests that bind to the `IAccount` interface and can be used to test any of the bank components that are created.

Programmer's Point: Interfaces are just promises

An interface is less of a binding contract, and more a promise. Just because a class has a method called `PayInFunds` does not mean that it will pay money into the account; it just means that a method with that name exists within the class. Nothing in C# allows you to enforce a particular behaviour on a method; that is down to how much you trust the programmer that made the class that you are using, and how good your tests are. In fact, we sometimes use this to good effect when building a program, in that we can create "dummy" components which implement the interface but don't have the behaviour as such.

The interface mechanism gives us a great deal of flexibility when making our components and fitting them together. It means that once we have found out what our bank account class needs to hold for us we can then go on to consider what we are going to ask the accounts to do. This is the real detail in the specification. Once we have set out an interface for a component we can then just think in terms of what the component must do, not precisely how it does it.

For example, the manager has told us that each bank account must have an account number. This is a very important value, in that it will be fixed for the life of the account and can never be changed. No two accounts should ever have the same number.

From the point of view of interface design this means that the account number will be set when the account is created and the account class will provide a method to let us get the value (but there will not be a method to set the account number).

We don't care what the method `GetAccountNumber` actually does, as long as it always returns the value for a particular account. So this requirement ends up being expressed in the interface that is implemented by the account class.

```
interface IAccount
{
    int GetAccountNumber ();
}
```

This method returns the integer which is the account number for this instance. By placing it in the interface we can say that the account must deliver this value, but we have not actually described how this should be done. The design of the interfaces in a system is just this. They state that we have a need for behaviours, but they do not necessarily state how they are made to work. I have to add comments to give more detail about what the method does.

The need for things like account numbers, which really need to be unique in the world, has resulted in the creation of a set of methods in the C# libraries to create things called *Globally Unique Identifiers* or *GUIDs*. These are data items which are created based on the date, time and certain information about the host computer. Each GUID is unique in the world. We could use these in our `Account` constructor to create a GUID which allows each account to have a unique number.

4.9 Inheritance

Inheritance is another way we can implement creative laziness. It is a way that we can pick up behaviours from classes and just modify the bits we need to make new ones. In this respect you can regard it as a mechanism for what is called *code reuse*. It can also be used at the design stage of a program if you have a set of related objects that you wish to create.

Inheritance lets a class pick up behaviours from the class which is its parent. You can regard an interface as a statement by a class that it has a set of behaviours because it implements a given interface. If a class is descended from a particular parent class this means that it has a set of behaviours because it has *inherited* them from its parent. In short:

Interface: "I can do these things because I have told you I can"
Inheritance: "I can do these things because my parent can"

4.9.1 Extending a parent class

We can see an example of a use for inheritance in our bank account project. We have already noted that a `BabyAccount` must behave just like a `CustomerAccount` except in respect of the cash withdrawal method. Customer accounts can draw out as much as they want. Baby accounts are only allowed to draw up to 10 pounds out at a time.

We have solved this problem from a design point of view by using interfaces. By separating the thing that does the job from the description of the job (which is what an interface lets you do) we can get the whole banking system thinking in terms of `IAccount` and then plug in accounts with different behaviours as required. We can even create brand new accounts at any time after the system has been deployed. These can be introduced and work alongside the others because they behave correctly (i.e. they implement the interface).

But this does make things a bit tiresome when we write the program. We need to create a `BabyAccount` class which contains a lot of code which is duplicated in the `CustomerAccount` class. "This is not a problem" you probably think "I can use the editor block copy to move the program text across". But:

Programmer's Point: Block Copy is Evil

I still make mistakes when I write programs. You might think that after such a huge number of years in the job I get everything right every time. Wrong. And a lot of the mistakes that I make are caused by improper use of block copy. I write some code and find that I need something similar, but not exactly the same, in another part of the program. So I use block copy. Then I change most, but not all, of the new code and find that my program doesn't work properly.

Try not to do this. A great programmer writes every piece of code once, and only once. If you need to use it in more than one place, make it a method.

What we really want to do is pick up all the behaviours in the `CustomerAccount` and then just change the one method that needs to behave differently. It turns out that we can do this in C# using inheritance. When I create the `BabyAccount` class I can tell the compiler that it is based on the `CustomerAccount` one:

```csharp
public class BabyAccount : CustomerAccount, IAccount
{
}
```

The key thing here is the highlighted part after the class name. I have put the name of the class that `BabyAccount` is *extending*. This means that everything that `CustomerAccount` can do, `BabyAccount` can do.

I can now write code like:

```csharp
BabyAccount b = new BabyAccount();
b.PayInFunds(50);
```

This works because, although `BabyAccount` does not have a `PayInFunds` method, the parent class does. This means that the `PayInFunds` method from the `CustomerAccount` class is used at this point.

So, instances of the `BabyAccount` class have abilities which they pick up from their parent class. In fact, at the moment, the `BabyAccount` class has no behaviours of its own; it gets everything from its parent.

4.9.2 Overriding methods

We now know that we can make a new class based on an existing one. The next thing we need to be able to do is change the behaviour of the one method that we are interested in. We want to replace the `WithdrawFunds` method with a new one. This is called *overriding* a method. In the `BabyAccount` class I can do it like this:

```csharp
public class BabyAccount : CustomerAccount, IAccount
{
    public override bool WithdrawFunds (decimal amount)
    {
        if (amount > 10)
        {
            return false ;
        }
        if (balance < amount)
        {
            return false ;
        }
        balance = balance - amount ;
        return true;
    }
}
```

The keyword override means "use this version of the method in preference to the one in the parent". This means that code like:

```csharp
BabyAccount b = new BabyAccount();
b.PayInFunds(50);
b.WithdrawFunds(5);
```

The call of `PayInFunds` will use the method in the parent (since that has not been overridden) but the call of `WithdrawFunds` will use the method in `BabyAccount`.

Virtual Methods

Actually, there is one other thing that we need to do in order for the overriding to work. The C# compiler needs to know if a method is going to be overridden. This is because it must call an overridden method in a slightly different way from a "normal" one. In other words, the above code won't compile properly because the compiler has not been told that `WithDrawFunds` might be overridden in classes which are children of the parent class.

To make the overriding work correctly I have to change my declaration of the method in the `CustomerAccount` class.

```
public class CustomerAccount : Account
{
   private decimal balance = 0;

   public virtual bool WithdrawFunds ( decimal amount )
   {
      if ( balance < amount )
      {
         return false ;
      }
      balance = balance - amount ;
      return true;
   }

}
```

The keyword `virtual` means "I might want to make another version of this method in a child class". You don't have to override the method, but if you don't have the word present, you definitely can't.

This makes `override` and `virtual` a kind of matched pair. You use `virtual` to mark a method as able to be overridden and `override` to actually provide a replacement for the method.

Protection of data in class hierarchies

It turns out that the code above still won't work. This is because the balance value in the `CustomerAccount` class is `private`. We carefully made it `private` so that methods in other classes can't get hold of the value and change it directly.

However, this protection is too strict, in that it stops the `BabyAccount` class from being able to change the value. To get around this problem C# provides a slightly less restrictive access level called `protected`. This makes the member visible to classes which extend the parent. In other words, methods in the `BabyAccount` class can see and use a protected member because they are in the same *class hierarchy* as the class containing the member.

A class hierarchy is a bit like a family tree. Every class has a parent and can do all the things that the parent can do. It also has access to all the protected members of the classes above it.

```
public class CustomerAccount : IAccount
{
   protected decimal balance = 0;

   .....
}
```

I'm not terribly happy about doing this, the `balance` is very important to me and I'd rather that nobody outside the `CustomerAccount` class could see it. However, for now making this change will make the program work. Later we will see better ways to manage this situation.

```csharp
IAccount[] accounts = new IAccount[MAX_CUST];

accounts[0] = new CustomerAccount();
accounts[0].PayInFunds(50);
Console.WriteLine("Balance: " + accounts[0].GetBalance());

accounts[1] = new BabyAccount();
accounts[1].PayInFunds(20);
Console.WriteLine("Balance: " + accounts[1].GetBalance());

if (accounts[0].WithdrawFunds(20))
{
    Console.WriteLine("Withdraw OK");
}
if (accounts[1].WithdrawFunds(20))
{
    Console.WriteLine("Withdraw OK");
}
```

Code Sample 39 Using Inheritance

The code above shows how we can create and use different types of account, with the `BabyAccount` based on the parent `CustomerAccount` type. If you are having a sense of deja vu here, it is because this is exactly the same code as we saw in the previous sample. Code that uses these objects will work in exactly the same way as it always did, except that the objects themselves work in a slightly different way, making the program smaller (which we don't particularly care about) and much easier to debug (because a fault in any of the shared methods only has to be fixed once).

BANK NOTES: OVERRIDING FOR FUN AND PROFIT

The ability to override a method is very powerful. It means that we can make more general classes (for example the `CustomerAccount`) and customise it to make them more specific (for example the `BabyAccount`). Of course this should be planned and managed at the design stage. This calls for more *metadata* to be gathered from the customer and used to decide which parts of the behaviour need to be changed during the life of the project. We would have made the `WithDrawFunds` method `virtual` because the manager would have said "We like to be able to customise the way that some accounts withdraw funds". And we would have written this down in the specification.

4.9.3 Using the base method

Remember that programmers are essentially lazy people who try to write code only once for a given problem. Well, it looks as if we are breaking our own rules here, in that the `WithDrawFunds` method in the `BabyAccount` class contains all the code of the method in the parent class.

We have already noted that we don't like this much, in that it means that the balance value has to be made more exposed than we might like. Fortunately the designers of C# have thought of this and have provided a way that you can call the *base* method from one which overrides it.

The word base in this context means "a reference to the thing which has been overridden". I can use this to make the `WithDrawFunds` method in my `BabyAccount` much simpler:

```csharp
public class BabyAccount : CustomerAccount, IAccount
{
    public override bool WithdrawFunds (decimal amount)
    {
        if (amount > 10)
        {
            return false ;
```

```
        }
        return base.WithdrawFunds(amount);
    }
}
```

Code Sample 40 Overriding the base method

The very last line of the `WithDrawFunds` method makes a call to the original `WithDrawFunds` method in the parent class, i.e. the one that the method overrides.

It is important that you understand what I'm doing here, and why I'm doing it:

- I don't want to have to write the same code twice
- I don't want to make the `balance` value visible outside the `CustomerAccount` class.

The use of the word `base` to call the overridden method solves both of these problems rather beautifully. Because the method call returns a `bool` result I can just send whatever it delivers. By making this change I can put the `balance` back to `private` in the `CustomerAccount` because it is not changed outside it.

Note that there are other useful spin-offs here. If I need to fix a bug in the behaviour of the `WithDrawFunds` method I just fix it once, in the top level class, and then it is fixed for all the classes which call back to it.

4.9.4 Making a Replacement Method

This bit is rather painful, but don't worry too much since it actually does make sense when you think about it. If you play around with C# you will find out that you don't actually seem to need the `virtual` keyword to override a method. If I leave it out (and leave out the `override` too) the program seems to work fine.

This is because in this situation there is no overriding, you have just supplied a new version of the method (in fact the C# compiler will give you a warning which indicates that you should provide the keyword `new` to indicate this):

```
public class BabyAccount : CustomerAccount,IAccount
{
    public new bool WithdrawFunds (decimal amount)
    {
        if (amount > 10)
        {
            return false ;
        }
        if (balance < amount)
        {
            return false ;
        }
        balance = balance - amount ;
        return true;
    }
}
```

Programmer's Point: Don't Replace Methods

I am very against replacing methods rather than overriding them. If you want to have a policy of allowing programmers to make custom versions of classes in this way it is much more sensible to make use of overriding since this allows a well-managed way of using the method that you over-rid. In fact, I'm wondering why I mentioned this at all..

4.9.5 Stopping Overriding

Overriding is very powerful. It means that a programmer can just change one tiny part of a class and make a new one with all the behaviours of the parent. This goes well with a design process which means that as you move down the "family tree" of classes you get more and more specific.

However, overriding/replacing is not always desirable. Consider the `GetBalance` method. This is never going to need a replacement. And yet a naughty programmer could write their own and override or replace the one in the parent:

```
public new decimal GetBalance ()
{
    return 1000000;
}
```

This is the banking equivalent of the bottle of beer that is never empty. No matter how much cash is drawn out, it always returns a balance value of a million pounds!

A naughty programmer could insert this into a class and give himself a nice spending spree. What this means is that we need a way to mark some methods as not being able to be overridden. C# does this by giving us a `sealed` keyword which means "You can't override this method any more".

Unfortunately this is rather hard to use. The rules are that you can only seal an overriding method (which means that we can't seal the `GetBalance` virtual method in the `CustomerAccount` class) and a naughty person could always replace a sealed method in the parent with one that has the same name in the child.

Another use for `sealed`, which has a bit more potential, is that you can mark a class as sealed. This means that the class cannot be extended, i.e. it cannot be used as the basis for another class.

```
public sealed class BabyAccount : CustomerAccount,IAccount
{
    .....
}
```

The compiler will now stop the `BabyAccount` from being used as the basis of another account.

BANK NOTES: PROTECT YOUR CODE

As far as the bank application is concerned, the customer will not have particularly strong opinions on how you use things like `sealed` in your programs. But they will want to have confidence in the code that you make. One of the unfortunate things about this business is that you will have to allow for the fact that people who use your components might not all be nice and trustworthy. This means that you should take steps when you design the program to decide whether or not methods should be flagged as virtual and also make sure that you seal things when you can do so.

For a programming course at this level it is probably a bit heavy handed of me to labour this point just right now, and if it didn't all make sense there is no particular need to worry, just remember that when you create a program this is another risk that you will have to consider.

4.9.6 Constructors and Hierarchies

A constructor is a method which gets control during the process of object creation. It is used by a programmer to allow initial values to be set into an object:

```
babyrobsAccount = new BabyAccount("Baby Rob Miles", 100);
```

In this case we want to create a new baby account for Baby Rob Miles with an initial balance of 100 pounds.

The code above will only work if the `BabyAccount` class has a constructor which accepts a string as first parameter and a decimal value as the second.

You might think that I could solve this by writing a constructor a bit like this:

```
public BabyAccount (string inName, decimal inBalance)
{
    name = inName;
    balance = inBalance;
}
```

But the `BabyAccount` class is an extension of the `CustomerAccount` class. In other words, to make a `BabyAccount` I have to make a `CustomerAccount`. And the account is the class which will have a constructor which sets the name and the initial balance. In this situation the constructor in the child class will have to call a particular constructor in the parent to set that up before it is created. The keyword `base` is used to make a call to the parent constructor. In other words, the proper version of the baby account constructor is as follows:

```
public BabyAccount (string inName, decimal inBalance) :
                        base ( inName, inBalance)
{
}
```

The `base` keyword is used in the same way as `this` is used to call another constructor in the same class. The constructor above assumes that the `CustomerAccount` class which `BabyAccount` is a child of has a constructor which accepts two parameters, the first a string and the second a decimal value.

Constructor Chaining

When considering constructors and class hierarchies you must therefore remember that to create an instance of a child class an instance of the parent must first be created. This means that a constructor in the parent must run before the constructor in the child. In other words, to create a `BabyAccount` you must first create a `CustomerAccount`. The result of this is that programmers must take care of the issue of *constructor chaining*. They must make sure that at each level in the creation process a constructor is called to set up the class at that level.

Programmer's Point: Design your class construction process

The means by which your class instances are created is something you should design into the system that you build. It is part of the overall architecture of the system that you are building. I think of these things as a bit like the girders that you erect to hold the floors and roof of a large building. They tell programmers who are going to build the components which are going to implement the solution how to create those components. It is of course very important that you have these designs written down and readily available to the development team.

4.9.7 Abstract methods and classes

At the moment we are using overriding to modify the behaviour of an existing parent method. However, it is also possible to use overriding in a slightly different context. I can use it to force a set of behaviours on items in a class hierarchy. If there are some things that an account must do then we can make these abstract and then get the child classes to actually provide the implementation.

For example, in the context of the bank application we might want to provide a method which creates a warning letter to the customer that their account is overdrawn. This will have to be different for each type of account (we don't want to use the same language to a baby account holder as we do for an older one). This means that at the time we create the bank account system we know that we need this method, but we don't know precisely what it does in every situation.

We could just provide a "standard" method in the `CustomerAccount` class and then rely on the programmers overriding this with a more specific message but we then have no way of making sure that they really do provide the method.

C# provides a way of flagging a method as `abstract`. This means that the method body is not provided in this class, but will be provided in a child class:

```
public abstract class Account
{
    public abstract string RudeLetterString();
}
```

The fact that my new `Account` class contains an `abstract` method means that the class itself is `abstract` (and must be marked as such). It is not possible to make an instance of an abstract class. If you think about it this is sensible. An instance of `Account` would not know what to do if the `RudeLetterString` method was ever called.

An abstract class can be thought of as a kind of template. If you want to make an instance of a class based on an abstract parent you must provide implementations of all the abstract methods given in the parent.

Abstract classes and interfaces

You might decide that an abstract class looks a lot like an interface. This is true, in that an interface also provides a "shopping list" of methods which must be provided by a class. However, abstract classes are different in that they can contain fully implemented methods alongside the abstract ones. This can be useful because it means you don't have to repeatedly implement the same methods in each of the components that implement a particular interface.

The problem is that you can only inherit from one parent, so you can only pick up the behaviours of one class. If you want to implement interfaces as well, you may have to repeat methods as well.

Perhaps at this point a more fully worked example might help. If we consider our bank account problem we can identify two types of behaviour:

- those which every type of bank account must provide (for example `PayInFunds` and `GetBalance`)
- those which each type of bank account must provide in a way specific to that particular account type (for example `WithdrawFunds` and `RudeLetterString`)

The trick is to take all the methods in the first category and put them inside the parent class. The methods in the second category must be made abstract. This leads us to a class design a bit like this:

```
public interface IAccount
{
   void PayInFunds ( decimal amount );
   bool WithdrawFunds ( decimal amount );
   decimal GetBalance ();
   string RudeLetterString();
}


public abstract class Account : IAccount
{
   private decimal balance = 0;

   public abstract string RudeLetterString();
```

```csharp
public virtual bool WithdrawFunds ( decimal amount )
{
    if ( balance < amount )
    {
        return false ;
    }
    balance = balance - amount ;
    return true;
}

public decimal GetBalance ()
{
    return balance;
}

public void PayInFunds ( decimal amount )
{
    balance = balance + amount ;
}
}

public class CustomerAccount : Account
{
    public override string RudeLetterString()
    {
        return "You are overdrawn" ;
    }
}

public class BabyAccount : Account
{
    public override bool WithdrawFunds ( decimal amount )
    {
        if (amount > 10)
        {
            return false ;
        }
        return base.WithdrawFunds(amount);
    }
    public override string RudeLetterString()
    {
        return "Tell daddy you are overdrawn";
    }
}
```

Code Sample 41 Using an Abstract method

This code repays careful study. Note how I have moved all the things that all accounts must do into the parent `Account` class. Then I have added customised methods into the child classes where appropriate. Note also though that I have left the interface in place. That is because; even though I now have this abstract structure I still want to think of the account objects in terms of their "accountness" rather than any particular specific type.

If we make any new kinds of account classes which are based on the `Account` parent each new class must provide its own version of the `RudeLetterString` method.

References to abstract classes

References to abstract classes work just like references to interfaces. A reference to an `Account` class can refer to any class which extends from that parent. This might seem useful, as we can consider something as an "account" rather than a `BabyAccount`.

However, I much prefer it if you manage references to abstract things (like accounts) in terms of their interface instead.

4.9.8 Designing with Objects and Components

For the purpose of this part of the text you now have broad knowledge of all the tools that can be used to design large software systems. If you understand what an interface and abstract classes are intended to achieve this will stand you in very good stead for your programming career. Broadly:

Interface: lets you identify a set of behaviours (i.e. methods) which a component can be made to implement. Any component which implements the interface can be thought of in terms of a reference of that interface type. A concrete example of this would be something like `IPrintHardCopy`. Lots of items in my bank system will need to do this and so we could put the behaviour details into the interface for them to implement in their own way. Then our printer can just regard each of the instances that implement this interface purely in this way. Interfaces let me describe a set of behaviours which a component can implement. Once a component can implement an interface it can be regarded purely in terms of a component with this ability. Objects can implement more than one interface, allowing them to present different faces to the systems that use them.

Abstract: lets you create a parent class which holds template information for all the classes which extend it. If you want to create a related set of items, for example all the different kinds of bank account you might need to deal with, including credit card, deposit account, current account etc. then the best way to do this is to set up a parent class which contains abstract and non-abstract methods. The child classes can make use of the methods from the parent and override the ones that need to be provided differently for that particular class.

Use Interface References

One important consideration is that even if you make use of an abstract parent class I reckon that you should still make use of interfaces to reference the data objects themselves. This gives you a degree of flexibility that you can use to good effect.

BANK NOTES: MAKING GOOD USE OF INTERFACE AND ABSTRACT

If our bank takes over another bank and wants to share account information we might need a way to use their accounts. If their accounts are software components too (and they should be) then all we have to do is implement the required interfaces at each end and then our systems understand each other. In other words the other bank must create the methods in the `IAccount` interface, get their account objects (whatever they are called) to implement the interface and, hey presto, I can now use their accounts.

This would be much more difficult if my entire system thought in terms of a parent Account class – since their classes would not fit into this hierarchy at all.

4.9.9 Don't Panic

This is all deep stuff. If you don't get it now, don't worry. These features of C# are tied up with the process of software design which is a very complex business. The important point to bear in mind is that the features are all provided so that you can solve one problem:

Create software which is packaged in secure, interchangeable components.

Interfaces let me describe what each component can do. Class hierarchies let me re-use code inside those components.

And that is it.

4.10 Object Etiquette

We have considered objects "in the large", in that we know how they can be used to design and implement large software systems. What we need to do now is take a look at some smaller, but very important, issues that relate to how we use objects in our programs.

4.10.1   Objects and ToString

We have taken it as read that objects have a magical ability to print themselves out. If I write the code:

```
int i = 99;
Console.WriteLine(i);
```

This will print out:

```
99
```

The integer somehow seems to know how to print itself out. Now it is time to find out how this is achieved, and also how we can give our own objects the same magical ability.

It turns out that this is all provided by the "objectness" of things in C#. We know that an object can contain information and do things for us. (in fact we have seen that the whole basis of building programs is to decide what the objects should do and then make them do these things). We have also seen that you can extend a parent object to create a child which has all the abilities of the parent, plus the new ones that we add. Now we are going to see how these abilities of objects are used in making parts of the C# implementation itself work.

The Object class

When you create a new class this is not actually created from nowhere. It is in fact a child of the object class. In other words, if I write:

```
public class Account {
```

- this is equivalent to writing:

```
public class Account : object {
```

The object class is a part of C#, and everything is a child of the `object` class. This has a couple of important ramifications:

- Every object can do what an object can do.
- A reference to an object type can refer to any class.

For the purpose of this part of the notes, the first point is the one which has the most importance here. It means that all classes that are made have a number of behaviours that they inherit from their ultimate parent, the object. If you look inside the actual code that makes an object work you will find a method called `ToString`. The object implementation of `ToString` returns a string description of the type of that object.

The ToString method

The system knows that `ToString` exists for every object, and so if it ever needs the string version of an object it will call this method on the object to get the text.

In other words:

```
object o = new object();
Console.WriteLine(o);
```

- would print out:

```
System.Object
```

You can call the method explicitly if you like:

```
Console.WriteLine(o.ToString());
```

- and the results would be exactly the same.

The nice thing about `ToString` is that it has been declared `virtual`. This means that we can override it to make it behave how we would like:

```
class Account
{
  private string name;
  private decimal balance;

  public override string ToString()
  {
    return "Name: " + name + " balance: " + balance;
  }

  public Account (string inName, decimal inBalance)
  {
    name = inName;
    balance = inBalance;
  }
}
```

In the tiny `Account` class above I've overridden the `ToString` method so that it prints out the name and balance value. This means that the code:

```
Account a = new Account("Rob", 25);
Console.WriteLine(a);
```

Code Sample 42 ToString method

- would print out:

```
Name: Rob balance: 25
```

So, from the point of view of good etiquette, whenever you design a class you should provide a `ToString` method which provides a text version of the content of that class.

Getting the string description of a parent object

If you want to get hold of a string description of the parent object, you can use the base mechanism to do this. This is sometimes useful if you add some data to a child class and want to print out the content of the parent first:

```
public override string ToString()
{
   return base.ToString() + " Parent : " + parentName;
}
```

The method above is from a `ChildAccount` class. This class extends the `CustomerAccount` and holds the name of the child's parent. The code above uses the `ToString` method in the parent object and then tacks the name of the parent on the end before returning it. The nice thing about this is that if the behaviour of the parent class changes, i.e. new members are added or the format of the string changes, the `ChildAccount` class does not have to change, since it will just make use of the upgraded method.

4.10.2   Objects and testing for equals

We have seen that when object references are compared a test for equals does not mean the same as it does for values. We know that objects are managed by named tags which refer to unnamed items held in memory somewhere. When we perform an equals test the system simply checks to see if both references refer to the same location.

To see how this might cause us problems we need to consider how we would implement a graphical computer game (makes a change from the bank for a while). In the game the various objects in it will be located at a particular place on the screen. We can express this position as a coordinate or point, with an x value and a y value. We then might want to test to see if two items have collided.

```
class Point
{
    public int x;
    public int y;
}
```

This is my point class. I can now create instances of `Point` and use them to manage my game objects:

```
Point spaceshipPosition = new Point();
spaceshipPosition.x = 1;
spaceshipPosition.y = 2;

Point missilePosition = new Point();
missilePosition.x = 1;
missilePosition.y = 2;

if ( spaceshipPosition == missilePosition )
{
    Console.WriteLine("Bang");
}
```

Note that I've made the `x` and `y` members of the `Point` class `public`. This is because I'm not that concerned about protecting them, but I do want my program to run quickly. The problem is that the above program code does not work. Even though I have put the spaceship and the missile at the same place on the screen the word Bang is not printed.

This is because although the two `Point` objects hold the same data, they are not located at the same address in memory, which means that the equals test will fail.

Programmer's Point: Make sure you use the right equals

As a programmer I must remember that when I'm comparing objects to see if they contain the same data I need to use the Equals method rather than the == operator. Some of the nastiest bugs that I've had to fix have revolved around programmers who have forgotten which test to use. If you find that things that contain the same data are not being compared correctly, take a look at the test that is being performed.

Adding your own Equals method

The way that you solve this problem is to provide a method which can be used to compare the two points and see if they refer to the same place. To do this we must override the standard `Equals` behaviour and add one of our own:

```
public override bool Equals(object obj)
{
    Point p = (Point) obj;
    if ( ( p.x == x ) && ( p.y == y ) )
    {
        return true;
    }
    else
    {
        return false;
    }
}
```

The `Equals` method is given a reference to the thing to be compared. Note that this reference is supplied as a reference to an object. The first thing we need to do is create a reference to a `Point`. We need to do this because we want to get hold of the x and y values from a `Point` (we can't get them from an object).

The object is cast into a `Point` and then the x and y values are compared. If they are both the same the method returns `true` to the caller. This means that I can write code like:

```
if ( missilePosition.Equals(spaceshipPosition) )
{
    Console.WriteLine("Bang");
}
```

Code Sample 43 Equals Method

This test will work, because the `Equals` method actually compares the content of the two points rather than just their references.

Note that I didn't actually need to override the `Equals` method; I could have written one called `TheSame` which did the job. However, the `Equals` method is sometimes used by C# library methods to see if two objects contain the same data and so overriding `Equals` makes my class behave correctly as far as they are concerned.

Programmer's Point: Equals behaviours are important for testing

The customer for our bank account management program is very keen that every single bank account that is created is unique. If the bank ever contains two identical accounts this would cause serious problems. The fact that everything in the system is required to be unique might lead you to think that there is no need to provide a way to compare two Account instances for equality. "If the system will never contain two things that are the same, why should I waste time writing code to compare them in this way?"

However, there is a very good reason why you might find an equals behaviour very useful. When you write the part of the program which stores data and brings it back again you will find it very useful to have a way of testing that what comes back from the store is identical to what you put there. In this situation an equals behaviour is important, and so I reckon you should always provide one.

BANK NOTES: GOOD MANNERS ARE A GOOD IDEA

It is considered good manners to provide the `Equals` and `ToString` methods in the classes that you create. These will allow your classes to fit in with others in the C# system. It is also very useful to make appropriate use of `this` when writing methods in classes. When you start to create your bank account management system you should arrange a meeting of all the programmers involved and make them aware that you will be insisting on good mannered development like this. In fact, for a professional approach you should set out standards which establish which of these methods you are going to provide. You will expect all programmers to write to these standards if they take part in the project.

4.10.3 Objects and `this`

By now you should be used to the idea that we can use a reference to an object to get hold of the members of that object. Consider:

```
public class Counter
{
   public int Data=0;
   public void Count ()
   {
      Data = Data + 1;
   }
}
```

The class above has a single data member and a single method member. The data is a counter. Each time the `Count` method is called the counter is made one larger. I can use the class as follows:

```
Counter c = new Counter();
c.Count();
Console.WriteLine("Count : " + c.Data);
```

This calls the method and then prints out the data. We know that in this context the . (dot) means "follow the reference to the object and then use this member of the class".

`this` as a reference to the current instance

I **hate** explaining this. I want to use the word this to mean this, but this also has a special meaning within your C# programs. Perhaps the best way to get around the problem is to remember that when I use the word `this` I mean "a reference to the currently executing instance of a class". When a method in a class accesses a member variable the compiler automatically puts a `this.` in front of each use of a member of the class. In other words, the "proper" version of the `Counter` class is as follows:

```
public class Counter
{
   public int Data=0;
   public void Count ()
   {
      this.Data = this.Data + 1;
   }
}
```

We can add a `this.` if we like to make it explicit that we are using a member of a class rather than a local variable.

Passing a reference to yourself to other classes

Another use for `this` is when an instance class needs to provide a reference to itself to another class that wants to use it. A new bank account could store itself in a bank by passing a reference to itself to a method that will store it:

```
bank.Store(this);
```

When the Store method is called it is given a reference to the currently executing account instance. The `Store` method accepts this and then stores this somehow. Of course, in this situation we are not passing an account into the bank, instead we are passing a reference to the account.

If this hurts your head, then don't worry about it for now.

Confusion with `this`

I reckon that using `this` is a good idea. It means that people reading my code can tell instantly whether I am using a local variable or a member of the class. However it might take a bit of getting used to. If I have a member of my class which contains methods, and I want to use one of those methods, I end up writing code like this:

```
this.account.SetName("Rob");
```

This means "I have a member variable in this class called `account`. Call the `SetName` method on that member to set the name to 'Rob'".

4.11 The power of strings and chars

It is probably worth spending a few moments considering the string type in a bit more detail. This is because it gives you a lot of nice extra features which will save you a lot of work. These are exposed as methods which you can call on a string reference. The methods will return a new string, transformed in the way that you ask. You can sort out the case of the text, trim spaces off the start and end and extract sub-strings using these methods.

4.11.1   String Manipulation

Strings are rather special. I regard them as a bit like bats. A bat can be regarded as either an animal or a bird in many respects. A string can be regarded as either an object (referred to by means of a reference) or a value (referred to as a value).

This hybrid behaviour is provided because it makes things easier for us programmers. However it does mean that we have to regard strings as a bit special when you are learning to program, because they seem to break some of the rules that we have learnt.

It is very important that you understand what happens when you transform a string. This is because, although strings are objects, they don't actually behave like objects all the time.

```
string s1="Rob";
string s2=s1;
s2 = "different";
Console.WriteLine(s1 + " " + s2);
```

If you think you know about objects and references, you should be expecting s1 to change when s2 is changed. The second statement made the reference s2 refer to the same object as s1, so changing s2 should change the object that s1 refers to as well. To find out more about this, take a look at section 4.4.1.

This does not happen though, because C# regards an instance of a string type in a special way. It calls it *immutable*. This is because programmers want strings to behave a bit like values in this respect.

4.11.2 Immutable strings

The idea is that if you try to change a string, the C# system instead creates a new string and makes the reference you are "changing" refer to the changed one. In other words, when the system sees the line:

```
s2 = "different";
```

- it makes a new string which contains the text "different" and makes s2 refer to that. The thing that s1 is referring to is unchanged. So, after the assignment s1 and s2 no longer refer to the same object. This behaviour, never allowing a thing to be changed by making a new one each time it is required, is how the system implements immutable.

You might ask the question: "Why go to all the trouble?" It might seem all this hassle could be saved by just making strings into value types. Well, no. Consider the situation where you are storing a large document in the memory of the computer. By using references we only actually need one string instance with the word "the" in it. All the occurrences in the text can just refer to that one instance. This saves memory and it also makes searching for words much faster.

4.11.3 String Comparison

The special nature of strings also means that you can compare strings using equals and get the behaviour you want:

```
if ( s1 == s2 )
{
    Console.WriteLine("The same");
}
```

If s1 and s2 were proper reference types this comparison would only work if they referred to the same object. But in C# the comparison works if they contain the same text. You can use an equals method if you prefer:

```
if ( s1.Equals(s2) )
{
    Console.WriteLine("Still the same");
}
```

4.11.4 String Editing

You can read individual characters from a string by indexing them as you would an array:

```
char firstCh = name[0];
```

This would set the character variable `firstCh` to the first character in the string. However, you can't change the characters:

```
name[0] = 'R';
```

- would cause a compilation error because strings are immutable.

You can pull a sequence of characters out of a string using the `SubString` method:

```
string s1="Rob";
s1=s1.Substring(1,2);
```

The first parameter is the starting position and the second is the number of characters to be copied. This would leave the string "ob" in `s1`.(remember that strings are indexed starting at location 0).

You can leave out the second parameter if you like, in which case all the characters up to the end of the string are copied:

```
string s1="Miles";
s1=s1.Substring(2);
```

- would leave "les" in `s1`.

4.11.5 String Length

All of the above operations will fail if you try to do something which takes you beyond the length of the string. In this respect strings are just like arrays. It is also possible to use the same methods on them to find out how long they are:

```
Console.WriteLine ( "Length: " + s1.Length);
```

The `Length` property gives the number of characters in the string.

4.11.6 Character case

Objects of type string can be asked to create new, modified, versions of themselves in slightly different forms. You do this by calling methods on the reference to get the result that you want:

```
s1=s1.ToUpper();
```

The `ToUpper` method returns a version of the string with all the letters converted to UPPER CASE. No other characters in the string are changed. There is a corresponding `ToLower` method as well.

4.11.7 Trimming and empty strings

Another useful method is `Trim`. This removes any leading or trailing spaces from the string.

```
s1=s1.Trim();
```

This is useful if your users might have typed "   Rob   " rather than "Rob". If you don't trim the text you will find equals tests for the name will fail. There are `TrimStart` and `TrimEnd` methods to just take off leading or trailing spaces if that is what you want. If you trim a string which contains only spaces you will end up with a string which contains no characters (i.e. its length is zero).

4.11.8 Character Commands

The `char` class also exposes some very useful methods which can be used to check the values of individual characters. These are `static` methods which are called on the character class and can be used to test characters in a variety of ways:

`char.IsDigit(ch)`	returns true if the character is a digit (0 to 9)
`char.IsLetter(ch)`	returns true if the character is a letter (a to z or A to Z)
`char.IsLetterOrDigit(ch)`	returns true if the character is a letter or a digit
`char.IsLower(ch)`	returns true if the character is a lower case letter
`char.IsUpper(ch)`	returns true if the character is an upper case letter
`char.IsPunctuation(ch)`	returns true if the character is a punctuation character
`char.IsWhiteSpace(ch)`	returns true if the character is a space, tab or newline

You can use these when you are looking through a string for a particular character.

4.11.9 String Twiddling with `StringBuilder`

If you really want to twiddle with the contents of your strings you will find the fact that you can't assign to individual characters in the string a real pain. The reason you are suffering is that strings are really designed to hold strings, not provide a way that they can be edited. For proper string editing C# provides a class called `StringBuilder`. It is found in the `System.Text` namespace.

It works a lot like a string, but you can assign to characters and even replace one string with another. It is also very easy to convert between `StringBuilder` instances and strings. You should look this up if you have a need to do some proper editing.

4.12 Properties

Properties are useful. They are a bit like the `switch` keyword, which lets us select things easily. We don't need properties, but C# provides them because they make programs slightly easier to write and simpler to read.

4.12.1 Properties as class members

A property is a member of a class that holds a value. We have seen that we can use a member variable to do this kind of thing, but we need to make the member value public. For example, the bank may ask us to keep track of staff members. One of the items that they may want to hold is the age of a member of staff. I can do it like this:

```
public class StaffMember
{
    public int Age;
}
```

The class contains a public member. I can get hold of this member in the usual way:

```
StaffMember s = new StaffMember();
s.Age = 21;
```

I can access a public member of a class directly; just by giving the name of the member. The problem is that we have already decided that this is a bad way to manage our objects. There is nothing to stop things like:

```
s.Age = -100210232;
```

This is very naughty, but because the Age member is public we cannot stop it.

4.12.2 Creating Get and Set methods

To get control and do useful things we can create get and set methods which are public. These provide access to the member in a managed way. We then make the Age member private and nobody can tamper with it:

```csharp
public class StaffMember
{
   private int age;
   public int GetAge()
   {
      return this.age;
   }
   public void SetAge( int inAge )
   {
      if ( (inAge > 0) && (inAge < 120) )
      {
         this.age = inAge;
      }
   }
}
```

We now have complete control over our property, but we have had to write lots of extra code. Programmer's who want to work with the age value now have to call methods:

```csharp
StaffMember s = new StaffMember();
s.SetAge(21);
Console.WriteLine ( "Age is : " + s.GetAge() );
```

4.12.3 Using Properties

Properties are a way of making the management of data like this slightly easier. An age property for the StaffMember class would be created as follows:

```csharp
public class StaffMember
{
   private int ageValue;

   public int Age
   {
      set
      {
         if ( (value > 0) && (value < 120) )
         {
            this.ageValue = value;
         }
      }
      get
      {
         return this.ageValue;
      }
```

```
    }
}
```

The age value has now been created as a property. Note how there are get and set parts to the property. These equate directly to the bodies of the get and set methods that I wrote earlier. The really nice thing about properties is that they are used just as the class member was:

```
StaffMember s = new StaffMember();
s.Age = 21;
Console.WriteLine ( "Age is : " + s.Age );
```

Code Sample 44 Using Properties

When the **Age** property is given a value the `set` code is run. The keyword `value` means "the thing that is being assigned". When the **Age** property is being read the `get` code is run. This gives us all the advantages of the methods, but they are much easier to use and create.

I can do other clever things too:

```
public int AgeInMonths
{
    get
    {
        return this.ageValue*12;
    }
}
```

This is a new property, called `AgeInMonths`. It can only be read, since it does not provide a set behaviour. However, it returns the age in months, based on the same source value as was used by the other property. This means that you can provide several different ways of recovering the same value.

You can also provide read-only properties by leaving out the set behaviour. Write only properties are also possible if you leave out the get.

4.12.4 Properties and interfaces

Interfaces are a way that you can bring together a set of behaviours. They are packaged as a list of methods which a class must contain if it implements the interfaces. It is also possible to add properties to interfaces. You do this by leaving out the statements which are the body of the get and set behaviours:

```
interface IStaff
{
    int Age
    {
        get;
        set;
    }
}
```

This is an interface that specifies that classes which implement it must contain an **Age** property with both get and set behaviours.

4.12.5 Property problems

Properties are really neat, and they are used throughout the classes in the .NET libraries. But there are a few things that you need to be aware of when deciding whether or not to use them:

Property Assignment Failure

We have seen that the set behaviour can reject values if it thinks they are out of range. This is OK, but it has no way of telling the user of the property that this has happened. With our Age property above the code:

```
s.Age = 121;
```

- would fail. However, the person performing the assignment would not be aware of this, since there is no way that the property can return a value which indicates success or failure. The only way that a property set method could do this would be to throw an exception, which is not a good way to go on.

A SetAge method on the other hand could return a value which indicates whether or not it worked:

```
public bool SetAge( int inAge )
{
   if ( (inAge > 0) && (inAge < 120) )
   {
      this.age = inAge;
      return true;
   }
   return false;
}
```

A programmer setting the age value can now find out if the set worked or failed.

If there is a situation where a property assignment can fail I **never** expose that as a property. I suppose that it would be possible to combine a set method and a get property, but I reckon that would be madness.

Properties Run Code

When you assign a value to a property you are actually calling a method. Unfortunately there is no way you can tell that from the code which does the assignment:

```
s.Age = 99;
```

This looks very innocent, but could result in a thousand lines of code running inside the set property. It is possible to use this to advantage, in that an object can react to and track property changes. But it can also be made very confusing.

4.12.6   Using Delegates

Events and delegates are a very important part of C#. Therefore you should read this text carefully and make sure you understand what is going on.

Delegates are useful because they let us manipulate references to methods. We can manage which particular method is going to be called in a given situation in terms of a lump of data which we can move around.

Delegates are an important part of how events are managed in a C# program. Events are things that happen which our program may need to respond to. They include stuff like people pressing buttons in our user interface, clocks going tick and messages arriving via the network. In each case we need to tell the system what to do when the event occurs. The way that C# does this is by allowing us to create instances of delegate classes which we give the event generators. When the event occurs (this is sometimes called the event "firing") the method referred to by the event is called to deliver the message. I call a delegate "A way of telling a piece of program what to do when something happens". A posh description would have the form:

A delegate is a type safe reference to a method in a class.

Type safe delegates

The phrase *type safe* in this context means that if the method accepts two integer parameters and returns a string, the delegate for that method will have exactly the same appearance and cannot be used in any other way. This word is used to distinguish a delegate from things like pointers which are used in more primitive languages like C.

In C you can create pointers to methods, but the C environment does not know (or even care) what the methods really look like. This means that you can call them in the wrong way and cause your program to explode. Don't worry about this too much. Just remember that delegates are safe to use.

Using a Delegate

As an example, consider the calculation of fees in our bank. The bank will have a number of different methods which do this, depending on the type of customer and the status of that customer. It might want to have a way in which a program can choose which fee calculation method to use as it runs.

We have seen that things like overriding let us create methods which are specific to a particular type of object, for example we provided a custom `WithdrawFunds` for the `BabyAccount` class which only lets us draw out a limited amount of cash. These techniques are very useful, but they are hard wired into the code that I write. Once I've compiled the class the methods in it cannot change.

A delegate is a "stand in" for a method. If you call the delegate it calls the method it presently refers to. This means I can use it as a kind of method selector. A delegate type is created like this:

```
public delegate decimal CalculateFee (decimal balance);
```

Note that I've not created any delegates yet, I've just told the compiler what the delegate type `CalculateFee` looks like. This delegate can stand in for a method which accepts a single decimal parameter (the balance on the account) and returns a decimal value (the amount we are going to charge the customer). An example of a method we might want to use with this delegate you could consider is this one:

```
public decimal RipoffFee (decimal balance)
{
   if ( balance < 0 )
   {
      return 100;
   }
   else
   {
      return 1;
   }
}
```

This is a rather evil fee calculator. If you are overdrawn the fee is 100 pounds. If you are in credit the fee is 1 pound. If I want to use this in my program I can make an instance of `CalculateFee` which refers to it:

```
CalculateFee calc = new CalculateFee (RipoffFee);
```

Now I can "call" the delegate and it will actually run the ripoff calculator method:

```
fees = calc(100);
```

The `calc` delegate presently refers to a delegate instance which will use the `RipoffFee` method. I can change that by making another delegate:

```
    calc = new CalculateFee (FriendlyFee);
```

Now when I "call" `calc` it will run the `FriendlyFee` method. This of course only works if `FriendlyFee` is a method which returns a value of type decimal and accepts a single decimal value as a parameter.

```
    using System;

public delegate decimal CalculateFee(decimal balance);

public class DelegateDemo
{
    public static decimal RipoffFee(decimal balance)
    {
        Console.WriteLine("Calling the Ripoff Method");
        if (balance < 0)
        {
            return 100;
        }
        else
        {
            return 1;
        }
    }

    public static decimal FriendlyFee(decimal balance)
    {
        Console.WriteLine("Calling the Friendly Method");
        if (balance < 0)
        {
            return 10;
        }
        else
        {
            return 1;
        }
    }

    public static void Main()
    {
        CalculateFee calc;

        calc = new CalculateFee(RipoffFee);
        calc(-1); // this will call the Ripoff method
        calc = new CalculateFee(FriendlyFee);
        calc(-1); // this will call the Friendly method
    }
}
```

Code Sample 45 Using Delegates

The sample above shows how all this fits together. The important point to note is that in the main method there are two calls of the calc delegate. Each call will actually result in the execution of different code.

An instance of a delegate is an object like any other. This means that it can be managed in terms of references, so I can build structures which contain delegates and I can also pass delegates in and out of methods. You can regard a list of delegates as a list of methods that I can call.

This gives us another layer of abstraction and means that we can now design programs which can have behaviours which change as the program runs. For now however, it is best just to consider them in terms of how we use delegates to manage the response of a program to events.

Programmer's Point: Use Delegates Sensibly

Allowing programs to change what they do as they run is a rather strange thing to want to do. I'm presenting this as an example of how delegates let a program manipulate method references as objects, rather than as a good way to write programs. Delegates are used a lot in event handlers and also to manage threads (as you will see below). I don't use them much beyond this in programs that I write.

4.13 Building a Bank

We are now in a situation where we can create working bank accounts. We can use interfaces to define the behaviour of a bank account component. This gives us a way of creating new types of account as the bank business develops. What we now need is a way of storing a large number of accounts. This *container* class will provide methods which allow us to find a particular account based on the name of the holder. We can express the behaviour that we need from our bank in terms of an interface:

```
interface IBank
{
    IAccount FindAccount (string name);
    bool StoreAccount (IAccount account);
}
```

A class which implements these methods can be used for the storage of accounts. I can put an account into it and then get it back again:

```
IBank friendlyBank = new ArrayBank (50);
IAccount account = new CustomerAccount("Rob", 0);
if (friendlyBank.StoreAccount(account)) {
    Console.WriteLine ( "Account stored OK" );
}
```

The code above creates a bank and then puts an account into it, printing out a message if the storage worked.

4.13.1   Storing Accounts in an array

The class `ArrayBank` is a bank account storage system which works using arrays. When you create an instance of an `ArrayBank` you tell it how many accounts you want to store by means of the constructor. In the code above we are creating a bank with enough room for references to 50 accounts. The constructor creates an array of the appropriate size when it is called:

```
private IAccount [] accounts ;

public ArrayBank( int bankSize )
{
    accounts = new IAccount[bankSize];
}
```

Note that it is very important that you understand what has happened here. We have not created any accounts at all. What we have created is an array of references. Each reference in the array can refer to an object which implements the `IAccount` interface. But at the moment none of the references refer anywhere, they are all set to `null`. When we add an account to the bank we simply make one of the references refer to that account instance. We never place an account "in" the array; instead we put a reference to that account in the array.

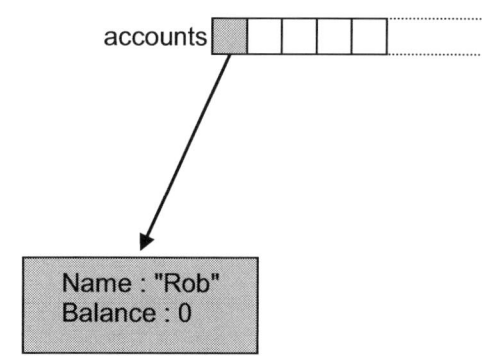

The diagram shows the state of the accounts array after we have stored our first account. The light coloured elements are set to `null`. The element at the start of the array contains a reference to the account instance.

The method to add an account to our bank has to find the first empty location in the array and set this to refer to the account that has been added:

```csharp
public bool StoreAccount (IAccount account)
{
    int position = 0;
    for (position = 0; position<accounts.Length; position++)
    {
        if (accounts[position] == null)
        {
            accounts[position] = account;
            return true;
        }
    }
    return false;
}
```

This method works through the array looking for an element containing null. If it finds one it sets this to refer to the account it has been asked to store and then returns `true`. If it does not find a `null` element before it reaches the end of the array it returns `false` to indicate that the store has failed.

When we want to work on an account we must first find it. The bank interface provides a method called `FindAccount` which will find the account which matches a particular customer name:

```csharp
IAccount fetchedAccount = arrayBank.FindAccount("Rob");
```

This will either return the account with the required name, or `null` if the account cannot be found. In the array based implementation of the bank this is achieved by means of a simple search:

```csharp
public IAccount FindAccount ( string name )
{
    int position=0 ;
    for (position=0 ; position<accounts.Length ; position++)
    {
        if ( accounts[position] == null )
        {
            continue;
        }
        if ( accounts[position].GetName() == name )
        {
            return accounts[position];
        }
```

```
        }
        return null;
}
```

This code works its way through the accounts array looking for an entry with a name which matches the one being looked for. If it finds an element which contains a `null` reference it skips past that onto the next one. If it reaches the end of the array without finding a match it returns `null`, otherwise it returns a reference to the account that it found.

```
class BankProgram
{

    public static void Main()
    {
        ArrayBank ourBank = new ArrayBank(100);

        Account newAccount = new Account("Rob", "Robs House",
                                        1000000);

        if(ourBank.StoreAccount(newAccount) == true)
            Console.WriteLine("Account added to bank");

        IAccount storedAccount = ourBank.FindAccount("Rob");
        if(storedAccount!=null)
            Console.WriteLine("Account found in bank");

    }
}
```

Code Sample 46 Storing accounts in an array

The sample code above shows how this would be used. It creates an `ArrayBank` that can hold 100 accounts. It then creates a new account and stores it in the bank. It then searches for that account by name and finds it.

4.13.2   Searching and Performance

The solution above will work fine, and could be used as the basis of a bank. However, it becomes very slow as the size of the bank increases. Each time we add a new account the searching gets slower as the `FindAccount` method must look through more and more items to find that one. On a bank with only fifty accounts this is not a problem, but if there are thousands of accounts this simple search will be much too slow.

4.13.3   Storing Accounts using a Hash Table

Fortunately for us we can use a device called a "hash table" which allows us to easily find items based on a key. This is much faster than a sequential search, since it uses a technique which will take us straight to the required item.

The idea is that we do something mathematical (called "hashing") to the information in the search property to generate a number which can then be used to identify the location where the data is stored.

For example, we could take all the letters in the account name string, look up the ASCII code for each letter and then add these values up. The name "Rob" could be converted to 82+111+98 = 291. We could look in location 291 for our account.

Of course this hash code is not fool proof, the name "Rpa" would give the same total (82+112+97) and refer to the same location. This is poetically referred to as a "hash clash". We can do clever things with the way we combine the values to reduce the chances of this happening, but we can't completely avoid clashes.

Clashes can be resolved by adding a test when we are storing an account. If we find the location we would like to use is not null we simply work our way down looking for the first free location on from that point.

When we want to find a given item we use the hash to take us to the starting position for the search and then look for the one with the matching name.

In short, the hash function gives us a starting point for our search, rather than always looking from the beginning of the array in our simple array-based code above. This greatly speeds up access to the data.

4.13.4 Using the C# Hashtable collection

Fortunately for us the designers of the C# have created a hash table class for us to use. This will store items for us based on a particular object which is called the *key*. It turns out to be very easy to create a bank storage mechanism based on this:

```csharp
class HashBank : IBank
{
    Hashtable bankHashtable = new Hashtable();

    public IAccount FindAccount(string name)
    {
        return bankHashtable[name] as IAccount;
    }

    public bool StoreAccount(IAccount account)
    {
        bankHashtable.Add(account.GetName(), account);
        return true;
    }
}
```

Code Sample 47 A hash table bank

The `Hashtable` class can be found in the `System.Collections` namespace. It provides a method called `Add` which is given the value of the key and a reference to the item to be stored on that hash code. It also allows you to use a reference to the key (in this case the name) to locate an item:

```csharp
return bankHashtable[name] as IAccount;
```

We have to use the "as" part of this code as the collection will return a reference to an `object`. We want to return a reference to an instance which implements the `IAccount` interface. The `as` operator is a form of casting (where we force the compiler to regard an item as being of a particular type). It is used in preference to the code:

```csharp
return (IAccount) bankHashtable[name];
```

The `as` operator has the advantage that if `bankHashtable[name]` does not return an account, or returns something of the wrong type, the `as` operator will generate a `null` reference. Since this is just what the caller of our `FindAccount` method is expecting this can be returned back directly. If a cast fails (i.e. at run time the bank hash table returns the wrong thing) our program will fail with an exception.

It is interesting to note that because we have implemented our bank behaviour using an interface, we can very easily change the way that the account storage part of the program works without changing anything else.

BANK NOTES: KEY PROPERTIES ARE IMPORTANT

The action that is being performed here is exactly the same as what happens when you use your cash card to draw some money from the bank. The cash machine uses information on the card as a key to find your account record so that it can check your balance value and then update it when the money has been withdrawn.

In our simple bank we only have a single key, which is the name of the account holder. In a real bank the key will be more complex, and there may well be more than one, so that they can search for an account holder by name, address or account number depending on the information they have available.

When gathering metadata about a system you will often need to consider which of the properties of an item will be key fields.

5 Advanced Programming

5.1 Generics and Collections

Generics are very useful. This statement probably doesn't tell you much about them or what they do, but it does indicate that they are very useful. They sound a bit scary; telling people you learned about "generics" probably conjures up images of people with white coats and test tubes, at least amongst those who can't spell very well. But I digress. I think the root of Generics is probably "general", in that the idea of them is that you specify a general-purpose operation and then apply it in different contexts in a way appropriate to each of them. If this sounds a bit like abstraction and inheritance you are sort of on the right track. If it doesn't, then it might be worth re-reading those bits of the book until they make sense.

Perhaps the best way to talk about generics is to see how they can help us solve a problem for the bank. We have just seen that we can store `Account` references in an Array. But we know that when an array is created the programmer must specify exactly how many elements it contains. This leads to a "straw that breaks the camel's back" problem, where adding the 10,001st customer to the bank is not actually a cause for celebration, because the array size was set at 10,000 and our program crashes.

One way to solve this problem is to use a really big array, but we aren't that keen on that because it means that for smaller banks the program might be wasting a lot of memory. Fortunately, the C# libraries provide a number of solutions, starting with the simple `ArrayList`.

5.1.1 The ArrayList class

The `ArrayList` is a cousin of the `HashTable` we have just seen, in that it lives in the same `System.Collections` namespace. It lets us create something very useful, an array that can grow in size. We can always add new elements to the `ArrayList`, and some very clever code in the library makes sure that this works.

Creating an ArrayList

It is very easy to create an `ArrayList`:

```
ArrayList store = new ArrayList();
```

Note that you don't have to set the size of the `ArrayList`, although there are overloaded constructors that let you give this information and help the library code along a bit:

```
ArrayList storeFifty = new ArrayList(50);
```

The `ArrayList` called `storeFifty` is initially able to store 50 references, but it can hold more or less as required.

Adding Items to an ArrayList

Adding items to an `ArrayList` is also very easy. The class provides an **Add** method:

```
Account robsAccount = new Account ();
store.Add(robsAccount);
```

It is important to remember what is going on here. We are not putting an `Account` into the arraylist; we are instead making one element of the arraylist refer to that account. In this respect the word `Add` can be a bit misleading, in that what it actually does is add a reference, not the thing itself.

Remember that it would be perfectly possible to have `robsAccount` in multiple arraylists, just like your name can appear on multiple lists in the real world. It might be that the bank has many lists of customers. It will have a list of all the customers, along with a list of "special" customers and perhaps another list of those who owe it the most money. So, an item "in" an arraylist is never actually in it, the list actually contains a reference to that item. When an item is removed from an arraylist, it is not necessarily destroyed; it is just no longer on that list.

Accessing Items in an ArrayList

Items in arraylists can be accessed in just the same way as array elements, but with a tricky twist. It would be very nice if we could just get hold of the account from the arraylist and use it.

```
Account a = store[0];
a.PayInFunds(50);
```

Unfortunately this won't work. If you write this code you will get a compilation error. The reason for this is that an arraylist holds a list of `object` references. If you think about it, this is the only thing that it could hold. The designers of the `ArrayList` class had no idea precisely what type of object a programmer will want to use it with and so they had to use the `object` reference.

You will no doubt remember from the discussion of object hierarchies that an `object` reference can refer to an instance of any class (since they are all derived from `object`) and so that is the only kind of reference that the arraylist works with.

This is not actually a huge problem, because a program can use a cast to change the type of the item the arraylist returns:

```
Account a = (Account) store[0];
a.PayInFunds(50);
```

This would get the element at the start of the arraylist, cast it into an `Account` class and then pay fifty pounds into it.

A slightly larger problem is that an arraylist is not *typesafe*. This means that I can't be sure that an arraylist you give me has nothing other than accounts in it:

```
KitchenSink k = new KitchenSink();
store.Add(k);
```

This puts a reference to a `KitchenSink` instance into our bank storage. This will cause problems (and an exception) if we ever try to use it as an `Account`. To get a properly typesafe `Account` storage we have to take a look at generics in detail a bit later.

Removing Items from an ArrayList

It is not really possible to remove things from an array, but the arraylist class provides a really useful `Remove` behaviour. This is given a reference to the thing to be removed:

```
store.Remove(robsAccount);
```

This removes the **first** occurrence of the reference `robsAccount` from the `store` arraylist. If the `store` contained more than one reference to `robsAccount` then each of them could be removed individually. Note that if the reference given is not actually in the arraylist (i.e. if I ran the code above when store did not contain `robsAccount`) this does not cause an error. If you remove an item the size of the arraylist is decreased.

Finding the size of an ArrayList

You can use the property `Count` to find out how many items there are in the list:

```
if (store.Count == 0)
{
    Console.WriteLine("The bank is empty");
}
```

Checking to see if an ArrayList contains an item

The final trick I'm going to mention (but there are lots more things an arraylist can do for you) is the `Contains` method. This is simply a quick way of finding out whether or not an arraylist contains a particular reference.

```
if (a.Contains(robsAccount))
{
    Console.WriteLine("Rob is in the bank");
}
```

The `Contains` method is given a reference to an object and returns true if the arraylist contains that reference. You could of course write this behaviour yourself, but having it built into the class makes it much easier.

ArrayLists and Arrays

Arraylists and arrays look a lot the same. They both let you store a large number of items and you can use subscripts (the values in square brackets) to get hold of elements from either. They also throw exceptions if you try to access elements that are not in the array. If you wish you can use arraylists in place of arrays and have the benefits of storage that will grow and shrink as you need it, the only problem that you have is that an arraylist will always hold references to objects, not any particular class. However, this can be fixed when you move over to the `List` class.

5.1.2 The List class

The `List` class gives you everything that an arraylist gives you, with the advantage that it is also *typesafe*. It is newer than the `ArrayList` class, being based on the generic features provided by a more recent version of the C# language. To understand how it works you have to understand a bit of generics.

Generics and Behaviours

If you think about it, the fundamental behaviours of arrays are always the same. Whether you have an `int`, `string`, `float` or `Account` array the job that it does is exactly the same. It holds a bunch of things in one place, and provides you with some means to work with them. The abilities an array gives you with an array of integers are exactly the same as those you have with an array of `Accounts`. And because each array is declared as holding values of a particular type, C# can make sure that an array always holds the appropriate type of values. The way that the system works, there is just no way that you can take an `Account` reference and place it in an array of integers. This is all to the good, but the `ArrayList` breaks things a bit.

The `ArrayList` was added afterwards, and because it is not quite as much a part of the language as an array is, it has to use a compromise to allow it to hold references to any kind of item in a program. It does this by using references to objects, but this can lead to programs which are dangerous, in that there is nothing to stop references of any type being added to an arraylist.

If you give me an array of `Accounts` I can be absolutely sure that everything in the array is an account. However, if you give me an `ArrayList` there is no way I can be sure that accounts are all it contains. It could contain a whole bunch of `KitchenSink` references for all I know. And I only really find out when I start trying to process elements as `Accounts` and my program starts to go wrong.

One way to solve this problem would have been to find a way of making the `ArrayList` strongly typed, so that it becomes as much a part of C# as the array is. However, that is not what the designers of C# did. Instead they introduced a new language feature, generics.

Generics let me write code that deal with objects as "things of a particular type". It doesn't matter what the thing I'm dealing with is, we can sort that out when we actually want to work with something.

This sounds a bit confusing, how about an example.

If you wanted to share out marbles amongst you and your friends you could come up with way of doing that. Something like: "Divide the number of marbles by the number of friends and then distribute the remainder randomly". You now have a system that lets you share marbles. However, you could also use it to share out sweets, cakes or even cars. What the system works on is not particularly important. You could take your universal sharing algorithm and use it to share most anything. The sharing algorithm could have been invented without worrying about the type of the thing being shared; it can be a general sharing behaviour that is then applied to the things we want to share. In this respect, generics can be regarded as another form of abstraction.

Generics and the List

In the case of generics, the behaviour you want is that of a list. What the list stores is not important when making the list, just as long as you have a way of telling it what to store. The C# features that provide generics add a few new notations to allow you to express this. The `List` class lives in the `System.Collections.Generic` namespace and works like this:

```
List<Account> accountList = new List<Account>();
```

The above statement creates a list called `accountList` which can hold references to `Accounts`. The type between the `<` and `>` characters is how we tell the list the kind of things it can store. We could create a `List` that can hold integers in a similar way:

```
List<int> scores = new List<int>();
```

Because we have told the compiler the type of things the list can hold it can perform type validation and make sure that nothing bad happens when the list is used:

```
KitchenSink k = new KitchenSink();
accountList.Add(k);
```

The above statements would cause a compilation error, since the `accountList` variable is declared as holding a list of `Account` references, and will not accept the kitchen sink.

Since the compiler knows that `AccountList` holds `Account` references, this means that you can write code like this:

```
accountList[0].PayInFunds(50);
```

There is no need to cast the item in the list as the type has already been established.

You can do everything with a `List` (Add, Count, Remove) that you can with an `ArrayList`, which makes them the perfect way to store a large number of items of a particular type.

5.1.3 The Dictionary class

Just as `ArrayList` has a more powerful, generically enhanced, cousin called `List`, so the `HashTable` has a more powerful cousin called `Dictionary`. This allows the key to your hashtable, and the items it stores, to be made typesafe. For example, we might want to use the name of an account holder as a way of locating a particular account. In other words, we have a string as the key and an `Account` reference as the value. We can create a dictionary to hold these key/value pairs as follows:

```
Dictionary<string,Account> accountDictionary =
    new Dictionary<string,Account>();
```

We can now add items into our dictionary:

```
accountDictionary.Add("Rob", robsAccount);
```

This looks just like the way the `HashTable` was used (and it is). However, using a `Dictionary` has the advantage that we can only add `Account` values which are located by means of a `string`. In other words statements like this would be rejected.

```
KitchenSink k = new KitchenSink();
accountDictionary.Add("Glug", k);
```

A further advantage is that we do not need to cast the results:

```
d["Rob"].PayInFunds(50);
```

This would find the element with the hash key `"Rob"` and then pay fifty pounds into it. The only problem with this use of a dictionary is that if there is no element with the key `"Rob"` the attempt to find one will result in a `KeyNotFoundException` being thrown. You can get around this by asking the dictionary if it contains a particular key:

```
if (d.ContainsKey("Rob")) {
    Console.WriteLine("Rob is in the bank");
}
```

The method returns true if the key is found. Note that you will also need to use this method to make sure that a key is present in the dictionary before you add a new element, because a dictionary will not allow two elements to have the same key.

```
class DictionaryBank
{
    Dictionary<string,IAccount> accountDictionary =
                  new Dictionary<string,IAccount>();

    public IAccount FindAccount(string name)
    {
        if (accountDictionary.ContainsKey(name))
            return accountDictionary[name];
        else
            return null;
    }

    public bool StoreAccount(IAccount account)
    {
        if (accountDictionary.ContainsKey(account.GetName()))
            return false;

        accountDictionary.Add(account.GetName(), account);
        return true;
    }
}
```

Code Sample 48 A dictionary bank

The code above shows how we can create `FindAccount` and `StoreAccount` methods using a dictionary. The methods check to make sure that the dictionary is used properly.

The `Dictionary` class is simply wonderful for storing keys and values in a typesafe manner, and I recommend it strongly to you.

5.1.4 Writing Generic Code

The `List` and `Dictionary` classes were of course written in C# and make use of the generic features of the language. How these features are used to create generic classes is a bit beyond the scope of this text, but you are strongly advised to find out more about generics as it can make writing code, particularly library routines, a lot easier.

Programmer's Point: Use Dictionary and List

You don't really have to know a lot about generics to be able to spot just how useful these two things are. Every time you need to hold a bunch of things, make a List. If you want to be able to find things on the basis of a key, use a Dictionary. Don't have any concerns about performance. The programmers who wrote these things are very clever folks . You should use these in preference to hashtables and arraylists.

5.2 Storing Business Objects

For our bank to really work we have to have a way of storing the bank accounts and bringing them back again. If we want to our program to be able to process a large number of accounts we know that we have to create an array to manage this. This means that our data storage requirements are that we should load all the accounts into memory when the program starts, and then save them when the program completes.

To start with, we'll consider how we save one account. Then we can move on to consider the code which will save a large number of them. The account that we are going to work with only has two members but the ideas we are exploring can be extended to handle classes containing much larger amounts of data. We can express the required account behaviour in terms of the following interface:

```csharp
public interface IAccount
{
    void PayInFunds ( decimal amount );
    bool WithdrawFunds ( decimal amount );
    decimal GetBalance ();
    string GetName();
}
```

All the accounts in the bank are going to be managed in terms of objects which implement this interface to manage the balance and read the name of the account owner.

We can create a class called `CustomerAccount` which implements the interface and contains the required method**s.** It also has a constructor which allows the initial name and balance values to be set when the account is created.

```csharp
public class CustomerAccount : IAccount
{
    public CustomerAccount(
        string newName,
        decimal initialBalance)
    {
```

```csharp
        name = newName;
        balance = initialBalance;
    }

    private decimal balance = 0;
    private string name;

    public virtual bool WithdrawFunds ( decimal amount )
    {
        if ( balance < amount )
        {
            return false;
        }
        balance = balance - amount ;
        return true;
    }

    public void PayInFunds ( decimal amount )
    {
        balance = balance + amount ;
    }

    public decimal GetBalance ()
    {
        return balance;
    }

    public string GetName()
    {
        return name;
    }
}
```

Note that this version of the class does not perform any error checking of the input values, so it is not what I would call "production" code, but it is just here to illustrate how the data in the class can be saved and restored.

5.2.1 Saving an Account

The best way to achieve the saving behaviour is to make an account responsible for saving itself. In fact, if you think about it, this is the only way that we can save an account, since any save mechanism would need to save data in the account which is private and therefore only visible to methods inside the class.

We can add a Save method to our CustomerAccount class:

```csharp
public bool Save ( string filename )
{
    try
    {
        System.IO.TextWriter textOut =
            new System.IO.StreamWriter(filename);
        textOut.WriteLine(name);
        textOut.WriteLine(balance);
        textOut.Close();
    }
    catch
    {
        return false;
    }
```

```
        return true;
    }
```

This method is given the name of the file that the account is to be stored in. It writes out the name of the customer and the balance of the account. So I could do things like:

```
if (Rob.Save ("outputFile.txt"))
{
    Console.WriteLine ("Saved OK");
}
```

This would ask the account referred to by Rob to save itself in a file called "outputFile.txt". Note that I have written the code so that if the file output fails the method will return false, to indicate that the save was not successful.

5.2.2 Loading an Account

Loading is slightly trickier than saving. When we save an account we have an account which we want to save. When we load there will not be an account instance to load from. A way to get around this is to write a static method which will create an account given a filename:

```
public static CustomerAccount Load(string filename)
{
    CustomerAccount result = null;
    System.IO.TextReader textIn = null;

    try
    {
        textIn = new System.IO.StreamReader(filename);
        string nameText = textIn.ReadLine();
        string balanceText = textIn.ReadLine();
        decimal balance = decimal.Parse(balanceText);
        result = new CustomerAccount(nameText,balance);
    }
    catch
    {
        return null;
    }
    finally
    {
        if (textIn != null) textIn.Close() ;
    }
    return result;
}
```

This method opens a file, fetches the balance value and then creates a new CustomerAccount with the balance value and name.

```
class SaveDemo
{
    public static void Main()
    {
        CustomerAccount test = new CustomerAccount("Rob",
                                                   1000000);
        test.Save("Test.txt");

        CustomerAccount loaded = CustomerAccount.Load(
                                     "Test.txt");
        Console.WriteLine(loaded.GetName());
    }
}
```

Code Sample 49 Account Save and Load

The code sample shows how a program can save an account into a file and then load it back.

The `Load` method above takes great pains to ensure that if anything bad happens it does a number of things:

- It does not throw any exceptions which the caller must catch.
- It returns `null` to indicate that the load failed if anything bad happens.
- It makes sure that the file it opens is always closed.

This is what I would call a "professional" level of quality, and is something you should aim for when writing code you are going to sell.

We can use this as follows:

```
test = CustomerAccount.Load( "test.txt" );
```

This kind of method is sometimes called a "factory" method, in that it creates an instance of a class for us. If the factory fails (because the file cannot be found or does not contain valid content) it will return a `null` result, which we can test for:

```
if (test == null)
{
    Console.WriteLine( "Load failed" );
}
```

Programmer's Point: There is only so much you can do

Note that if an incompetent programmer used my Load method above they could forget to test the result that it returns and then their program would follow a null reference if the customer is not found. This means that their program will fail in this situation. And they will probably try and blame me for the problem (which would be very unfair).

The way around this is to make sure that you document the null return behaviour in big letters so that users are very aware of how the method behaves. You can also get code analysis tools which are bit like "compilers with attitude" (a good one is called FxCop). These scan programs for situations where the results of methods are ignored and flag these up as potential errors. At the end of the day though there is not a great deal you can do if idiots use your software, you just have to make sure that, whatever happens, your part doesn't break.

Actually, as I grow older I become more inclined to make my programs throw exceptions in situations like this, since that makes sure that a failure is brought to the attention of the system much earlier. However, you can argue this either way, the best place to do it is at the pub.

5.2.3 Multiple Accounts

The above code lets us store and load single accounts. However, at the moment we can only store one account in a file. We could create a new file for each account, but this would be confusing and inefficient, with large numbers of file open and close actions being required (bear in mind that our bank may contain thousands of accounts).

Using streams

A better solution is to give the file save method a stream to save itself, rather than a filename. A *stream* is the thing that the C# library creates when we open a connection to a file:

```csharp
System.IO.TextWriter textOut =
    new System.IO.StreamWriter( "Test.txt" );
```

The reference `textOut` refers to a stream which is connected to the file Test.txt. We can create a save method which accepts the stream reference as a parameter instead of a filename:

```csharp
public void Save(System.IO.TextWriter textOut)
{
    textOut.WriteLine(name);
    textOut.WriteLine(balance);
}
```

This save method can be called from our original file save method:

```csharp
public bool Save ( string filename )
{
    System.IO.TextWriter textOut = null;
    try
    {
        textOut = new System.IO.StreamWriter(filename);
        Save(textOut);
    }
    catch
    {
        return false;
    }
    finally
    {
        if (textOut != null)
        {
            textOut.Close();
        }
    }
    return true;
}
```

This method creates a stream and then passes it to the save method to save the item. Note that this is an example of *overloading* in that we have two methods which share the same name.

The load method for our bank account can be replaced by one which works in a similar way.

```csharp
public static CustomerAccount Load(
    System.IO.TextReader textIn)
{
    CustomerAccount result = null;

    try
    {
        string name = textIn.ReadLine();
        string balanceText = textIn.ReadLine();
        decimal balance = decimal.Parse(balanceText);
        result = new CustomerAccount(name, balance);
    }
    catch
    {
        return null;
    }
    return result;
}
```

This method is supplied with a text stream. It reads the name and the balance from this stream and creates a new `CustomerAccount` based on this data.

Programmer's Point: Streams are wonderful

Using streams is a very good idea. The C# input/output system lets us connect streams to all manner of things, not just files on a disk. For example, you can create a stream which is connected to a network port. This means that if you make your business objects save and load themselves using streams they can then be sent over network connections with no extra work from you.

Saving and loading bank accounts

Now that we have a way of saving multiple accounts to a single stream we can write a save method for the bank. This will open a stream and save all the accounts to it:

```csharp
public void Save(System.IO.TextWriter textOut)
{
    textOut.WriteLine(bankHashtable.Count);
    foreach (CustomerAccount account in bankHashtable.Values)
    {
        account.Save(textOut);
    }
}
```

This is the `Save` method which would be added to our `Hashtable` based bank. It gets each account out of the hash table and saves it in the given stream. Note that we are using a new C# loop construction here, `foreach`. This is very useful when dealing with collections of data. It works its way through a *collection*, in this case the `Values` property of the `bankHashtable`, and supplies each item in turn.

Note that before it writes anything it writes out the number of customers in the bank. This can be obtained via the `Count` property of the `Hashtable`. We do this so that when the bank is read back in the load method knows how many accounts are required. We could just write out the data and then let the load method stop when it reaches the end of the file, but this would not allow us to detect if the file had been shortened.

The `Load` method for the entire bank is as follows:

```csharp
public static HashBank Load(System.IO.TextReader textIn)
{
    HashBank result = new HashBank();
    string countString = textIn.ReadLine();
    int count = int.Parse(countString);

    for (int i = 0; i < count; i++)
    {
        CustomerAccount account = CustomerAccount.Load(textIn);
        result.bankHashtable.Add(account.GetName(), account);
    }
    return result;
}
```

This reads the size of the bank and then reads each of the accounts in turn and adds it to the hash table. Note that this load method does not handle errors. A production version of the program would check that each account was loaded correctly before adding it to the hash table.

```csharp
class BankProgram
{
    public static void Main()
    {
        DictionaryBank ourBank = new DictionaryBank();

        Account newAccount = new Account("Rob", 1000000);
```

```csharp
            if (ourBank.StoreAccount(newAccount) == true)
                Console.WriteLine("Account added to bank");

            ourBank.Save("Test.txt");

            DictionaryBank loadBank =
                            DictionaryBank.Load("Test.txt");

            IAccount storedAccount = ourBank.FindAccount("Rob");
            if (storedAccount != null)
                Console.WriteLine("Account found in bank");
        }
    }
```

Code Sample 50 Saving an entire bank

This code sample shows how it all works in a Dictionary powered bank. The sample above only stores one account, but it could be extended to hold as many as needed.

BANK NOTES: LARGE SCALE DATA STORAGE

What we have done is created a way that we can store a large number of bank account values in a single file. We have done this without sacrificing any *cohesion*, in that only the `CustomerAccount` class is responsible for the content. We have also been very careful to make sure that whenever we save and load data we manage the way that this process can fail.

5.2.4 Handling different kinds of accounts

The code above will work correctly if all we want to save and load are accounts of a particular type, in that everything is written in terms of the `CustomerAccount` class. However, we have seen that our customer needs the program to be able to handle many different kinds of account.

Health Warning

This is complicated stuff. I don't expect you to understand this at first reading. The reason that it is here is for completeness. Having told you all about class hierarchies and how useful it is to be able to base a new class on an existing one (as we did with `BabyAccount`) it would be most unfair of me to leave you guessing as to how these things can be stored and retrieved. This material is provided to give you an idea of how you really could make a working bank, but it assumes a very good understanding of class hierarchies, method overriding/overloading and constructor chaining.

The good news is that when you do understand this stuff you really can call yourself a fully-fledged C# programmer.

Banks and Flexibility

We know that when our system is actually used in a bank there will be a range of different kinds of account class, some of which will be based on others. As an example, we have previously discussed the `BabyAccount`, a special account for young people which limits the amount that can be withdrawn to no more than 10 pounds. The customer has also asked that the `BabyAccount` class contains the name of the "parent" account holder. We could implement such behaviour by creating an account which extends the `CustomerAccount` class and adds the required behaviours and properties:

```csharp
    public class BabyAccount : CustomerAccount
    {
```

```csharp
        private string parentName;

        public string GetParentName()
        {
            return parentName;
        }

        public override bool WithdrawFunds(decimal amount)
        {
            if (amount > 10)
            {
                return false;
            }
            return base.WithdrawFunds(amount);
        }

        public BabyAccount(
            string newName,
            decimal initialBalance,
            string inParentName)
            : base(newName, initialBalance)
        {
            parentName = inParentName;
        }
    }
```

This is a complete `BabyAccount` implementation. It contains an additional property, `parentName`, and overrides the `WithdrawFunds` method to provide the new behaviour. Note that I have created a constructor which is supplied with the name of the account holder, the starting balance and the name of the parent. This makes use of the constructor in the parent to set the balance and name, and then sets the parent name. I can create a `BabyAccount` as follows:

```csharp
BabyAccount babyJane = new BabyAccount ("Jane", 20, "John");
```

This would create a new `BabyAccount` instance and set the reference `babyJane` to refer to it.

Saving a child class

When we want to save a `BabyAccount` we also need to save the information from the parent class. This turns out to be very easy, as long as we use the save method which sends the information to a stream:

```csharp
public override void Save(System.IO.TextWriter textOut)
{
    base.Save(textOut);
    textOut.WriteLine(parentName);
}
```

This method overrides the `Save` method in the parent `CustomerAccount`. However, it first calls the overridden method in the parent to save the `CustomerAccount` data. Then it performs the save behaviour required by the `BabyAccount` class. This is very good design, as it means that if the data content and save behaviour of the parent class changes we don't need to change the behaviour of the child.

Loading a child class

We could create a `static` load method for the `BabyAccount` which reads in the information and constructs a new `BabyAccount`:

```csharp
public static BabyAccount Load(
    System.IO.TextReader textIn)
{
```

```
        BabyAccount result = null;

        try
        {
            string name = textIn.ReadLine();
            string balanceText = textIn.ReadLine();
            decimal balance = decimal.Parse(balanceText);
            string parent = textIn.ReadLine();
            result = new BabyAccount (name, balance, parent);
        }
        catch
        {
            return null;
        }
        return result;
    }
```

However, I'm not particularly keen on this approach. This method breaks one of the rules of good design, in that we now have a *dependency* between the two classes which means that when I change the `CustomerAccount` class (perhaps to add a new field called `customerPIN`) I also have to update the `Load` method in the `BabyAccount` class to make sure that this extra data is loaded. If I forget to do this the program will compile, but when it runs it will not work correctly.

What we really want to do is make the `CustomerAccount` responsible for loading its data and the `BabyAccount` just look after its content; in a similar way to the way the save method uses the `base` keyword to save the parent object.

The way to do this is to go back to the construction process. We know that a constructor is a method which gets control when an instance of a class is being created. A constructor can be used to set up the data in the instance, and it can be passed information to allow it to do this. In the code above there is a constructor for the `BabyAccount` class which accepts the three data items that the `BabyAccount` holds and then sets the instance up with these values.

What we do is create constructors for the `CustomerAccount` and `BabyAccount` classes which read their information from a stream that is supplied to them:

```
public CustomerAccount(System.IO.TextReader textIn)
{
    name = textIn.ReadLine();
    string balanceText = textIn.ReadLine();
    balance = decimal.Parse(balanceText);
}
```

This constructor sets up the new `CustomerAccount` instance by reading the values from the stream that it is supplied with. I can therefore write code like this:

```
System.IO.TextReader textIn =
    new System.IO.StreamReader(filename);
result = new CustomerAccount(textIn);
textIn.Close();
```

This creates a new `CustomerAccount` from the stream. Now I can create a constructor for the `BabyAccount` which uses the constructor of the parent class:

```
public BabyAccount(System.IO.TextReader textIn) :
    base (textIn)
{
    parentName = textIn.ReadLine();
}
```

This removes the dependency relationship completely. If the behaviour of the `CustomerAccount` constructor changes we do not have to change the `BabyAccount` at all.

Note that these constructors do not do any error checking, they just throw exceptions if something goes wrong. Bearing in mind that the only way that a constructor can fail is to throw an exception anyway, this is reasonable behaviour.

Interfaces and the save operation

When we started this account development we set out an interface which describes all the things which an instance of an account should be able to do. At the start this did not include the save behaviours, but it could be updated to include them:

```csharp
public interface IAccount
{
    void PayInFunds ( decimal amount );
    bool WithdrawFunds ( decimal amount );
    decimal GetBalance ();
    string GetName();

    bool Save(string filename);
    void Save(System.IO.TextWriter textOut);
}
```

We can now ask any item which implements the `IAccount` interface to save itself to either a file or a stream. This is very useful when we store our collection of accounts, since the account container will not have to behave differently depending on what kind of account it is saving, it just has to call the save method for the particular instance. This is a good idea.

Loading and factories

When it comes to loading our classes back, things get a little trickier. You might think it would be sensible to add load methods to the `IAccount` interface, so that we can ask instances of a particular kind of account to load themselves. However, there is a problem here, in that when we are loading the accounts we don't actually have an instance to call any methods on. Also, bearing mind we are reading from a stream of data, we don't actually know what kind of item we are loading.

The solution to this problem is to identify the type of each instance in the stream when we save the classes. The save method for our bank could look like this:

```csharp
public void Save(System.IO.TextWriter textOut)
{
    textOut.WriteLine(bankHashtable.Count);
    foreach (CustomerAccount account in bankHashtable.Values)
    {
        textOut.WriteLine(account.GetType().Name);
        account.Save(textOut);
    }
}
```

This looks very like our original method, except that it has an additional line, which has been highlighted. This writes out the name of the class. It makes use of the method `GetType()`, which can be called on an instance of a class to get the type of that class. Having got the type we can then get the **Name** property of this type and print that. In other words, if the account is of type `CustomerAccount` the program will output:

```
CustomerAccount
Rob
100
```

The output now contains the name of the type of each class that has been written. This means that when the stream is read back in this information can be used to cause the correct type of class to be created. The neatest way to do this is to create a *factory* which will produce instances of the required class:

```
class AccountFactory
{
    public static IAccount MakeAccount(
        string name, System.IO.TextReader textIn)
    {
        switch (name)
        {
            case "CustomerAccount":
                return new CustomerAccount(textIn);
            case "BabyAccount":
                return new BabyAccount(textIn);
            default:
                return null;
        }
    }
}
```

This class only contains a single method, which is `static`. The method is given two parameters, the name of the class to be created and a stream to read from. It uses the name to decide which item to make, creates one, and then returns that to the caller. If the name is not recognized it returns `null`. The bank load method can use this factory to create instances of accounts as they are loaded:

```
public static HashBank Load(System.IO.TextReader textIn)
{
    HashBank result = new HashBank();
    string countString = textIn.ReadLine();
    int count = int.Parse(countString);

    for (int i = 0; i < count; i++)
    {
        string className = textIn.ReadLine();
        IAccount account =
            AccountFactory.MakeAccount(className, textIn);
        result.bankHashtable.Add(account.GetName(), account);
    }
    return result;
}
```

Again, this looks very like our original load method, except that it uses the factory to make account instances once it has read the name of the class from the stream.

```
class BankProgram
{
    public static void Main()
    {
        DictionaryBank ourBank = new DictionaryBank();

        CustomerAccount newAccount = new CustomerAccount("Rob",
                                                    1000000);

        if (ourBank.StoreAccount(newAccount))
            Console.WriteLine("CustomerAccount added to bank");

        BabyAccount newBabyAccount = new BabyAccount("David",
                                                    100,"Rob");

        if (ourBank.StoreAccount(newBabyAccount))
```

```
            Console.WriteLine("BabyAccount added to bank");

        ourBank.Save("Test.txt");

        DictionaryBank loadBank =
                        DictionaryBank.Load("Test.txt");

        IAccount storedAccount = loadBank.FindAccount("Rob");
        if (storedAccount != null)
            Console.WriteLine("CustomerAccount found in bank");
        storedAccount = loadBank.FindAccount("David");
        if (storedAccount != null)
            Console.WriteLine("BabyAccount found in bank");
    }
}
```

Code Sample 51 Factory class in action

The code above shows how I tested my factory. It creates a bank, adds two different accounts and then loads them back.

Factory Dependencies

Note that we now have a genuine dependency between our system and the factory class. If we ever add a new type of account we need to update the behaviour of the factory so that it contains a case to deal with the new account type. There is in fact a way of removing the need to do this. It involves writing code which will search for C# classes which implement particular interfaces and creating them automatically. However this kind of stuff is beyond the scope of this text.

BANK NOTES: MESSY CODE

You might think that the solutions above are rather messy. The way that we manage the saving of items (by using a method in the class) and loading (by using a constructor) is not symmetrical. However, there is no dishonour in this way of working. When you want to move from objects to storage and back you will find that you hit these issues and this solution is as good as any I've found.

5.3 Business Objects and Editing

We have seen how to design a class which can be used to hold information about the customers in our bank. We now also know how to save the information in a class instance, and also perform this for a large number of items of a range of different types. Now we need to consider how we can make our account management system genuinely useful, by providing a user interface which lets people interact with our business objects to run the bank.

Programmer's Point: Production Code

From now on all the code examples are going to be given in the context of *production code*. This is code which I would be happy to have supplied in a product. This means that I will be considering what things you should look at when you are writing code for real customers. This might make the examples a bit more complex than you might like, but I reckon this is worth doing since it is important you start to understand that what you are writing now, and the problems you are grappling with, are just those that "real" programmers are up against.

5.3.1 The role of the Business Object

We have taken a very strict line in our banking system to stop any of the bank account components from actually talking to the user. This is because classes like `CustomerAccount` are what is called *business objects*. It is not their job to talk to users; they are strictly concerned with keeping track of the information in the bank account of the customer. The job of the business object is to make sure that the data that it holds is always correct. The editing behaviours should make use of the methods that the business object exposes.

Managing a bank account name

As an example, consider the name of the bank account holder. It is important that this is always stored safely but people may want to change their name from time to time. This means that the business object must provide a way that the name can be changed.

However, there is more to it than just changing one string for another. The new name must be a valid one. This means that the account must be able to reject names it doesn't like. If it is going to reject names it would be very useful to the user if they could be told why a given name was not valid, so the validation process should provide feedback as to why it did not work.

A good software engineer would provide something like this:

```
private string name;

public string GetName()
{
   return this.name;
}

public static string ValidateName ( string name )
{
   if ( name == null ) {
      return "Name parameter null";
   }
   string trimmedName = name.Trim();
   if ( trimmedName.Length == 0 )
   {
      return "No text in the name";
   }
   return "";
}

public bool SetName ( string inName )
{
   string reply ;
   reply = ValidateName(inName);
   if ( reply.Length > 0 )
   {
      return false;
   }

   this.name = inName.Trim();
   return true;
}
```

The name is stored as a `private` member of the account class. The programmer has provided three methods which let the users of my `Account` class deal with names. There is a method to **get** the name, another to **set** it and another to **validate** it. The validate method is called by the set method so that my business object makes sure that an account never has an invalid name. The validate method will reject a name string which is empty, or just contains spaces. It trims off all the spaces before and after the name text and then checks to see if the length of the resulting string is empty. If it is, the string is rejected.

I provide the validate method so that users of my class can check their names to make sure that they are valid. This does not involve me in much extra work, since I also use the method myself when I validate the name. The validate method returns a string which gives an error message if the string is rejected. There may be several reasons why a name is not valid, at the moment I've just given two. The reasons why a name is invalid are of course part of the *metadata* for the project. I've also made this method `static` so that names can be validated without needing to have an actual instance of the account.

Testing Name Handling

Of course, once we have these methods, the natural thing to do is create tests for them:

```csharp
int errorCount=0;
string reply;
reply = CustomerAccount.ValidateName(null);
if (reply != "Name parameter null")
{
    Console.WriteLine("Null name test failed");
    errorCount++;
}
reply = CustomerAccount.ValidateName("");
if (reply != "No text in the name")
{
    Console.WriteLine("Empty name test failed");
    errorCount++;
}
reply = CustomerAccount.ValidateName("   ");
if (reply != "No text in the name")
{
    Console.WriteLine("Blank string name test failed");
    errorCount++;
}
CustomerAccount a = new CustomerAccount("Rob", 50);
if (!a.SetName("Jim"))
{
    Console.WriteLine("Jim SetName failed");
    errorCount++;
}
if ( a.GetName() != "Jim" ) {
    Console.WriteLine("Jim GetName failed");
    errorCount++;
}
if (!a.SetName("   Pete   "))
{
    Console.WriteLine("Pete trim SetName failed");
    errorCount++;
}
if ( a.GetName() != "Pete" )
{
    Console.WriteLine("Pete GetName failed");
    errorCount++;
}
if (errorCount > 0 )
{
    SoundSiren();
}
```

Code Sample 52 Testing the name setting

These are all the tests I could think of. First I test `ValidateName` to make sure that it rejects both kinds of empty string. Then I make sure that I can set the name on an account. Finally I check that the space trimming for the names works correctly.

Programmer's Point: Use Numbers Not Messages

There is one issue which I have not addressed in my sample programs which stops them from being completely perfect. And that is the matter of error handling. At the moment the errors supplied by my validation methods are strings. In a genuine production environment the errors would be numeric values. This is because they are much easier to compare in tests and it also means that my program could be made to work in a foreign language very easily. All I would need is a lookup table to convert the message number to an appropriate string in the currently active language. You should consider issues like this as part of the *metadata* in your project. The fact that the system must work in France and Germany is something you need to be aware of right at the start.

Editing the Name

We now have a business object that provides methods which let us edit the name value. I can now write code to edit this property:

```
while (true)
{
   Console.Write ( "Enter new name : " ) ;
   newName = Console.ReadLine();
   string reply;
   reply = account.ValidateName(newName);

   if ( reply.Length == 0 )
   {
      break;
   }
   Console.WriteLine( "Invalid name : " + reply );
}
account.SetName(newName);
```

This code will perform the name editing for an account instance referred to by `account`. It will read a new name in. If the name is valid the loop is broken and the name is set. If the name is not valid the message is printed and the loop repeats. This is not the most elegant solution, but it does keep the user informed of what it is doing and it does work. Now that we have our edit code we need to put it somewhere.

Creating an Editor class

The best way to do this is to create a class which has the job of doing the editing. This class will work on a particular account that needs to be edited. There will be a dependency between the editor class and the account class, in that if the account class changes the editor may need to be updated, but this is something we will just have to live with.

When I want to edit an account I create an editor instance and pass it a reference to the account instance:

```csharp
public class AccountEditTextUI
{
   private IAccount account;

   public AccountEditTextUI(Account inAccount)
   {
      this.account = inAccount;
   }

   public void EditName ()
   {
      string newName;
      Console.WriteLine( "Name Edit" );
      while (true)
      {
         Console.Write ( "Enter new name : " ) ;
         newName = Console.ReadLine();
         string reply;
         reply = this.account.ValidateName(newName);

         if ( reply.Length == 0 )
         {
            break;
         }
         Console.WriteLine( "Invalid name : " + reply );
      }
      this.account.SetName(newName);
   }
}
```

This is my account editor class. At the moment it can only edit the name, but I will add other edit methods later. The class keeps track of the account it is editing, I pass it a reference to this account when I construct it. I would use the name editor as follows:

```csharp
CustomerAccount a = new CustomerAccount("Rob", 50);
AccountEditTextUI edit = new AccountEditTextUI(a);
edit.EditName();
```

Code Sample 53 Name Editing

This code creates an instance of a customer account. It then creates an editor object and asks it to edit the name of that account.

Note that the editor class is passed a reference to the `IAccount` interface, not a reference to the account class. This means that anything which behaves like an account can be edited using this class. Note also that the editor remembers the account class that is being edited so that when I call `EditName` it can work on that reference.

Programmer's Point: Get used to passing references around

It is important that you get used to the idea of passing references between methods. If I want to "give" a class something to work on I will do this by calling a method in that class and passing the reference as a parameter to this method. You will use this technique when you create different editing forms

5.3.2 A Text Based Edit System

We now have a single method in our editor class which can be used to edit the name of a bank account. What we really want is a menu system which takes a command from the user and performs that function:

```
Editing account for Pete
    Enter name to edit name
    Enter pay to pay in funds
    Enter draw to draw out funds
    Enter exit to exit program
Enter command :
```

The user types in the name of the command that is required and then the program selects that function. My edit class contains a method which does this:

This is my edit method which repeatedly reads commands and dispatches them to the appropriate method. I've extended the account class to manage the account balance and added edit methods which pay in funds and withdraw them. Note that I trim the command string and convert it to lower case before using it to drive the switch construction which selects the command.

The edit method is passed a reference to the account which is being edited. It then passes that reference to the service methods which will do the actual work.

```csharp
public void DoEdit (CustomerAccount account)
{
    string command;
    do
    {
        Console.WriteLine ( "Editing account for {0}", account.GetName() );
        Console.WriteLine ( "    Enter name to edit name" );
        Console.WriteLine ( "    Enter pay to pay in funds" );
        Console.WriteLine ( "    Enter draw to draw out funds" );
        Console.WriteLine ( "    Enter exit to exit program" );
        Console.Write ("Enter command : ");
        command = Console.ReadLine();
        command = command.Trim();
        command = command.ToLower();
        switch ( command )
        {
            case "name" :
                EditName(account);
                break;
            case "pay" :
                PayInFunds(account);
                break;
            case "draw" :
                WithDrawFunds(account);
                break;
        }
    } while ( command != "exit" );
}
```

Programmer's Point: Every Message Counts

You should remember that every time your program sends text to the user you may have a problem with language. The menu for my bank account edit method sample code prints out text which is hard wired to English. In a properly written program this would be managed in terms of message numbers to make it easier to change the text which is output.

As a general rule in a production system you should **never** write out straight text to your user (this includes the names of commands that the user might type in). Everything should be managed in terms of message numbers. The only exception to this is the situation where the customer has assured you that the program will only ever be written for use in a particular language. The C# libraries contain a set of resources which help you manage the internationalization of your programs.

BANK NOTES: MORE THAN ONE USER INTERFACE

The bank may have a whole range of requirements for editing account details. These will range from an operator in a call centre, an operator on a dial up terminal, a customer on a mobile phone and a customer at a cash machine. I hope that you can see that the only way we can manage all these different ways of interacting with the bank account is to separate the business object (the account itself) from the input/output behaviour.

Note that we **never** do things like allow the user interface code to decide what constitutes a valid name. This question is not the responsibility of the front end. The only thing that can decide on the validity of a name is the account object itself. The user interface must always work on the basis that it will use the business object to perform this kind of validation.

5.4 Threads and Threading

If you want to call yourself a proper programmer you need to know something about threads. They can make programs much easier to create, but they can also be the source of really nasty bugs. In the future, where the speed of computer processors is going to be limited by irritating things like the speed of light and the size of atoms, they are the way that we will be able to keep on improving the performance of our computer systems.

5.4.1 What is a thread?

At the moment our programs are only using a single *thread* when they run. The thread usually starts in the `Main` method and finishes when the end of this method is reached. You can visualise a thread as a train running along a track. The track is the statements that the thread is executing. In the same way that you can put more than one train on a single track, a computer can run more than one thread in a single block of program code.

A computer can support multiple threads in two ways. The first is by rapidly switching between active threads, giving each thread the chance to run for a limited time before moving on to run another. When a thread is not running it is held in a "frozen" state, waiting for its turn to run. As far as the thread is concerned it is running continuously, but in reality a thread may only be active for a small fraction of a second every now and then.

The second way to support multiple threads is to actually have more than one processor. The first computers had only one processor and so were forced to use "time slicing" to support multiple threads. Newer machines now have "dual core" or even "quad core" processors which can actually run multiple threads simultaneously.

5.4.2 Why do we have threads?

Threads make it possible for your computer to do something useful while one program is held up. Your system can play music and download files while your program waits for you to press the next key. A modern computer can perform many millions of instructions per second; it makes sense to share this ability amongst several tasks.

The programs that you have been writing and running have all executed as threads in your computer. This is how your program can be active at the same time as other programs you may wish to use alongside it. You have not been aware of this because the operating system (usually Windows) does a very good job of sharing out the processing power.

Threads provide another level of "abstraction", in that if we wish to do more than one thing at the same time it is very useful just to send a thread off to perform the task, rather than try interleaving the second task with the first. If we wrote a word processor we might find it useful to create threads to perform time consuming tasks like printing or spell checking. These could be performed "in the background" while the user continues to work on the document.

Threads are also how Windows forms respond to events. You have seen that a "click" event from a Button component can be made to run an event handler method. The Windows system actually creates a new thread of execution which runs the event handler code.

Programmer's Point: Threads can be dangerous

In the same way that letting two trains share the same railway track can sometimes lead to problems, programs that use threads can also fail in spectacular and confusing ways. It is possible for systems to fail only when a certain sequence of events causes two previously well behaved threads to "fight" over a shared item of data. Bugs caused by threading are amongst the hardest ones to track down and fix because you have to make the problem happen before you can fix it, and the circumstances that cause the fault may only occur every now and then. I'm going to give some tips on how to make sure that your programs don't fall foul of threading related bugs, and I suggest that you follow these carefully.

5.4.3 Threads and Processors

Consider the following method:

```
static private void busyLoop()
{
    long count;
    for (count = 0; count < 1000000000000L; count = count+1)
    {
    }
}
```

Code Sample 54 Single Thread Busy Loop

This method does nothing, but it does do it many millions of times. If I run a program that calls this method the first thing that happens is that the program seems to stop. Then the fan in my computer comes on as the processor starts to heat up as it is now working hard. If I run the program within Visual Studio I get a rather handy display of how much of the central processor unit my program is using:

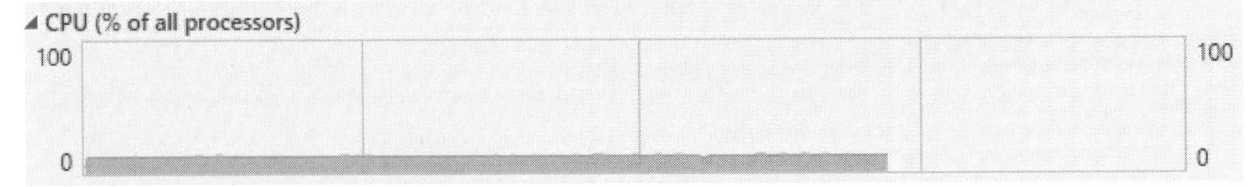

My desktop has eight processor cores, which means that it can run eight threads at a time. The graph shows that the program is using around an eighth of the PC, which is about right.

> **Programmer's Point: Multiple Threads Can Improve Performance**
>
> If you can work out how to spread your program over several threads this can make a big difference to the speed it runs at. The method above can only ever use a maximum of 25% of my system, since it only runs on one of the four available processors.

5.4.4 Running a Thread

Note that these descriptions of thread behaviour are for the Microsoft .NET environment and are not strictly part of the C# language itself. If you write programs for the Windows 8 operating system you may be creating software based on Windows RT. In this case you will find that threads are used in a slightly different way.

An individual thread is managed by your program as an instance of the Thread class. This class lives in the System namespace. We have used namespaces to locate resources before when we used files. The easiest way to make sure that we can use all the threading resources is to add a using directive at the start of our program:

```
using System.Threading;
```

The Thread class provides a link between your program and the operating system. One job of the operating system is to manage threads on your computer and decide exactly when each should get to run. By calling methods provided by the Thread class you can start and stop them.

Selecting where a Thread starts running

When you create a thread you need to tell the thread where to start running. This is like telling your younger brother where on the track you'd like him to place your train. You do this by using *delegates*. A delegate is a way of referring to a method in a class. The delegate type used by threads is the ThreadStart type. This delegate type can refer to a method that does not return a value or accept any parameters. If you take a look at the busyLoop method above you will find that this method fits the bill perfectly. You can create a ThreadStart delegate to refer to this method as follows:

```
ThreadStart busyLoopMethod = new ThreadStart(busyLoop);
```

Creating a Thread

Once you have your start point defined you can now create a Thread value:

```
Thread t1 = new Thread(busyLoopMethod);
```

The variable t1 now refers to a thread instance. Note that at the moment the thread is not running, it is waiting to be started. When we start running t1 it will follow the delegate busyLoopMethod and make a call to the busyloop method.

Starting a Thread

The Thread class provides a number of methods that your program can use to control what it does. To start the thread running you can use the Start method:

```
t1.Start();
```

This is the point at which the thread begins to run.

```
class ThreadDemo
{
```

```
static private void busyLoop()
{
    long count;
    for (count = 0; count < 1000000000000L; count = count+1)
    {
    }
}

static void Main()
{
    ThreadStart busyLoopMethod = new ThreadStart(busyLoop);

    Thread t1 = new Thread(busyLoopMethod);

    t1.Start();
    busyLoop();
}
```

Code Sample 55 Two Threaded Busy Loop

The above code creates a thread called `t1` and starts it running the `busyLoop` method. It also calls `busyLoop` directly from the `Main` method. This means that there are two processes active. This changes the Task Manager display:

Now more of the usage graphs are showing activity and the CPU usage is up from around 12% to 25% as our program is now using more processors.

Making lots of Threads

From the displays above you can see that if we create an additional thread we can use more of the power the computer gives us. In fact, we can create many more threads than this:

```
for (int i = 0; i < 100; i = i + 1)
{
    Thread t1 = new Thread(busyLoopMethod);
    t1.Start();
}
```

Code Sample 56 Hundred Thread Busy Loop

This loop will create 100 threads, all running the `busyLoop` method. Now our computer is really busy:

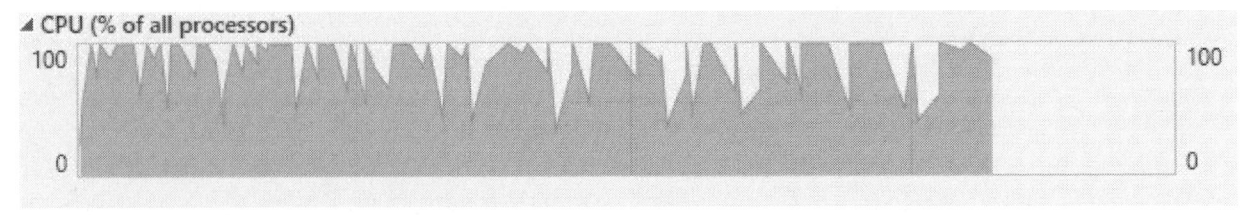

All the processors are now maxed out, and the CPU usage is up to 100%. If you run this code you might actually find that the machine becomes slightly less responsive, and that all the cooling fans come on full blast. The troughs in the graph above show when other processes are taking over the cpu.

Programmer's Point: Too Many Threads Will Slow Everything Down

Note that nothing has stopped your program from starting a large number of threads running. This is potentially dangerous. If you run too many threads at once you will slow everything down. This is actually the basis of a type of attack on your computer, called a *Denial of Service* attack. This makes your computer unusable by starting a huge number of threads which tie up the processor. Fortunately Windows boosts the priority of threads that deal with user input so you can usually get control and stop such wayward behaviour.

5.4.5 Threads and Synchronisation

You might be wondering why all the threads don't fight over the value of count that is being used as the loop counter. This is because the variable is *local* to the busyLoop method:

```
static private void busyLoop()
{
    long count;
    for (count = 0; count < 1000000000000L; count = count+1)
    {
    }
}
```

The count variable is declared within the body of the method. This means that each method has its own copy of this *local* variable. If you are still thinking about threads as trains, it is as if the data for each thread is held in trucks that are pulled along behind the train. We could make a tiny change to this code and make the count variable a member of the class:

```
static long count;
static private void busyLoop()
{
    for (count = 0; count < 1000000000000L; count = count + 1)
    {
    }
}
```

The method looks very similar, but now every thread running busyLoop is sharing the same count variable. This is potentially disastrous. It is now very hard to predict how long this multi-threaded program will take to finish. Consider the following sequence of actions:

1. Thread 1 fetches the value of the count variable so that it can add 1 to it.

2. Before the addition can be performed, Thread 1 is stopped and Thread 20 is allowed to run.

3. Thread 20 fetches the value of count, adds one to it and stores it back in memory.

4. Sometime later Thread 1 gets control again, adds 1 to the value it fetched before it was stopped and stores the result back in memory.

Because of the way that Thread 1 was interrupted during its calculation, it has overwritten the changes that Thread 20 made. As the threads run they are all loading, incrementing and storing the value of count and overwriting changes that they have made.

What we need is a way of stopping the threads from interrupting each other. The statement count = count + 1; must be allowed to complete without being interrupted. You can do this by using a feature called *mutual exclusion* or *mutex*. We can return to our train analogy here.

Using Mutual Exclusion to Manage Data Sharing

Allowing two threads to share the same variable is a bit like allowing two trains to share the same piece of track. Both are dangerous. The single-track problem was solved by using a single brass token which was held by the engine driver. When they entered the single track they were given the token. When the train left the single-track section the driver handed the token back. Anyone wanting to enter the track had to wait for their turn with the token.

Mutual exclusion works in just the same way by using an instance of an object to play the role of the token.

```
static object sync = new object();
```

This object doesn't actually hold any data. It is just used as the token which is held by the active process.

```
Monitor.Enter(sync);
count = count + 1;
Monitor.Exit(sync);
```

The code between the `Monitor.Enter` and `Monitor.Exit` calls can only be performed by one thread at a time. In other words, there is no chance of Windows interrupting the increment statement and switching to another process. All the increment operations will complete in their entirety. Once execution leaves the statements between the Monitor calls the thread can be suspended as usual.

Threads that aren't able to run are "parked" in a queue of waiting threads. This queue is held in order, so the first thread to get to the entry point will be the first to get the token, with the other threads lining up for their turn. The `Monitor` class looks after all this for us; we don't need to know how it works.

Programmer's Point: Threads can Totally Break your Program

If a thread grabs hold of a synchronisation object and doesn't let go of it, this will stop other threads from running if they need that object. This is a really good way to make your programs fail. Another one, called the "Deadly Embrace" is where thread a has got object x and is waiting for object y, and thread b has got object y and is waiting for object x. This is the computer version of "I'm not calling him to apologise, I'm going to wait for him to call me".

5.4.6 Thread Control

There are a number of additional features available for thread management. These let you pause threads, wait for a thread to finish, see if a thread is still active and suspend and remove threads.

Pausing Threads

As you can see above, one way to "pause" a thread is to create a loop with an enormous limit value. This will certainly pause your program, but at the expense of any other threads that want to run. If you just want your program to pause, perhaps to allow the user to read the output or to wait a little while for something to happen you should use the `Sleep` method which is provided by the `Thread` class:

```
Thread.Sleep(500);
```

This method is given the number of milliseconds (thousandth's of a second) that the execution is to pause. The above call would pause a program for half a second.

Joining Threads

You might want to make one thread wait for another to finish working. A thread finishes when it exits the method that was called when it started. In our examples above, each thread will end when the call of `busyloop` finishes. A thread instance provides a `Join` method that can be called to wait for another thread to complete operation.

```
t1.Join();
```

This would cause the executing thread to wait until the thread t1 finishes.

Thread Control

The Thread class provides a set of methods that you can use to control the execution of a thread. You can abort a thread by calling its `Abort` method:

```
t1.Abort();
```

This asks the operating system to destroy that thread and remove it from memory.

If you don't want to destroy a thread, but simply make it pause for a while, you can call the Suspend method on the thread:

```
t1.Suspend();
```

The thread is put to sleep until you call the `Resume` method on that thread.

```
t1.Resume();
```

Finding the state of a thread

You can find out the state of a thread by using its `ThreadState` property. This is an enumerated value which has a number of possible values.

The most useful are:

ThreadState.Running	the thread is running
ThreadState.Stopped	the thread has finished executing the thread method
ThreadState.Suspend	the thread has been suspended
ThreadState.WaitSleepJoin	the thread is executing a Sleep, waiting to join with another thread or waiting for a Monitor

As an example, to display a message if thread `t1` is running:

```
if ( t1.ThreadState == ThreadState.Running )
{
    Console.WriteLine("Thread Running");
}
```

5.4.7 Staying Sane with Threads

Threads are very useful. They let your program deal with tasks by firing off threads of execution. The best way to create a system that must support many users, for example a web server, is to create a multi-threaded application which starts up a thread to deal with each incoming request. This makes the code easier to manage and also means that your program can make the best use of the processing power available.

However, threads can also be a great source of frustration. We know that our programs sometimes produce errors when they run. This is mostly because we have done something wrong. When we get a problem we look at what has happened and then work out what the fault is. Up until now our programs have been single threaded and we have been able to put in the data which causes the problem. This will cause the program to fail, at which point we can begin to fix it.

Unfortunately when you add multi-threading to a solution this is no longer true. A program which works fine for 99.999% of the time may fail spectacularly, or just lock up completely, when a specific set of timing related events occur. Synchronisation problems like the "Deadly Embrace" described above may only appear when two users both request a particular feature at exactly the same time.

When you have problems with a multi-threaded system the biggest difficultly is always making the fault occur so you can fix it. Often the only way to investigate the problem is to add lots of write statements so that the program makes a log that you can examine after it has failed. Of course, time spent writing the log output affects the timing of events in the program and can often cause a fault to move or, if you are very lucky, vanish completely.

You should protect any variables shared between threads by using the Monitor class as described above. This will stop inadvertent data corruption. If variables sometimes get "out of step" then this is a sure sign that you have several threads fighting over data items.

You should try to avoid any "Deadly Embrace" situations by making your threads either *producers* or *consumers* of data. If consumers are always waiting for producers (and producers never wait for consumers) then you can be sure that you never get the situation where one thread waits for a thread that is waiting for it.

Finally you should design in the logging and debugging behaviour (you can always use conditional compilation to turn the logging off later) so that if you do have a problem it is easy to get some diagnostic information which will tell you what your program was doing at the time it went wrong.

Programmer's Point: Put Threads into your Design

I think what I am really saying here is that any thread use should be designed into your program, and not tacked on afterwards. If you want to use threads the way that they are managed and how they communicate should be decided right at the start of your design and your whole system should be constructed with them in mind.

5.4.8 Threads and Processes

You can regard different threads as all living in the computer together in the same way that a number of trains can share a particular railway. The next step up is to have more than one railway. In programming terms this is a move from threads to processes. Processes are different from threads, in that each process has its own memory space which is isolated from other processes.

When you are using a word processor and a web browser at the same time on your computer each of them is running on your computer as a different process. Your word processor may fire off several threads that run within it (perhaps one to perform spell checking), but nothing in the word processor program can ever directly access the variables in the browser.

In a C# program you can create a process and start it in a similar way to starting a thread. You can also use the Process class to start programs for you. This class is held in the System.Diagnostics namespace, so you can add a Using statement to make it easier to get hold of the class:

```
using System.Diagnostics;
```

To start a program on your system you can use the Start method on the Process class:

```
    Process.Start("Notepad.exe");
```

The `Start` method is supplied with the name of the program that you want to start. The above line of C# would start the Notepad program.

You can also create `Process` instances that you can control from within your program in a similar manner to threads.

5.5 Structured Error Handling

By now I hope that you are starting to think very hard about how programs fail. You should also be thinking that when you build a system you should consider how you are going to manage the way that it will fail. This is actually a very important part of the design process. When something bad happens the program must deal with this in a managed way. The key to achieving this is to think about making your own custom exceptions for your system.

We have been on the receiving end of exceptions already. We have seen that if something bad happens whilst a file is being read, or a `Parse` method is given an invalid string, the system will throw an exception to indicate that it is unhappy. This means that potentially badly behaved code like this has to be enclosed in a `try – catch` construction so that our program can respond sensibly. Now we are going to take a closer look at exceptions and see about creating our own exception types.

5.5.1 The Exception class

The C# System namespace holds a large number of different exceptions, but they are all based on the parent `Exception` class. If you want to throw your own exceptions you are strongly advised to create your own exception type which extends the system one. You can generate `System.Exception` when something goes wrong, but this means that exceptions produced by your code will get mixed up with those produced by other parts of the system. If you want your code to be able to explicitly handle your errors the best way forward is to create one or more of your own exceptions.

This means that, along with everything else in your system, you will need to design how your program will handle and generate errors. This all (of course) leads back to the metadata which you have gathered, in that the specification will give you information about how things can fail and the way that the errors are produced.

5.5.2 Creating your own exception type

Creating your exception type is very easy. It can be done by simply extending the `System.Exception` class:

```
    public class BankException : System.Exception
    {
    }
```

This works because the `System.Exception` class has a default constructor which takes no parameters. The default constructor in `BankException` (which is added automatically by the compiler), can just use this to make an `Exception` instance.

However, there is a version of the `Exception` constructor which lets us add a message to the exception. This can be picked up and used to discover what has gone wrong. To create a standard exception with a message I pass the constructor a string. If I want to use this with my bank exception I have to sort out the constructor chaining for my exception class and write code as follows:

```
    public class BankException : System.Exception
    {
```

```
    public BankException (string message) :
        base (message)
    {
    }
}
```

This makes use of the `base` keyword to call the constructor of the parent class and pass it the `string` message.

5.5.3 Throwing an Exception

The throw keyword throws an exception at that point in the code. The thing that is thrown must be based on the `System.Exception` class. For example, I might want to throw an exception if the name of my account holder is an empty string. I can do this with the code:

```
if ( inName.Length == 0 )
{
    throw new BankException( "Invalid Name" );
}
```

The throw keyword is followed by a reference to the exception to be thrown. In the code above I make a new instance of the bank exception and then throw that. At this point the execution would transfer to the "nearest" catch construction. This might be a catch of mine, or it might be one supplied by the system. If the exception is caught by the system it means that my program will be terminated. However, I can catch the exception myself as follows:

```
Account a;
try
{
    a = new Account(newName, newAddress);
}
catch (BankException exception)
{
    Console.WriteLine( "Error : " + exception.Message);
}
```

The code tries to create a new account. If doing this causes an exception to be thrown, the code in the exception handler is obeyed. The reference `exception` is set to refer to the exception which has been thrown. The `Message` member of an exception is the text which was given. This means that if I try to create an account with an empty name the exception will be thrown, the catch invoked, and the message printed.

Programmer's Point: Design your error exceptions yourself

An exception is an object which describes how things have gone wrong. It can contain a text message which you can display to explain the problem to the user. However, you should seriously consider extending the exception class to make error exceptions of your own which are even more informative. Errors should be numbered, i.e. your exceptions should be tagged with an error number. This helps a great deal in working with different languages. If the customer can say "Error number 25" when they are reporting a problem it makes it much easier for the support person to respond sensibly. Note that, as with just about everything else, you need to design in your handling of errors.

5.5.4 Multiple Exception Types

It is worth spending time thinking about how the exceptions and errors in your system are to be managed. We can have many catch constructions if we like, and the catch will be matched up to the type of exception that was thrown:

```
public class BankExceptionBadName : System.Exception
{
   public BankExceptionBadName (string message) :
      base (message)
   {
   }
}

public class BankExceptionBadAddress : System.Exception
{
   public BankExceptionBadAddress (string message) :
      base (message)
   {
   }
}
```

Now I can use different catches, depending on how the code fails:

```
Account a;
try
{
   a = new Account("Rob", "");
}
catch (BankExceptionBadName nameException)
{
   Console.WriteLine("Invalid name : " +
      nameException.Message);
}
catch (BankExceptionBadAddress addrException)
{
   Console.WriteLine("Invalid address : " +
      addrException.Message);
}
catch (System.Exception exception )
{
   Console.WriteLine("System exception : " +
      exception.Message);
}
```

Each of the catches matches a different type of exception. At the very end of the list of handlers I have one which catches the system exception. This will be called if the exception is not a name or an address one.

Programmer's Point: Programs often fail in the error handlers

If you think about it, error handlers are rather hard to test. They only get run when something bad happens, and most of the time you will be using test data which assumes everything is OK. This means that errors are more likely to get left in the error handlers themselves, since the code doesn't get exercised as much as the rest of the system. Of course this is a recipe for really big disasters, in that the error handler is supposed to put things right and if it fails it will usually make a bad situation much worse.

As a professional programmer you must make sure that your error handling code is tested at least as hard as the rest of the system. This might mean that you have to create special test versions of the system to force errors into the code. Believe me, it is worth the effort!

Error handling should be something you design in. When you create the system you decide how many and what kind of errors you are going to have to manage.

5.6 Program Organisation

At the moment we have put the entire program source that we have created into a single file, which we compile and run. This is fine for teeny tiny projects, but now we are starting to write much larger programs and we need a better way to organise things. This is especially important when you consider that a given project may have many people working on it.

To do this we have to solve two problems:

- how we *physically* spread the code that we write around a number of files
- how we *logically* identify the items in our program.

The two problems are distinct and separate and C# provides mechanisms for both. In this section we are going to see how a large program can be broken down into a number of different chunks.

5.6.1 Using Separate Source Files

In a large system a programmer will want to spread the program over several different source files. When you design your solution to a problem you need to decide where all the files live.

In our bank management program we have identified a need for a class to keep track of a particular account. The class will be called `Account`. Consider a really simple `Account` class:

```csharp
public class Account
{
    private decimal balance = 0;
    public void PayInFunds ( decimal amount )
    {
        balance = balance + amount;
    }
    public decimal GetBalance ()
    {
        return balance;
    }
    public bool WithDrawFunds ( decimal amount )
    {
        if ( amount < 0 )
        {
            return false ;
        }
        if ( balance >= amount )
        {
            balance = balance - amount ;
            return true;
        }
        else
        {
            return false ;
        }
    }
}
```

This is a fairly well behaved class in that it won't let us withdraw more money than we have in the account. We could put it into a file called "Account.cs" if we wanted to. However, we might want to create lots of other classes which will deal with bank accounts. So instead I have decided to put the class into a file called "AccountManagement.cs". As I add more account management elements I can put them in this file. The problem is that the compiler now gets upset when I try to compile the file:

```
error CS5001: AccountManagement.exe' does not have an entrypoint defined
```

The compiler is expecting to produce an executable program. These have an entry point in the form of the `Main` method. Our bank account class does not have a main method because the program will never start by actually running an account. Instead other programs will run and create accounts when they need them. So, the compiler cannot make an executable file, since it does not know where the program should start.

Note that I have made the `Account` class `public`. This is so that classes in other files can make use of it. You can apply the protection levels to classes in the same way that you can protect class members. Generally speaking your classes will be `public` if you want them to be used in libraries.

Creating a Library

I solve this problem by asking the compiler to produce a *library* instead. I use the target option to the compile command. Options are a way of modifying what a command does. The compiler can tell that it is being given an option because options always start with a slash character:

```
csc /target:library AccountManagement.cs
```

The compiler will not now look for a `Main` method, because it has been told to produce a library rather than a program. If I look at what has been created I find that the compiler has not made me an executable, instead it has made me a library file:

```
AccountManagement.dll
```

The language extension dll stands for *dynamic link library*. This means that the content of this file will be loaded *dynamically* as the program runs.

Using a Library

Now I have a library I next have to work out how to use it. Firstly I'm going to create another source file called `AccountTest.cs`. This contains a `Main` method which will use the `Account` class:

```csharp
using System;

class AccountTest
{
  public static void Main ()
  {
    Account test = new Account();
    test.PayInFunds (50);
    Console.WriteLine ("Balance:" + test.GetBalance());
  }
}
```

This makes a new account, puts 50 pounds in it and then prints out the balance. If I try to compile it I get a whole bunch of errors:

```
AccountTest.cs(5,3): error CS0246: The type or namespace name 'Account' could not be
found (are you missing a using directive or an assembly reference?)
AccountTest.cs(6,3): error CS0246: The type or namespace name 'test' could not be found
(are you missing a using directive or an assembly reference?)
```

```
AccountTest.cs(7,37): error CS0246: The type or namespace name 'test' could not be found
(are you missing a using directive or an assembly reference?)
```

The problem is that the compiler does not know to go and look in the file `AccountManagement.cs` to find the `Account` class. This means that it fails to create `test`, which causes further errors.

To solve the problem I need to tell the compiler to refer to `AccountManagement` to find the `Account` class:

```
csc /reference:AccountManagement.dll AccountTest.cs
```

The reference option is followed by a list of library files which are to be used. In this case there is just the one file to look at, which is the library that contains the required class. The compiler now knows where to find all the parts of the application, and so it can build the executable program.

Library References at Runtime

We have now made two files which contain program code:

`AccountManagement.dll`   the library containing the `Account` class code

`AccountTest.exe`   the executable program that creates an `Account` instance

Both these files need to be present for the program to work correctly. This is because of the "dynamic" in *dynamic link library*. It means that library is only loaded when the program runs, not when it is built.

Deleting System Components

This means that if I do something horrid like delete the `Acccountmanagement.dll` file and then run the program this causes all kinds of nasty things to happen:

```
Unhandled Exception: System.IO.FileNotFoundException: File or assembly name
AccountManagement, or one of its dependencies, was not found.
File name: "AccountManagement" at AccountTest.Main()
… lots of other stuff
```

This means that we need to be careful when we send out a program and make sure that all the components files are present when the program runs.

Updating System Components

Creating a system out of a number of executable components has the advantage that we can update part of it without affecting everything else. If I modify the `AccountManagement` class and re-compile it, the new version is picked up by `AccountTest` automatically. Of course this only works as long as I don't change the appearance of the classes or methods which `AccountTest` uses.

The good news is that I can fix the broken parts of the program without sending out an entire new version.

The bad news is that this hardly ever works. There is a special phrase, "dll hell", reserved for what happens. Unless the fixed code is **exactly** right there is a good chance that it might break some other part of the program. Windows itself works in this way, and the number of times that I've installed a new program (or worse yet an upgrade of an existing one) which has broken another program on the computer is too numerous to happily remember.

> **Programmer's Point: Use Version Control and Change Management**
>
> So many things end up being rooted in a need for good planning and management. And here we are again. When you think about selling your application for money you must make sure that you have a managed approach to how you are going to send out upgrades and fixes. The good news is that there are ways of making sure that certain versions of your program only work with particular program files. The bad news is that you have to plan how to use this technology, and then make sure you use it. If this sounds boring and pedantic then I'm very sorry, but if you don't do this you will either go mad or bankrupt. Or both.

5.6.2 Namespaces

We can use library files to break up our solution into a number of files. This makes management of the solution slightly easier. But we also have another problem. We don't just want to break things into physical chunks. We also want to use *logical* ones as well.

If you are not sure what I mean by this, consider the situation in our bank. We have decided that `Account` is a sensible name for the class which holds all the details of a customer account.

But if you consider the whole of the bank operations you find that the word "account" crops up all over the place. The bank will buy things like paper clips, rubber stamps, little pens on chains (pre-supplied with no ink in of course) and the like from suppliers.

You could say that the bank has an account with such a supplier. It may well wish to keep track of these accounts using a computer system. Perhaps the programmers might decide that a sensible name for such a thing would be `Account`. Arrgh! We are now heading for real problems. If the two systems ever meet up we can expect a digital fight to the death about what "Account" really means. Which would be bad.

We could solve the problem by renaming our account class `CustomerBankAccount`. But this would be messy, and mean that at design time we have to make sure that we name all our classes in a way which will always be unique.

A far better way would be to say that we have a `CustomerBanking` namespace in which the word `Account` has a particular meaning. We can also have an `EquipmentSupplier` namespace as well. This prevents the two names from clashing, in that they are not defined in the same namespace.

Putting a Class in a Namespace

Up until now every name we have used has been created in what is called the *global* namespace. This is because we have not explicitly set up a namespace in our source files. However, they are very easy to set up:

```csharp
namespace CustomerBanking
{
  public class Account
  {
    private decimal balance = 0;
    public void PayInFunds ( decimal amount )
    {
      balance = balance + amount;
    }
    public decimal GetBalance ()
    {
        return balance;
    }
    public bool WithDrawFunds ( decimal amount )
    {
```

```csharp
      if ( amount < 0 )
      {
        return false ;
      }
      if ( balance >= amount )
      {
        balance = balance - amount ;
        return true;
      }
      else
      {
        return false ;
      }
    }
  }
}
```

I have used the namespace keyword to identify the namespace. This is followed by a block of classes. Every class declared in this block is regarded as part of the given namespace, in this case `CustomerBanking`.

A given source file can contain as many namespace definitions and each can contain as many classes as you like.

Using a Class from a Namespace

A Global class (i.e. one created outside any namespace) can just be referred to by its name. If you want to use a class from a namespace you have to give the namespace as well.

```csharp
CustomerBanking.Account test;
```

This creates a variable which can refer to instances of the `Account` class. The `Account` class we use is the one in the `CustomerBanking` namespace.

A name like this, with the namespace in front, is known as a *fully qualified* name. If we want to create an instance of the class we use the fully qualified name again:

```csharp
test = new CustomerBanking.Account();
```

If I want to use the `Account` class from the `CustomerBanking` namespace I have to modify my test class accordingly.

Using a namespace

If you are using a lot of things from a particular namespace C# provides a way in which you can tell the compiler to look in that namespace whenever it has to resolve the name of a particular item. We do this with the using keyword:

```csharp
using CustomerBanking ;
```

When the compiler sees a line like:

```csharp
Account RobsAccount;
```

- it automatically looks in the `CustomerBanking` namespace to see if there is a class called `Account`. If there is it uses that. We have already used this technique a lot. The `System` namespace is where a lot of the library components are located. We can use these by means of fully qualified names:

```csharp
System.Console.WriteLine ( "Hello World" );
```

However, it is common for most programs to have the line:

```csharp
using System;
```

- at the very top. This means that the programmer can just write:

```csharp
Console.WriteLine ( "Hello World" );
```

The compiler goes "ah, I'll go and have a look for a thing called `Console` in all the namespaces that I've been told to use". If it finds one, and only one, `Console` then all is well and it uses that. If it finds two `Console` items (if I was an idiot I could put a `Console` class in my `CustomerBanking` namespace I suppose) it will complain that it doesn't know which to use.

Nesting Namespaces

You can put one namespace inside another. This allows you to break things down into smaller chunks. The System namespace is like this, there is a namespace which is part of the System namespace which is specifically concerned with Input/Output. You get to use the items in the `System.IO` namespace with an appropriate include:

```csharp
using System.IO ;
```

In terms of declaring the namespace you do it like this:

```csharp
namespace CustomerBanking {
  namespace Accounts {
    // account classes go here
  }
  namespace Statements {
    // statement classes go here
  }
  namespace RudeLetters {
    // rude letter classes go here
  }
}
```

Now I can use the classes as required:

```csharp
using CustomerBanking.RudeLetters ;
```

Of course the namespaces that you use should always be carefully designed. But then again, you'd probably figured that one out already.

5.6.3 Namespaces in Separate Files

There is no rule that says you have to put all the classes from a particular namespace in a particular file. It is perfectly OK to spread the classes around a number of different source files. You have to make sure that the files you want to use contain all the bits that are needed, and this means of course more planning and organising.

Programmer's Point: Fully Qualified Names are Good

There are two ways you can get hold of something. You can spell out the complete location by using a Fully Qualified Name (`CustomerBanking.RudeLetters.OverdraftWarning`) or you can get hold of items in a namespace with `using`. Of the two I much prefer the fully qualified name. I know that this makes the programs slightly harder to write, but it means that when I'm reading the code I can see exactly where a given resource has come from. If I just see the name `OverdraftWarning` in the code I have no idea where that came from and so I have to search through all the namespaces that I'm using to find it.

5.7 A Graphical User Interface

The programs that we have written up until now use a command line to interact with the user. That is the computer asks questions, the user types in their responses and the computer then processes the response to produce the required answer. Now we are going to move into Graphical User Interfaces.

A user interface is a posh name for the thing that people actually see when they use your program. It comprises the buttons, text fields, labels and pictures that the user actually works with to get their job done. Part of the job of the programmer is to create this "front end" and then put the appropriate behaviours behind the screen display to allow the user to drive the program and get what they want from it. In this section we are going to find out how to create a program that uses a graphical user interface.

We are going to create a Windows Presentation Foundation (WPF) application which uses a markup language called XAML to define the pages that the user sees. This is available on the Windows operating system, including Windows Vista, Windows 7 and the Windows 8 desktop environment. If you want to create Windows RT applications the fundamentals are similar, but you will need to make some modifications to the XAML files that you create.

There is a point in the Wizard of Oz where Dorothy looks at her dog, the yellow brick road, the munchkins and all and says "We're not in Kansas anymore". We are kind of at this point with C# here. This section is not really about the programming language C#, it is much more about how to create user interfaces using XAML as a markup language and C# to provide the behaviours. You can create programs that use a XAML based user interface using other languages, for example Visual Basic .NET.

We are going to discover that it is hard to talk about XAML without mentioning Visual Studio, the integrated development environment that lets programmers create applications which contain a XAML designed user interface connected to C# code behind.

Visual Studio can synchronise the XAML description of a user interface with the program code that is connected to it. It also contains graphical editor that can be used to design the interface itself.

It is perhaps best to regard C#, XAML and Visual Studio as a whole, as they were designed to work together to make it easy for programmers to create these kinds of applications.

Programmer's Point: Learn how to use Visual Studio

It is possible to create XAML files and complete applications by just writing the text files that contain the C# and XAML elements. However, this will take a very long time. At this point you should invest some time in learning how to use Visual Studio, which provides a very rich environment for the creation of programs like this. It will let you drag display elements around a design surface (if you must position things by hand) and automatically create event handlers for things like buttons.

5.7.1 The XAML Markup Language

We are going to use the eXtensible Application Markup Language (or XAML) which has been designed by Microsoft to make it easy to create a good looking application. To understand this we are going to have to learn a few things about how markup languages work. The good news is that this knowledge is extremely useful, lots of modern user interface systems work in a similar way.

XAML is a *declarative* language. This means that all it can do is give information to a computer about stuff. In the case of XAML the stuff is the design of the screen, or page, that the user sees.

Extensible Markup Languages

At this point you may be wondering what an eXtensible Application Markup Language actually is. Well, it is a markup language for applications that is extensible. I'm sure that helped. What we mean by this is that you can use the rules of the language to create constructions that describe anything. English is a lot like this. We have letters and punctuation which are the symbols of English text. We also have rules (called grammar) that set out how to make up words and sentences and we have different kinds of words. We have nouns that describe things and verbs that describe actions. When something new comes along we invent a whole new set of word to describe them. Someone had to come up with the word "computer" when the computer was invented, along with phrases like "boot up", "system crash" and "too slow".

XML based languages are extensible in that we can invent new words and phrases that fit within the rules of the language and use these new constructions to describe anything we like. They are called *markup* languages because they are often used to describe the arrangement of items on a page. The word markup was originally used in printing when you wanted to say things like "Print the name Rob Miles in very large font". The most famous markup language is probably HTML, HyperText Markup Language, which is used by the World Wide Web to describe the format of web pages.

Programmers frequently invent their own data storage formats using XML. As an example, a snippet of XML that describes a set of high scores might look as follows:

```
<?xml version="1.0" encoding="us-ascii" ?>
<HighScoreRecords count="2">
    <HighScore game="Breakout">
        <playername>Rob Miles</playername>
        <score>1500</score>
    </HighScore>
    <HighScore game="Space Invaders">
        <playername>Rob Miles</playername>
        <score>4500</score>
    </HighScore>
</HighScoreRecords>
```

This is a tiny XML file that describes some high score records for a video game system. The `HighScoreRecords` element contains two `HighScore` items, one for `Breakout` and one for `Space Invaders`. The two high score items are contained within the `HighScoreRecords` item. Each of the items has a property which gives the name of the game and also contains two further elements, the name of the player and the score that was achieved. This is quite easy to us to understand. From the text above it is not hard to work out the high score for the Space Invaders game.

The line at the very top of the file tells whatever wants to read the file the version of the XML standard it is based on and the encoding of the characters in the file itself. XAML takes the rules of an extensible markup language and uses them to create a language that describes components on a page of a display.

```
<TextBox Height="72" HorizontalAlignment="Left" Text="0" VerticalAlignment="Top"
Width="460" TextAlignment="Center" />
```

If we now take a look at the above description of a `TextBox` I think we can see that the designers of XAML have just created field names that match their requirements. We will see more XAML later in this section.

XML Schema

The XML standard also contains descriptions how to create a *schema* which describes a particular document format. For example, in the above the schema for the high score information would say that a `HighScore` must contain a `PlayerName` and a `Score` property. It might also say things like the

`HighScore` can contain a `Date` value (the date when the high score was achieved) but that this is not required for every `HighScore` value.

This system of standard format and schema means that it is very easy for developers to create data formats for particular purposes. This is helped by the fact that there are a lot of design tools to help create documents and schemas. The .NET framework even provides a way by which a program can save an object as a formatted XML document. In fact the Visual Studio solution file is actually stored as an XML document.

As far as we are concerned, it is worth remembering that XML is useful for this kind of thing, but at the moment I want to keep the focus on XAML itself.

XAML and display page design

A file of XAML can describe a complete page. When you create a brand new WPF application you get a page that just contains a few elements. As you put more onto the page the file grows as each description is added. Some elements work as *containers*. This means that they can hold other components. They are very useful when you want to lay things out, for example there is a Grid element which can hold a set of other elements in a grid arrangement. The XAML file can also contain the descriptions of animations and transitions that can be applied to items on the page to make even more impressive user interfaces. We are not going to spend too much time on the layout aspects of XAML; suffice it to say that you can create incredibly impressive front ends for your programs using this tool. There is also a special design tool called "Expression Blend" that can be used to make amazing displays.

Unfortunately it turns out that most programmers (including me) are not that good at designing attractive user interfaces (although I'm sure that you are). In real life a company will employ graphic designers who will create artistic looking front ends. The role of the programmer will then be to put the code behind these displays to get the required job done.

Microsoft designed XAML as a recognition of this issue. It enforces a very strong separation between the screen display design and the code that is controlled by it. This makes it easy for a programmer to create an initial user interface which is subsequently changed by a designer into a much more attractive one. It is also possible for a programmer to take a complete user interface design and then fit the behaviours behind each of the display components.

Describing XAML Elements

We can start to discover how XAML lets us design an application by taking a look at how you could construct a program using it. Consider the following screen.

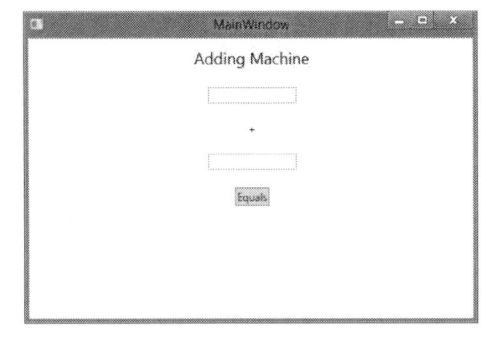

This is a very simple Windows program that I've called an "Adding Machine". You can use to perform very simple sums. You just enter two numbers into the two text boxes at the top and then press the equals button. It then rewards you with the sum of these two numbers. At the moment it is showing us that 0 plus 0 is 0. Each individual item on the screen is called a *UIElement* or User Interface element. I'm going to call these things elements from now on. There are six of them on the screen above:

1. The title "Adding Machine". This is a block of text with a font size of 18 so that it stands out.
2. The top textbox, where I can type a number.
3. A text item holding the character +.
4. The bottom textbox, where I can type another number.
5. A button, which we press to perform the sum.
6. A result textbox, which changes to show the result when the button is pressed. At the moment this is empty, as we haven't done any sums yet.

Each of these items has a particular position on the screen, particular size of text and lots of other properties too. We can change the colour of the text in a text box, whether it is aligned to the left, right or centre of the enclosing box and lots of other things too, by updating the XAML that describes the page. The actual XAML that describes the display is as follows:

```
<StackPanel>
    <TextBlock Text="Adding Machine" TextAlignment="Center"
      Margin="0,10" FontSize="18"></TextBlock>
    <TextBox Name="firstNumberTextBox" Width="100"
      Margin="0,10" TextAlignment="Center"></TextBox>
    <TextBlock Text="+" TextAlignment="Center" Margin="0,10"></TextBlock>
    <TextBox Name="secondNumberTextBox" Width="100"
      Margin="0,10" TextAlignment="Center"></TextBox>
    <Button Content="Equals" Name="equalsButton" HorizontalAlignment="Center"
      Margin="0,10" Click="equalsButton_Click"></Button>
    <TextBlock Name="resultTextBlock" Text="" TextAlignment="Center"
  Margin="0,10"></TextBlock>
</StackPanel>
```

If you look carefully you can map each of the elements in the list above into items in the XAML file. The only thing that is a bit confusing is the `StackPanel` element. This is very simple, and terribly useful. Rather than us having to define the position on the screen of each of the elements, a `StackPanel` just lets us "pile up" a series of display elements. The default arrangement is to stack the items down the screen, but you can also stack items across the screen. You can, and this is really useful, put a `StackPanel` inside a `StackPanel`, so you can make up a stack of rows. This nesting of elements is a recurring theme inside XAML files.

Programmer's Point: Use automatic layout as much as you can

I always worry when I start absolutely positioning things on the screen. As soon as you do this you are making assumptions about the size of the screen that you are using, and the dimensions of the text. Modern computers are supplied in a huge range of different screen sizes and users can also change the size of the text on the screen to zoom into the display. They may also change the orientation of their screen from landscape to portrait while using your program. If you fix the position of things on the screen this means that it may work well for one particular device, but will look very wrong on another. For this reason you should use the automatic layout features like StackPanel to dynamically position things for you. This makes your program much less likely to have display problems.

XAML Elements and Objects

From a programming point of view each of the XAML elements on the screen of a display is actually a software object. Objects are a great way to represent things we want to work with. It turns out that objects are also great for representing other things too, such as items on a display. If you think about it, a box displaying text on a screen will have properties such as the position on the screen, the colour of the text, the text itself and so on.

You are (or should be) familiar with the process of compilation, where the source code (i.e. what we type in) for a C# program is converted into a lower level set of instructions that will be executed by the computer. When a program that uses the XAML user interface is compiled the system also "compiles" the XAML description to create a set of C# objects, each of which represents a user interface element. There are three different types of element in the adding machine:

1. `TextBox` – allows the user to enter text into the program.
2. `TextBlock` – a block of text that just conveys information.
3. `Button` – something we can press to cause events in our program.

If you think about it, you can break the properties of each of these elements down into two kinds, those that all the elements need to have, for example position on the screen, and those that are specific to that type of element. For example only a `TextBox` needs to record the position of the cursor where text is being entered. From a software design point of view this is a really good use for a class hierarchy.

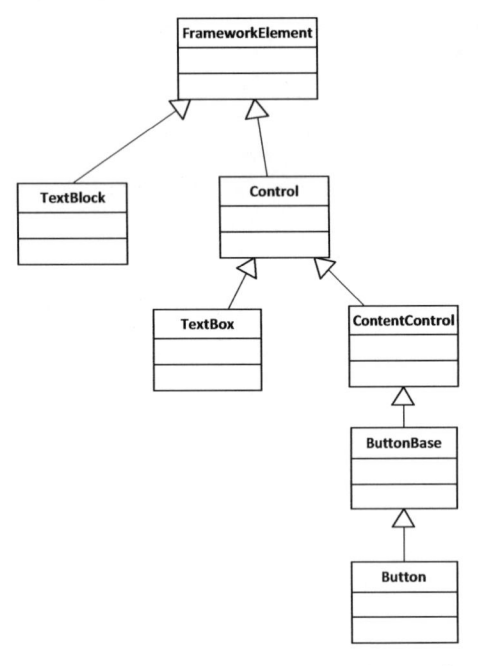

Above you can see part of the hierarchy that the XAML designers built. The top class is called `FrameworkElement`. It contains all the information that is common to all controls on the screen. Each of the other classes is a child of this class. Children pick up all the behaviours and properties of their parent class and then add some of their own. Actually the design is a bit more complex than shown above, the `FrameworkElement` class is a child of a class called `UIElement`, but it shows the principles behind the controls.

Creating a class hierarchy like this has a lot of advantages. If we want a custom kind of textbox we can extend the `TextBox` class and add the properties and behaviours that we need. As far as the software implementing the XAML system is concerned it can treat all the controls the same and then ask each control to draw itself in a manner appropriate to that component.

Our program will manipulate the elements as if they were C# objects, although they were actually defined in a XAML source file. This works because when the program is built the XAML system will create objects that match elements described in the XAML source file.

Managing Element Names

When we want to use the user interface elements in our program we need a way of referring to each of them. If we take a look at the XAML that implements our adding machine we can see that some of the components have been given a name property:

```
<TextBox Name="firstNumberTextBox" Width="100" Margin="0,10"
         TextAlignment="Center"></TextBox>
```

I have set the name of this textbox to `firstNumberTextBox`. You'll never guess what the second text box is called. Note that the name of a property in this context is actually going to set the name of the variable declared inside the adding machine program. In other words, as a result of what I've done above there will now be the following statement in my program somewhere:

```
TextBox firstNumberTextBox;
```

These declarations are created automatically when the program is built and so we don't need to actually worry about where the above statement is. We just have to remember that this is how the program works. Note that not all the elements in my user interface have got names, there is no point in giving a name to the `TextBlock` that holds the "+" character as I will never need to interact with this when the program runs.

Properties in Elements

Once we have given our `TextBox` variable a proper name we can move on to give it all the properties that are required for this application. We can also change lots of properties for the textbox including the width of the textbox, the margin (which sets the position) and so on.

When we talk about the "properties" of Silverlight elements on the page (for example the text displayed in a `TextBox`) we are actually talking about property values in the class that implements the `TextBox`. In other words, when a program contains a statement such as:

```
resultTextBlock.Text = "0";
```

- This will cause a `Set` method to run inside the `resultTextBlock` object which sets the text on the `TextBlock` to the appropriate value.

You may be asking the question "Why do we use properties in XAML elements?" It makes sense to use them in a bank account where I want to be able to protect the data inside my objects but in a XAML page, where I can put any text I like inside a `TextBlock`, there seems to be no point in having validation of the incoming value. In fact running this code will slow down the setting process. So, by making the `Text` value a public string we could make the program smaller and faster, which has to be a good thing. Right?

Well, sort of. Except that when we change the text on a `TextBlock` we would like the text on the XAML page in front of the user to change as well. This is how our adding machine will display the result. If a program just changed the value of a data member there would be no way the XAML system could know that the message on the screen needs to be updated.

However, if the `Text` member is a property when a program updates it the set behaviour in the `TextBlock` will get to run. The code in the set behaviour can update the stored value of the text field and it can also trigger an update of the display to make the new value visible. Properties provide a means by which an object can get control when a value inside the object is being changed, and this is extremely important. The simple statement:

```
resultTextBlock.Text = "0";
```

- may cause many hundreds of C# statements to run as the new value is stored in the TextBlock and an update of the display is triggered to make the screen change.

Page Design with XAML

XAML turns out to be very useful. Once you get the hang of the information used to describe components it turns out to be much quicker to add things to a page and move them about by just editing the text in the XAML file, rather than dragging things around or moving between property values. I find it particularly useful when I want a large number of similar elements on the screen. Visual Studio is aware of the syntax used to describe each type of element and will provide Intellisense support help as you go along.

If you read up on the XAML specification you will find that you can give elements graphical properties that can make them transparent, add images to their backgrounds and even animate them around the screen. At this point we have moved well beyond programming and entered the realm of graphic design. And I wish you the best of luck.

5.7.2 Creating a complete XAML Application

Now that we know that items on the screen are in fact the graphical realisation of software objects, the next thing we need to know is how to get control of these objects and make them do useful things for us in our application. To do this we will need to add some C# program code that will perform the calculation that the adding machine needs.

Whenever Visual Studio makes a XAML file that describes a page on the display it also makes a C# program file to go with it. This is where we can put code that will make our application work. If you actually take a look in the file `MainPage.xaml.cs` above you will find that it doesn't actually contain much code:

```csharp
using System;
using System.Collections.Generic;
using System.Linq;
using System.Text;
using System.Windows;
using System.Windows.Controls;
using System.Windows.Data;
using System.Windows.Documents;
using System.Windows.Input;
using System.Windows.Media;
using System.Windows.Media.Imaging;
using System.Windows.Navigation;
using System.Windows.Shapes;

namespace sample
{
    /// <summary>
    /// Interaction logic for MainWindow.xaml
    /// </summary>
    public partial class MainWindow : Window
    {
        public MainWindow()
        {
            InitializeComponent();
        }
    }
}
```

Most of the file is `using` statements which allow our program to make direct use of classes without having to give the fully formed name of each of them. For example, rather than saying `System.Windows.Controls.Button` we can say `Button`, because the file contains the line `using System.Windows.Controls`.

The only methods in the program are the constructor of the `MainWindow` class. As we know, the constructor of a class is called when an instance of the class is created. All the constructor does is call the method `InitializeComponent`. If you go take a look inside this method you will find the code that actually creates the instances of the display elements. This code is automatically created for you by Visual Studio, based on the XAML that describes your page. It is important that you leave this call as it is and don't change the content of the method itself as this will most likely break your program.

Note that at this point we are deep in the "engine room" of XAML. I'm only really telling you about this so that you can understand that actually there is no magic here. If the only C# programs you have seen so far start with a call of the `Main` method then it is important that you understand that there is nothing particularly special about a XAML one. There is a `Main` method at the base of a XAML application; it starts the process of building the components and putting them on the screen for the user to interact with.

The nice thing as far as we are concerned is that we don't need to worry about how these objects are created and displayed, we can just use the high level tools or the easy to understand XAML to design and build our display.

Building the Application

We can now see how to create the user interface for our number adding program. If we add all the components and then start the application it even looks as though it might do something for us. We can type in the numbers that we want to add, and even press the equals button if we like. We seem to have got a lot of behaviour for very little effort, which is nice. However, we need to add some business logic of our own now to get the program to work out the answer and display it.

Calculating the Result

At the moment our program looks good, but doesn't actually do anything. We need to create some code which will perform the required calculation and display the result. Something like this.

```
private void calculateResult()
{
    float v1 = float.Parse(firstNumberTextBox.Text);
    float v2 = float.Parse(secondNumberTextBox.Text);

    float result = v1 + v2;

    resultTextBlock.Text = result.ToString();
}
```

The `TextBox` objects expose a property called `Text`. This can be read from or written to. Setting a value into the `Text` property will change the text in the textbox. Reading the `Text` property allows our program to read what has been typed into the textbox.

The text is given as a string, which must be converted into a numeric value if our program is to do any sums. You have seen the `Parse` method before. This takes a string and returns the number that the string describes. Each of the numeric types (`int`, `float`, `double` etc.) has a `Parse` behaviour which will take a string and return the numeric value that it describes. The adding machine that we are creating can work with floating point numbers, so the method parses the text in each of the input textboxes and then calculates a result by adding them together.

Finally the method takes the number that was calculated, converts it into a string and then sets the text of the `resultTextBlock` to this string. `ToString` is the reverse of `Parse`, the "anti-parse" if you like. It provides the text that describes the contents of an object. In the case of the float type, this is the text that describes that value.

Now we have our code that works out the answer, we just have to find a way of getting it to run when the user presses the equals button.

Events and Programs

If you have done any kind of form based programming you will know all about events. If you haven't then don't worry, we now have a nice example of a situation where we need them, and they are not that frightening anyway. In the olden days, before graphical user interfaces and mice, a program would generally start at the beginning, run for a while and then finish.

But now we have complicated and rich user interfaces with lots of buttons and other elements for the user to interact with. The word processor I am using at the moment exposes hundreds of different features via buttons on the screen and menu items. In this situation it would be very hard to write a program which checked every user element in turn to see if the user has attempted to use that. Instead the system waits for these display elements to raise an event when they want attention. Teachers do this all the time. They don't go round the class asking each child in turn if they know the answer. Instead they ask the children to raise their hands. The "hand raising" is treated as an event which the teacher will respond to.

Using events like this makes software design a lot easier. Our program does not have to check every item on the screen to see if the user has done anything with it, instead it just binds to the events that it is interested in.

To make events work a programming language needs a way of expressing a reference to a method in an object. C# provides the *delegate* type which does exactly that. You can create a delegate type that can refer to a particular kind of method and then create instances of that delegate which refer to a method in an object. Delegates are very powerful, but can be a bit tricky to get your head around. Fortunately we don't have to worry about how delegates work just at the moment; because we can get Silverlight and Visual Studio to do all the hard work for us.

Events in XAML

In C# an event is delivered to an object by means of a call to a method in that object. In this respect you can regard an event and a message as the same thing. From the point of view of our adding machine we would like to have a particular method called when the "equals" button is pressed by the user. This is the only event that we are interested in. When the event fires we want it to call the `calculateResult` method above. If we take a look back at the XAML for the button we can see how this is achieved.

```
<Button Content="Equals" HorizontalAlignment="Center" Margin="0,10"
        Name="equalsButton" Click="equalsButton_Click"></Button>
```

The button element has a name, `equalsButton`, and a property called `Click`. This is set to the value `equalsButton_Click`. This is the link between the XAML (which is the *declarative* language that describes the page on the screen) and C# (which is the programming language that will actually do something for us).

For this to work the page which contains the `equalsButton` display element **must** contain a method called `equalsButton_Click`. Otherwise the program will not build correctly. This is the method that provides the behaviour for the equals button:

```
private void equalsButton_Click(object sender, RoutedEventArgs e)
{
```

```
        calculateResult();
    }
```

The event handler must have the correct *signature* so that it can be given parameters that describe the event.

If you are wondering how all this works, it actually uses *delegates* to manage the events that are passed from the Windows display manager into the program running on it. As you saw earlier, a delegate is an object that represents a method in an instance of a class. If you think about it; that is exactly what we need here. We need a way of telling the window management system in Windows that when the equals button is clicked we would like this method to be called. A delegate object is perfect for this task. The `Button` display element contains a property called `Click`. A program can add delegate objects to this property so that when the window manager detects that the button has been pressed it can call that method. In other words, somewhere in the code generated for the XAML above is the statement:

```
equalsButton.Click +=new RoutedEventHandler(equalsButton_Click);
```

The `+=` operator is a bit confusing here, but what it really means is "add a delegate object to the list of those that will be called when the button is clicked by the user". The delegate is of type `RoutedEventHandler` and when an instance of the delegate is constructed it is given the identifier of the method it is going to refer to. If a program ever needs to disconnect a handler from an event it can use the `-=` operator to do this.

Event Driven Applications

Note that this is quite a contrast with how programs used to run in "the good old days". Previously a program would run when the `Main` method was called and then stop when the end of the method was reached. Now we are in a situation where we never actually call the method to run the program. The method is called for us in response to a user action. What actually happens is that the event handler on the button creates a thread that calls the button method in our program.

If we have an application that uses lots of buttons we need to make sure that the program is able to deal with the buttons being pressed in any order. For example, if a user presses the Print button before they have loaded a document it is important that the program doesn't crash at this point.

Dealing with Errors

The solution that we have come up with does work, and it will provide a working adding machine. However it is not a very user friendly program.

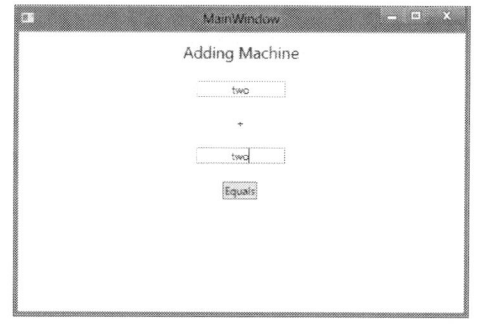

For example, the user might type in numbers as above. We already know that this will cause problems with the `Parse` method, which will promptly throw an exception and stop the program. We also know that we can catch exceptions and deal with them. In the case of the program above the best way to deal with these kinds of errors is to display a message box:

```csharp
private void calculateResult()
{
    try
    {
        float v1 = float.Parse(firstNumberTextBox.Text);
        float v2 = float.Parse(secondNumberTextBox.Text);

        float result = v1 + v2;
        resultTextBlock.Text = result.ToString();
    }
    catch
    {
        MessageBox.Show("Invalid number", "Adding machine");
    }

}
```

Code Sample 57 WPF Adding Machine

This version of `calculateResult` catches the exception that would be thrown by `Parse` and then uses the `MessageBox` class to display an error message.

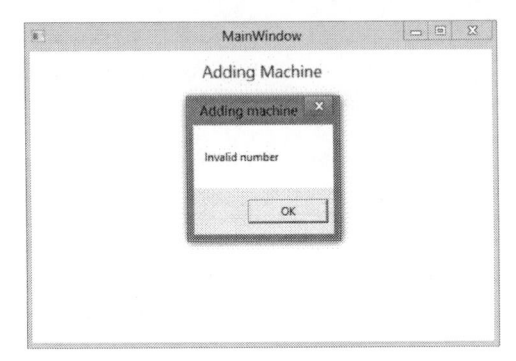

The `MessageBox` class is a static class that is part of the XAML library. There are several versions of the Show method so that you can display different versions of the message box. The one I used just accepts two strings. One is the title of the box. The other is the message to be displayed. The user can cancel the message by pressing the OK button.

Note that this method is not a very good one, in that it doesn't say which of the two numbers was in error.

Programmer's Point: Customers really care about the user interface

If there is one part of the system which the customer is guaranteed to have strong opinions about it is the user interface. The design of this should start at the very beginning of the product and be refined as it goes. Never, ever assume you know that the user interface should work in a particular way. I have had to spend more time re-working user interface code than just about any other part of the system. The good news is that with something like Visual Studio it is very easy to produce quite realistic looking prototypes of the front end of a system. These can then be shown to the customer (get them signed off even) to establish that you are doing the right thing.

5.8 Debugging

Some people are born to debug. Not everyone is good at debugging, some will always be better than others. Having said that there are techniques which you can use to ease the process, and we are going to explore some of these here. The good news is that if you use a test driven approach to your development the number of faults that are found by the users should be as small as possible, but there will still be some things that need to be fixed.

Incidentally, the reason why problems with programs are called bugs is that the original one was caused by an actual insect which got stuck in some contacts in the computer, causing it to fail. This is not however how most bugs are caused. It is very rarely that you will see your program fail because the hardware is faulty, I've been programming for many years and only seen this in a handful of occasions. The sad thing is that most of the bugs in programs have been put there by programmers. In other words, debugging is working very hard to find out how stupid you were in the first place.

5.8.1 Fault Reporting

We have already seen that a fault is something which the user sees as a result of an error in your program.

Faults are uncovered by the testing process or by users. If a program fails as part of a test, the steps taken to manifest it will be well recorded. However, if a user reports a fault the evidence may well be anecdotal, i.e. you will not be supplied with a sequence of steps which cause the fault to appear, you will simply be told "There's a bug in the print routine".

There is a strong argument for ignoring a fault report if you have not been given a sequence of steps to follow to make it happen. However, this approach will not make you popular with users. It is important to stress to users that any fault report will only be taken seriously if it is well documented.

Programmer's Point: Design Your Fault Reporting Process

Like just about everything else I've ever mentioned, the way in which you manage your fault reports should be considered at the start of the project. In other words, you should set up a process to deal with faults that are reported. In a large scale development fault reports are managed, assigned to programmers and tracked very carefully. The number of faults that are reported, and the time taken to deal with them, is valuable information about the quality of the thing that you are making. Also, if you formalize (or perhaps even automate) the fault reporting process you can ensure that you get the maximum possible information about the problem.

The two types of Fault

Faults split into two kinds, those which always happen and those which sometimes happen.

Faults which always happen are easy, you can perform the sequence which always causes the bug to manifest itself and then use suitable techniques to nail it (see later).

Faults which sometimes happen are a pain. What this means is that you do not have a definite sequence of events which causes the system to fail. This does not mean that there is no sequence (unless you are suffering from a hardware induced transient of some kind – which is rather rare) but that you have not found the sequence yet.

An example would be a print function which sometimes crashes and works at other times. You might track this down to the number of pages printed, or the amount of text on the page, or the size of the document which is being edited when the print is requested.

The manifestation of a fault may be after the error itself has actually occurred, for example a program may fail when an item is removed from a database, but the error may be in the routine which stored the item, or in code which overwrote the memory where the database lives.

A fault may change or disappear when the program itself is changed; errors which overwrite memory will corrupt different parts of the program if the layout of the code changes. This can lead to the most annoying kind of fault, where you put in extra print statements to find out more about the problem, and the problem promptly disappears!

If you suspect such an error, your first test is to change the code and data layout in some way and then re-run the program. If the fault changes in nature this indicates problems with program or data being corrupted.

5.8.2 Bugswatting

You can split faults into other categories, where the program crashes (i.e. stops completely) or when it does the wrong thing. Surprisingly, crashes are often easier to fix. They usually point to:

- a state which is not catered for (make sure that all selection statements have a default handler which does something sensible and that you use defensive programming techniques when values are passed between modules)
- programs that get stuck into loops, do – while constructions which never fail, for loops which contain code which changes the control variable, methods that call themselves by mistake and recurse their way into stack overflow
- an exception that is not caught properly

If your program does the wrong thing, this can be harder to find. Look for:

- use of un-initialised members of classes
- typographical errors (look for incorrectly spelt variable names, incorrect comparison operators, improperly terminated comments)
- logical errors (look for faults in the sequence of instructions, invalid loop termination's, wrongly constructed logical conditions)

As I said above, some folks are just plain good at finding bugs. Here are some tips:

Don't make any assumptions. If you assume that "the only way it could get here is through this sequence" or "there is no way that this piece of code could be obeyed" you will often be wrong. Rather than make assumptions, add extra code to prove that what you think is happening is really happening.

Talk to the Duck

Explain the problem to someone else - even if it is just the cat or a rubber duck! The act of explaining the problem can often lead you to deduce the answer. It is best if the person you are talking to is highly sceptical of your statements.

Look at all possible (if seemingly unrelated) factors in the manifestation of the bug. This is particularly important if the bug is intermittent. If the bug appears on Friday afternoons on your UNIX system, find out if another department uses the machine to do a payroll run at that time and fills up all the scratch space, or the loading department turn on the big hoist and inject loads of noise into the mains.

Leave the problem alone for a while. Go off and do something different and you may find that the answer will just appear. Alternatively you may find the answer as soon as you come back to the problem.

Remember that although the bug is of course impossible, it is happening. This means that either the impossible is happening, or one of your assumptions that it is impossible is wrong!

Can you get back to a state where the bug was not present, and then look at the changes made since? If the system is failing as a result of a change or, heaven forbid, a bug fix, try to move back to a point where the bug is not there, and then introduce the changes until the bug appears. Alternatively, look carefully at how the introduction of the feature affects other modules in the system. A good Source Code

Control System is very valuable here, in that it can tell you exactly what changes have been made from one version to the next.

One thing that I should make clear at this point is that the process of debugging is that of fixing faults in a solution which should work. In other words you must know how the program is supposed to work before you try and fix problems with what it actually does. I have been nearly moved to tears by the sight of people putting in another loop or changing the way their conditions operate to "see if this will make the program work". Such efforts are always doomed, just like throwing a bunch of electrical components at the wall and expecting a DVD player to land on the floor is also not going to work.

Rip it up and start again

In some projects it is possible that the effort involved in starting again is less than trying to find out what is wrong with a broken solution that you have created. If you have taken some time off from debugging, explained the code to a friend and checked all your assumptions then maybe, just maybe this might be the best way forward.

Programmer's Point: Bug Fixes Cause Bugs

The primary cause of bugs is probably the bug fixing process. This is because when people change the program to make one bit of it work the change that they make often breaks other features of the system. I have found statistics which indicate that "two for one" is frequently to be expected, in that every bug fix will introduce two brand new bugs. The only way round this is to make sure that your test process (which you created as a series of lots of unit tests) can be run automatically after you've applied the fix. This at least makes sure that the fix has not broken anything important.

5.8.3 Making Perfect Software

There is no such thing as perfect software. One of the rules by which I work is that "any useful program will have bugs in it". In other words I can write programs that I can guarantee will contain no bugs. However, such programs will be very small and therefore not be good for much. As soon as I create a useful program, with inputs, outputs and some behaviours, I start introducing bugs.

This does not mean that every program that I write is useless, just that it will not be perfect. When considering faults you must also consider their impact. Part of the job of a project manager in a development is deciding when a product is good enough to sell, and whether or not a fault in the code is a "stopper" or not.

A *stopper* is a fault which makes the program un-saleable. If the program crashes every third time you run it, or sometimes destroys the filestore of the host computer, this is probably the behaviour of a stopper bug. But if it does something like always output the first page twice if you do a print using the Chinese font and a certain kind of laser printer this might be regarded as a problem most users could live with.

This means that you need to evaluate the impact of the faults that get reported to you, prioritise them and manage how they are dealt with. You also need to be aware of the context of the development. For example, a fault in a video game is much less of a problem than one in an air traffic control system.

The key to making software that is as perfect as possible is to make sure that you have a good understanding of the problem that you are solving, that you know how to solve it before you start writing code and that you manage your code production process carefully. Read some of the recommended texts at the end of this document for more on this aspect of programming.

5.9 The End?

This is not all you need to know to be a programmer. It is not even all you need to know to be a C# programmer. However, it is quite a good start, but there are quite a few things missing from this text, because we don't have time to teach them all. You should take a look at the following things if you want to become a great C# programmer:

- serialisation
- attributes
- reflection
- networking

5.9.1 Continuous Development

A good programmer has a deliberate policy of constantly reviewing their expertise and looking at new things. If you are serious about this business you should be reading at least one book about the subject at any one time. I have been programming for as long as I can remember but I have never stopped learning about the subject. And I've never stopped programming, reading books about programming and looking at other people's code.

5.9.2 Further Reading

Code Complete Second Edition:
Steve McConnell

Published by Microsoft: ISBN 0-7356-1967-0

Not actually a book about C#. More a book about everything else. It covers a range of software engineering and programming techniques from the perspective of "software construction". If you have any serious intention to be a proper programmer you should/must read/own this book.

How to be a programmer

This web site is also worth a read, as it covers the behaviours of a programmer very well indeed:

http://samizdat.mines.edu/howto/HowToBeAProgrammer.html

6 Glossary of Terms

Abstract

Something which is abstract does not have a "proper" existence as such. When writing programs we use the word to mean "an idealised description of something". In the case of component design an abstract class contains descriptions of things which need to be present, but it does not say how they are to be realised. In C# terms a class is abstract if it is marked as such, or if it contains one or more method which is marked as abstract.

You can't make an instance of an abstract class, but you can use it as the basis of, or template for, a concrete one. For example, we may decide that we need many different kinds of receipt in our transaction processing system: cash receipt, cheque receipt, wholesaler receipt etc. We don't know how each particular receipt will work inside, but we do know those behaviours which it must have to make it into a receipt.

We can therefore create an abstract Receipt class which serves as the basis of all the concrete ones. Each "real" receipt class is created by extending the parent, abstract one. This means that it is a member of the receipt family (i.e. it can be treated as a Receipt) but it works in its own way.

Accessor

An accessor is a method which provides access to the value managed within a class. Effectively the access is read only, in that the data is held securely in the class but code in other classes may need to have access to the value itself. An accessor is implemented as a public method which will return a value to the caller. Note that if the thing being given access to is managed by reference the programmer must make sure that it is OK for a reference to the object is passed out. If the object is not to be changed it may be necessary to make a copy of the object to return to the caller.

Base keyword

`base` is a C# keyword which has different meanings depending on the context in which it is given. It is used in a constructor of a child class to call the constructor in the parent. It is also used in overriding methods to call the method which they have overridden.

Calling methods

When you want to use a method, you call it. When a method is called the sequence of execution switches to that method, starting at the first statement in its body. When the end of the method, or the return statement, is reached the sequence of execution returns to the statement immediately following the method call.

Class in C#

A class is a collection of behaviours (methods) and data (properties). It can be used to represent a real world item in your program (for example bank account). Whenever you need to collect a number of things into a single unit you should think in terms of creating a class.

Code Reuse

A developer should take steps to make sure that a given piece of program is only written once. This is usually achieved by putting code into methods and then calling them, rather than repeating the same statements at different parts of a program. The use of class hierarchies is also a way of reusing code. You only need to override the methods that you want to update.

Cohesion

A class has high cohesion if it is not dependent on/coupled to other classes.

Collection

The C# library has the idea of a collection as being a bunch of things that you want to store together, for example all the players in a football team or all the customers in a bank. One form of a collection is an array. Another is the hashtable, which allows you to easily find a particular item based on a key value in that item. A collection class will support *enumeration* which means that it can be asked to provide successive values to the C# foreach construction.

Whenever you want to store a number of things together you should consider using a collection class to do this for you. The collection classes can be found in the System.Collections namespace.

Compiler

A compiler takes a source file and makes sense of it. The compiler will produce an executable file which is run. Writing compilers is a specialised business, they used to be written in assembly language but are now constructed in high level languages (like C#!). A compiler is a large program which is specially written for a particular computer and programming language. Most compilers work in several phases. The first phase, the pre-processor, takes the source which the user has written and then finds all the individual keywords, identifiers and symbols producing a stream of program source which is fed to the "parser" which ensures that the source adheres to the grammar of the programming language in use. The final phase is the code generator, which produces the executable file which is later run by the host.

Component

A component is a class which exposes its behaviour in the form of an interface. This means that rather than being thought of in terms of what it is (for example a `BabyCustomerAccount`) it is thought of in terms of what it can do (implement the `IAccount` interface to pay in and withdraw money). When creating a system you should focus on the components and how they interact. Their interactions are expressed in the interfaces between them.

Constructor

A constructor is a method in a class which is called as a new instance of that class is created. Programmers use constructors to get control when an instance is created and set up the values inside the class. If a class is a member of a hierarchy, and the parent class has a constructor, it is important when making the child that you ensure the parent constructor is called correctly. Otherwise the compiler will refuse to compile your program.

Coupling

If a class is *dependent* on another the two classes are said to be *coupled*. Generally speaking a programmer should strive to have as little coupling in their designs as possible, since it makes it harder to update the system.

Coupling is often discussed alongside cohesion, in that you should aim for high cohesion and low coupling.

Creative Laziness

It seems to me that some aspects of laziness work well when applied to programming. Code reuse, where you try and pick up existing code, is a good example of this. Making sure the spec. is right before you do anything is another way of saving on work. However, structuring the design so that you can get someone else to do a lot of the work is probably the best example of creative laziness in action.

Declarative language

A declarative language tells a computer system about stuff. It doesn't give instructions that explain how to perform an action; it just makes the system aware of the fact that something exists and has a particular set of properties.

C# contains declarations; this is how a program can create variables.

```
int i;
```

This declaration creates an integer variable which is identified by the name `i`. However, a C# program also contains statements which tell the computer how to perform an action.

```
i = i + 1;
```

This statement changes the value in `i`, making it larger by 1. The ability to do this means that C# is not a declarative language. The markup language XAML however, is declarative. XAML was designed to express the design of a page. All a XAML source file contains is descriptions of items.

```xml
<TextBox Name="firstNumberTextBox" Text="0"
 VerticalAlignment="Top" Width="460"
 TextAlignment="Center">
</TextBox>
```

This chunk of XAML describes a TextBox display element. It gives the width, the initial text, the alignment and the name of the element. However, it does not, and can never, tell the system what to do with the element, or any behaviour that it has. This is because XAML does not provide a way of expressing behaviour; it is simply there to tell the display system about stuff.

Delegate

A delegate is a type safe reference to a method. A delegate is created for a particular method signature (for example this method accepts two integers and returns a float). It can then be directed at a method in a class which matches that signature. Note that the delegate instance holds two items, a reference to the instance/class which contains the method and a reference to the method itself. The fact that a delegate is an object means that it can be passed around like any other.

Delegates are used to inform event generators (things like buttons, timers and the like) of the method which is to be called when the event they generate takes place.

Dependency

In general, too much dependency in your designs is a bad thing. A dependency relationship exists between two classes when a change in code in one class means that you might have to change the other as well. It usually means that you have not properly allocated responsibility between the objects in your system and that two objects are looking after the same data. As an example see the discussion of the `CustomerAccount` and `ChildAccount` Load method on page 162.

Dependency is often directional. For example a user interface class may be dependent on a business object class (if you add new properties to the business object you will need to update the user interface). However, it is unlikely that changes to the way that the user interface works will mean that the business object needs to be altered.

Event

An event is some external occurrence which your program may need to respond to. Events include things like mouse movement, keys being hit, windows being resized, buttons being pressed, timers going tick etc. Many modern programs work on the basis of events which are connected to methods. When the event occurs the method is called to deliver notification. Windows components make use of delegates (a delegate is a type safe reference to a method) to allow event generators to be informed of the method to be called when the event takes place.

Exception

An exception is an object that describes something bad that has just happened. Exceptions are part of the way that a C# program can deal with errors. When a running program gets to a position where it just can't continue (perhaps a file cannot be opened or an input value makes no sense) it can give up and "throw" an exception:

```
throw new Exception("Oh Dear");
```

The `Exception` object contains a Message property that is a string which can be used to describe what has gone wrong. In the above example the message would be set to "Oh Dear".

If the exception is not "caught" the program will end at that point. You can make a program respond to exceptions by enclosing code that might throw an exception in a try – catch construction. When the exception is thrown the program transfers execution to the code in the catch clause:

```
try
{
    // code that might throw an exception
}
catch (Exception e)
{
```

```
        // code that is obeyed if an exception is thrown
        // e is a reference to the exception that was thrown
    }
    finally
    {
        // code in here is always obeyed, whether the exception
        // was thrown or not
    }
```

A try – catch construction can also contain a finally clause, which contains code that is executed whether or not the exception is thrown.

Functional Design Specification

Large software developments follow a particular path, from the initial meeting right up to when the product is handed over. The precise path followed depends on the nature of the job and the techniques in use at the developer; however, all developments must start with a description of what the system is to do. This is the most crucial item in the whole project, and is often called the Functional Design Specification, or FDS.

Globally Unique Identifier (GUID)

This is something which is created with the intention of it being unique in the world. It gives an identifier by which something can be referred to. GUID creation involves the use of random values and the date and time, amongst other things. GUIDs are used for things like account references and tags which must be unique. Most operating systems and programmer libraries provide methods which will create GUIDs.

Hierarchy

A hierarchy is created when a parent class is extended by a child to produce a new class with all the abilities of the parent plus new and modified behaviours specific to the requirements of the child. Extending the child produces a further level of hierarchy. The classes at the top of the hierarchy should be more general and possibly abstract (for example `BankAccount`) and the classes at the lower levels will be more specific (for example `ChildBankAccount`).

Immutable

An immutable object cannot be changed. If an attempt is made to change the content of an immutable object a new object is created with the changed content and the "old" one remains in memory. The `string` class is immutable. This gives strings a behaviour similar to value types, which makes them easier to use in programs.

Inheritance

Inheritance is the way in which a class extends a parent to allow it to make use of all the behaviours and properties the parent but add/customise these for a slightly different requirement. For more detail see the description of hierarchy.

Interface

An interface defines a set of actions. The actions are defined in terms of a number of method definitions. A class which implements an interface must contain code for each of the methods. A class which implements an interface can be referenced purely in terms of that interface. Interfaces make it possible to create components. We don't care precisely what the component is, as long as it implements the interface it can be thought of purely in terms of that ability.

Library

A library is a set of classes which are used by other programs. The difference between a library and a program is that the library file will have the extension .dll (dynamic link library) and will not contain a main method.

Machine code

Machine Code is the language which the processor of the computer actually understands. It contains a number of very simple operations, for example move an item from the processor into memory, or add one to an item in the processor. Each particular range of computer processors has its own specific machine code, which means that machine code written for one kind of machine cannot be easily used on another.

Member

A member of a class is declared within that class. It can either do something (a method) or hold some data (variable). Methods are sometimes called behaviours. Data members are sometimes called properties.

Metadata

Metadata is data about data. It operates at all kinds of levels. The fact that the age value is held as an integer is metadata. The fact that it cannot be negative is more metadata. Metadata must be gathered by the programmer in consultation with the customer when creating a system.

Method

A method is a block of code preceded by a *method signature*. The method has a particular name and may return a value. It may also accept a parameter to work on. Methods are used to break a large program up into a number of smaller units, each of which performs one part of the task. They are also used to allow the same piece of program to be used in lots of places in a large development. If a method is public it can be called by code other classes. A public method is how an object exposes its behaviours. A message is delivered to an object by means of a call of a method inside that object.

Mutator

A mutator is a method which is called to change the value of a member inside an object. The change will hopefully be managed, in that invalid values will be rejected in some way. This is implemented in the form of a public method which is supplied with a new value and may return an error code.

Namespace

A namespace is an area within which a particular name has a particular meaning. Namespaces let you reuse names. A programmer creating a namespace can use any name in that namespace. A fully qualified name of a resource is prefixed by the namespace in which the name exists. A namespace can contain another namespace, allowing hierarchies to be set up. Note that a namespace is purely logical in that it does not reflect where in the system the items are physically located, it just gives the names by which they are known. C# provides the `using` keyword to allow namespaces to be "imported" into a program.

Overload

A method is overloaded when one with the same name but a different set of parameters is declared in the same class. Methods are overloaded when there is more than one way of providing information for a particular action, for example a date can be set by providing day, month, year information or by a text string or by a single integer which is the number of days since 1st Jan. Three different, overloaded, methods could be provided to set the date, each with the same name. In that case the SetDate method could be said to have been overloaded.

Override

Sometimes you may want to make a more specialized version of an existing class. This may entail providing updated versions of methods in the class. You do this by creating a child class which extends the parent and then overriding the methods which need to be changed. When the method is called on instances of the child class, the new method is called, not the overridden one in the parent. You can use the `base` keyword to get access to the overridden method if you need to.

Portable

When applied to computer software, the more portable something is the easier it is to move it onto a different type of computer. Computers contain different kinds of processors and operating systems which can only run programs specifically written for them. A portable application is one which can be transferred to a new processor or operating system with relative ease. High Level languages tend to be portable, machine code is much harder to transfer.

Private

A private member of a class is only visible to code in methods inside that class. It is conventional to make data members of a class private so that they cannot be changed by code outside the class. The programmer can then **provide methods or C# properties to manage the values** which may be assigned **to the private members. The only reason for no**t making a data member private is to remove the performance hit of using a method to access the data.

Property

A property is an item of data which is held in an object. An example of a property of a BankAccount class would be the balance of the account. Another would be the name of the account holder. The C# language has a special construction to make the management of properties easy for programmers.

Protected

A protected member of a class is visible to methods in the class and to methods in classes which extend this class. It is kind of a half way house between private (no access to methods outside this class) and public (everyone has access). It lets you designate members in parent classes as being visible in the child classes.

Public

A public member of a class is visible to methods outside the class. It is conventional to make the method members of a class public so that they can be used by code in other class. A public method is how a class provides services to other classes.

Reference

A reference is a bit like a tag which can be attached to an instance of a class. The reference has a particular name. C# uses a reference to find its way to the instance of the class and use its methods and data. One reference can be assigned to another. If you do this the result is that there are now two tags which refer to a single object in memory.

Signature

A given C# method has a particular signature which allows it to be uniquely identified in a program. The signature is the name of the method and the type and order of the parameters to that method:

`void Silly(int a, int b)` – has the signature of the name Silly and two int parameters.

`void Silly(float a, int b)` – has the signature of the name Silly and an float parameter followed by an integer parameter. This means that the code:

`Silly(1, 2) ;`

- would call the first method, whereas:

`Silly(1.0f, 2) ;`

- would call the second.

Note that the type of the method has no effect on the signature.

Source file

You prepare a source file with a text editor of some kind. It is text which you want to pass through a compiler to produce a program file for execution.

Static keyword

In the context of C# the keyword `static` makes a member of a class part of a class rather than part of an instance of the class. This means that you don't need to create an instance of a class to make use of a static member. It also means that static members are accessed by means of the name of their class rather than a reference to an instance. Static members are useful for creating class members which are to be shared with all the instances, for example interest rates for all the accounts in your bank.

Stream

A stream is an object which represents a connection to something which is going to move data for us. The movement might be to a disk file, to a network port or even to the system console. Streams remove the need to modify a program depending on where the output is to be sent or input received from.

Structure

A structure is a collection of data items. It is not managed by reference, and structures are copied on assignment. Structures are also passed by value into methods. Structures are useful for holding chunks of related data in single units. They are not as flexible as objects managed by reference, but they are more efficient to use in that accessing structure items does not require a reference to be followed in the same way as for an object.

Subscript

This is a value which is used to identify the element in an array. It must be an integer value. Subscripts in C# always start at 0 (this locates, confusingly, the first element of the array) and extend up to the size of the array minus 1. This means that if you create a four element array you get hold of elements in the array by subscript values of 0,1,2 or 3. The best way to regard a subscript is the distance down the array you are going to move to get the element that you want. This means that the first element in the array must have a subscript value of 0.

Syntax Highlighting

Some program editors (for example Visual Studio) display different program elements in different colours, to make it easier for the programmer to understand the code. Keywords are displayed in blue, strings in red and comments in green. Note that the colours are added by the editor, and there is nothing in the actual C# source file that determines the colour of the text.

Test harness

The test harness will contain simulations of those portions of the input and output which the system being tested will use. You put your program into a test harness and then the program thinks it is in the completed system. A test harness is very useful when debugging as it removes the need for the complete system (for example a trawler!) when testing.

This keyword

this is a C# keyword which has different meanings depending on the context in which it is given. It is used in a constructor of a class to call another constructor. It is also used as a reference to the current instance, for use in non-static methods running inside that instance.

Typesafe

We have seen that C# is quite fussy about combining things that should not be combined. Try to put a float value into an int variable and the compiler will get cross at this point. The reason for this is that the designers of the language have noticed a few common programming mistakes and have designed it so that these mistakes are detected before the program runs, not afterwards when it has crashed. One of these mistakes is the use of values or items in contexts where it is either not meaningful to do this (put a string into a bool) or could result in loss of data or accuracy (put a double into a byte). This kind of fussiness is called *type safety* and C# is very big on it. Some other languages are much more relaxed when it comes to combining things, and work on the basis that the programmer knows best. They assume that just because code has been written to do something, that thing must be the right thing.

C# is very keen on this (as am I). I think it is important that developers get all the help they can to stop them doing stupid things, and a language that stops you from combining things in a way that might not be sensible is a good thing in my book.

Of course, if you really want to impose your will on the compiler and force it to compile your code in spite of any type safety issues you can do this by using casting.

Unit test

A unit test is a small test which exercises a component and ensures that it performs a particular function correctly. Unit tests should be written alongside the development process so that they can be applied to code just after (or in test drive development just before) the code is written.

Value type

A value type holds a simple value. Value types are passed as values into method calls and their values are copied upon assignment; i.e. x = y causes the value in y to be copied into x. Changes to the value in x will not affect the value of y. Note that this is in contrast to reference types where the result of the assignment would make x and y refer to the same instance.

Virtual Method

A method is a member of a class. I can call the method to do a job. Sometimes I may want to extend a class to produce a child class which is a more specialized version of that class. In that case I may want to replace (override) the method in the parent with a new one in the child class. For this to take place the method in the parent class must have been marked as `virtual`. Only virtual methods can be overridden. Making a method virtual slightly slows down access to it, in that the program must look for any overrides of the method before calling it. This is why not all methods are made virtual initially.

Index

(
() 17, 19

/
/* 36

;
; 18

{
{ 17

+
+ 21

A

abstract
    classes and interfaces 127
    methods 126
    references to abstract classes 129
accessor 101, 139
argument 53
ArrayList 149
    access element 150
    find size 151
    remove element 150
    search 151
arrays 64
    elements 65
    subscripts 65
    two dimensional 67
assignment 18
assignments 48

B

base method 123, 132
block 40
boolean 28
brace 17
break 45
Button 192

C

camel case 30
case 75
casting 32
chain saw 11
char 26, 135
    case 137
    tests 138
class members 98
Close 77

code reuse 120
column printing 50
comments 36
compiler 12
components 113
computer
    data processing 3
    embedded system 4
    hardware & software 2
    program 4
condition 38
Console 18
constants 40
constructor 106
    chaining 125
    custom 107
    default 106
    failure 111
    management 109
    overloading 109
    parameters 107
context 21
continue 46
custom constructors 107

D

data 3, 23
data protection 122
default 75
default constructor 106
delegate 196
delegates 141
    pointers 142
Dictionary 153
double 17

E

elements 65
enumerated types 83
Equals method 133
escape sequence 27
events 141
exception 179
    class 179
    multiple catches 181
    throwing 180
    type 179
expressions 30
    data types 33
    operands 31
    operators 31

F

files
    streams 157
foreach 159

fridge 2
fully qualified name 78

G

Generics 149, 151
global namespace 185
gozzinta 18
GUID 120

H

hash table... 146
Hashtable 147
HTML.. 189

I

identifier 14, 29
if 37
immutable 136
information 3
inheritance 120
integers 24
interface
    abstraction 113
    design 119
    implementing 115
    implementing multiple 118
    reference 116

K

keyword 14

L

Length 137
library 183
List class 151
literal values 23, 33
loops.. 42
    break 45
    continue 46
    do - while 42
    for... 43
    while.. 43

M

member protection 98
metadata 7
methods 51
    base method 123
    Main 14
    overriding 121
    replace 124
    sealed 125
    stopping overriding 125
    virtual 122
mutator 99, 139

N

namespace 16, 185
    global 185
    nesting 187
    separate files 187
    using 186
namespaces..78
narrowing 32
nested blocks..61
nesting namespaces 187
new 92, 106

O

object class 130
object oriented 12
objects 90, 97, 125
    container 144
    equals 132
    factory method...157
    key 148
    properties..138
    this 134
operands..31
operating system 3
operators...31
    combining logical 39
    priority...31
    relational 38
    unary 47
out parameters...59
overflow...25
overloading
    constructors 109
overriding 121

P

parameters 20, 52
Parse 19
pause 176
pointers 142
print formatting..49
print placeholders 49
priority...31
private 98, 100
program flow..37
programmer 2
Programmers Point
    Always provide an equals behaviour.............134
    Avoid Many Dimensions........................69, 72, 73
    Block Copy is Evil 120
    Break Down Your Conditions......................39, 40
    Bug fixes cause bugs.......................................201
    Casts Add Clarity..34
    Check your maths 25
    Choose Variable Types Carefully 29

Clever is not always Clever	44
Construction Should Be Planned	111, 112
Data Structures are Important	96
Delegates are strong magic	172, 173
Design wth Methods	55
Design Your Class Construction Process	126
Design your error exceptions yourself	180
Design your fault reporting	199
Document your Side Effects	58
Don't use new fangled stuff just because it is there	154
Don't Replace Methods	124
Enums are Good	82, 84
Every Message Counts	170
Flipping Conditions	46
Fully Qualified Names are Good	187
Give Your Variables Sensible Names	30
Good Communicators	10
Great Programmers	13
Importance of Hardware	4
Importance of Specification	6
Interfaces are just promises	119
Internationalise your code	113, 115
Know Your Data Source	18
Langauges do Help	59
Learn to use Visual Studio	188
Make sure you use the right equals	133
Metadata	7
Metadata members Members and Methods	99
Not everything should be possible	97
Pace Your Comments	37
Plan for Failure	61
Plan Your Variables	64, 68
private data and public methods	100, 101, 102
Production Code	165
Program Layout	23
Programming Languages	10
Programs often fail in the error handlers	181
Static Data Members are Useful and Dangerous	104
Static Method Members can be used to make libraries	106
Streams are wonderful	159
Strive for Simplicity	48
Structures are Crucial	89, 90
Stupid Computers	11
Switches are Good	76
There is only so much you can do	157
Try to avoid the garbage man	94
Use break With Care	45
Use Numbers Not Messages	168
Use Simple Variable Types	26
Users have strong opinions about the user interface	198
Version Control and Change Management	185, 199, 201
programming languages	10
properties	98, 138
in interfaces	140
public	100
punctuation	22

R

ReadLine	18
recipie	13
reference	92, 93, 95
parameters	58
to abstract class	129
replacing methods	124
return	52

S

schema	190
scope	82, 94
sealed	125
searching	146
semicolon	18
source files	182
StackPanel	191
Star Trek	3
statement	14
returning values	48
static	102
data	103
methods	104
story telling	36
stream	76
streams	157
StreamWriter	77
string	26, 135
comparison	136
editing	137
immutable	136
Length	137
literal	21
StringBuilder	138
structures	85
accessing	86
defining	86
subscripts	65
switch	73, 74
case	75
System namespace	16

T

text based editing	170
TextBox	192
this	134
Thread	173
Monitor	176
mutex	175
Sleep	176
Start	173
threads	171
ThreadStart	173
ToString	130

ToUpper 137
Trim 137

U

unicode 27
user 2

V

value parameters 57
variable scope 61
variables 13, 23
   arrays 64
   assignment 30
   bool 28
   char 26
   double 17
   float 25
   list 17
   string 28
   structures 85
   text 26
   types 23
verbatim 28
virtual methods 122
Visual Studio 188
void 16

W

widening 32
Wizard of Oz 188
WriteLine 20

X

XAML 188
XML 189

Printed in Great Britain
by Amazon